LAWYERS
IN
CORPORATE
DECISION-MAKING

_____

ROBERT ELI ROSEN

___

Classic Dissertation Series

qpp

Quid Pro Books
New Orleans, Louisiana

Lawyers in Corporate Decision-Making

Published by Quid Pro Books. Printed in the United States of America.

ISBN: 1-61027-039-8
ISBN-13: 978-1-61027-039-7

Quid Pro Books
Quid Pro, LLC
5860 Citrus Blvd., Suite D-101
New Orleans, Louisiana 70123
www.quidprobooks.com

qP

Publisher's Cataloging-in-Publication

Rosen, Robert Eli.

  Lawyers in corporate decision-making / Robert Eli Rosen.

      p. cm.
    Includes 2010 foreword and preface.
    Series: *Classic Dissertation.*

ISBN: 1610270398 (pbk.)
ISBN: 1610270401 (Kindle)
ISBN: 161027041X (ePub)

1. Practice of Law—United States—Corporate Representation. 2. Attorney and Client—United States. 3. Lawyers—United States—Corporate Law. 4. Sociology—Professional Roles. 5. Practice of Law—United States—Sociological Aspects. 6. Lawyers—United States—Biography. I. Title. II. Series.

KF300.R35 2010   340'.06'077—dc20

Early reviews for *Lawyers in Corporate Decision-Making...*

"*Lawyers in Corporate Decision-Making* should be read by everyone interested in how law matters to organizations of all kinds."

— *Jonathan Simon*
Adrian A. Kragen Professor of Law,
UC Berkeley, School of Law, and
MacCormick Fellow,
Edinburgh University

"Rob Rosen's study of in house counsel is a deft, subtle dissection of a complex world where nothing is as it quite seems. In interviewing in house counsel, outside counsel, and clients, Rosen captures, in a Rashomon-like way, the moral character of lawyers' work—their choices, their pitches, their claims—by which they justify what they do. We see inside the professional black box."

— *John Flood*
Professor of Law and Sociology,
University of Westminster, London

"In *Lawyers in Corporate Decision-Making*, Robert Rosen takes us inside large law firms to explore how corporate lawyers advise their clients and how that advice can go wrong. The case studies he describes—including four situations in which the legal advice failed—show how important it is for lawyers to frame the clients' needs appropriately. Rosen's ability to weave together the importance of organizational hierarchy, coordination of responsibility, thoroughness of communication, and business acumen makes this book a 'must-read' for lawyers and law students alike."

— *Nancy B. Rapoport*
Gordon Silver Professor of Law,
William S. Boyd School of Law, UNLV, and
Coauthor of *Enron and Other Corporate Fiascos*

"Rob Rosen's book captures the personal and organizational complexity of the effective in-house counsel's experience. As a former GC of two large industrial businesses, I know how right he is when he disdains the simple either/or characterizations of inside lawyers as counselors, cops, and entrepreneurs. Inside lawyers (with few exceptions) are the only ones in a position to operate in the Venn diagram overlap between pure business and pure legal decisions; the best ones operate with equal credibility on business and law. 'No' is rare, but when an inside lawyer who knows the business speaks, people listen."

— *Jeffrey Lipshaw*
Associate Professor,
Suffolk University Law School

The *Classic Dissertation Series* offers high-quality print and digital renditions of influential scholarship in law, history and the social sciences, drawn from doctoral theses occasionally available in libraries or microfiche but not previously published. All works in the Series are recognized in their fields, having been passed around in manuscript form for years and repeatedly cited as authority by later scholars. In addition, new Forewords by contemporary experts place the works in context and provide scholarly background.

TABLE OF CONTENTS

Foreword

On one sunny spring day in Santa Monica in 1999, I stepped into the office of my major client to meet with the company's officers. But instead of meeting them in my capacity as the principal outside corporate lawyer, a role that I had happily occupied for four years, I met them as a fellow employee—the new inside general counsel. On that first day as a corporate employee, I had only an inkling of what my new role would entail. I knew then that I would continue to assist the company in navigating the laws and regulations that constrained their business activities. What I did not anticipate, however, were the tremendous social, political, and ethical challenges inherent to the in-house role.

Only years later, after launching an academic career focused on inside counsel and business corporations, did I stumble on Professor Robert Eli Rosen's path-breaking Ph.D. dissertation, completed in 1984. Although *Lawyers in Corporate Decision-Making* was unpublished at the time, it was widely regarded by experts in the field as a pioneering work in the sociology of the legal profession and a foundational piece in the slowly emerging canon of empirical research on inside counsel.[1] Indeed, I have since used his work in my own writing on corporate legal ethics in context.[2] Professor Rosen's study provides a rich, detailed account of the roles of inside and outside lawyers in corporate ethical decision-making. It is jam-packed with anecdotes and direct quotations from an astonishing number (70) of in-depth interviews with inside and outside lawyers and business persons.

---

[1] *See, e.g.*, Clyde Spillenger, *Elusive Advocate: Reconsidering Brandeis as People's Lawyer*, 105 Yale L.J. 1445, 1503 n.205 (1996) ("Rosen's important manuscript is widely cited in recent literature on legal professionalism."); David Luban, *Asking the Right Questions*, 72 Temp. L. Rev. 839, 855 (1999) ("Some years ago, Robert Eli Rosen completed an important study of in-house counsel...."); Robert W. Gordon, *Corporate Law Practice as a Public Calling*, 49 Md. L. Rev. 255, 281 (1990) ("Robert Rosen on the sociology of in-house counsel's work is particularly suggestive"); Mary C. Daly, *The Cultural, Ethical, and Legal Challenges in Lawyering for a Global Organization: The Role of the General Counsel*, 46 Emory L.J. 1057, 1070 (1997) ("According to Rosen, successful legal risk analysis enables its practitioners to become influential within the corporation. Articles in the popular legal press strongly support Rosen's thesis."); Tanina Rostain, *General Counsel in the Age of Compliance: Preliminary Findings and New Research Questions*, 21 Geo. J. Legal Ethics 465, 471 (2008); Robert L. Nelson & Laura Beth Nielsen, *Cops, Counsel, and Entrepreneurs: Constructing the Role of Inside Counsel in Large Corporations*, 34 Law & Society Rev. 457, 458-59, 470-72, 482-83, 486-87 (2000); Lawrence M. Friedman, et al., *The Growth of Large Law Firms and its Effect on the Legal Profession and Legal Education: Law, Lawyers, and Legal Practice in Silicon Valley: A Preliminary Report*, 64 Ind. L.J. 555, 559 (1989); Robert W. Gordon, *The Independence of Lawyers*, 68 B.U.L. Rev. 1, 27, 30 (1988).

[2] Sung Hui Kim, *The Ethics of In-House Practice*, in Lynn Mather & Leslie Levin, eds., Lawyers in Practice: Ethical Decision Making in Context, ch. 10 (Univ. of Chicago Pr., fthcg. 2011).

As one example of the many gems embedded in this text's pages, consider Rosen's masterful case study about how four professionals handled an employment discrimination issue [pp. 151-153]. A divisional personnel officer was disturbed to learn that a corporate manager who had recently transferred to a new business unit wanted to terminate a female Black employee because she was "difficult" [p. 151]. The personnel officer strongly suspected racial motivations because the employee had worked in the unit for five years without incident and had good relationships with past superiors. As a result, the personnel officer brought in an inside lawyer and asked him to "explain to [the manager] the law on firing members of protected classes" [p. 151]. The inside lawyer, who was relatively new to the company and unfamiliar with employment law, brought in an outside law firm specializing in employment matters. The law firm immediately focused on "how" and not "whether"; in other words, it advised the manager on how to create the necessary paper trail before firing. Frustrated by this course of advice, the personnel officer brought in a second inside lawyer, and together they reminded the manager of the company's commitment to rewarding loyal employees. They pointed out to the manager that this employee had been a trusted colleague for five years. Due to this intervention, the manager reversed his decision to terminate the employee.

According to Professor Rosen, the first inside counsel and outside counsel "assumed a decision had been made and they were simply conduits for it" [p. 152]. Since neither was certain that the manager harbored an illicit motive, neither felt it was part of his job to second-guess the manager. "To avoid a power struggle between themselves and the manager, both these lawyers relied on the law's potential sanctions to discipline the manager" [p. 153]. In other words, these lawyers did not see it as their role to dissuade the manager; if anything , that was anti-discrimination law's job.

By contrast, the personnel officer and second inside lawyer had a much more political understanding of their roles. They understood that the corporation had created their professional positions in part to constrain managerial discretion without supplanting it. Accordingly, their job was not to simply obey hierarchical commands issued by the "corporate bureaucracy" but, rather, to use their discretion to participate in the conflicts, compromises, and bargaining from which corporate goals and decisions emerge. Through this and many other in-depth accounts, Rosen unpacks the complex role of inside counsel—its transformative potential, its educative function, its limitations, its conundrums, and the hard moral choices that it presents.

But *Lawyers in Corporate Decision-Making*'s contributions are not limited to rich, thick description. The study also normatively challenges the legal profession's ideology of moral "independence"—the claim that lawyers are morally firewalled from and thus not morally responsible for their clients' objectives or actions. To avoid misunderstanding, this claim of independence is not that the lawyer should exercise independent moral judgment; to the contrary, it means that the immorality of the client's ends cannot be linked back to the lawyer, which in turn licenses the lawyer to be dependent and servile to the client's wishes without fear of moral taint or social reprimand. This claim of moral independence has long been used to justify providing legal advice in the service of ethically problematic ends and the profession's collective retreat away from the role of "influential counselor," as exemplified by lawyer-statesmen, such as Elihu Root or Louis Brandeis. It has been used to disclaim lawyers' responsibilities to broader social concerns. As one outside lawyer in Rosen's study snidely put it, "Let's find out what makes us guardians of the public interest and write it out of our retainer agreement" [p. 83].

Most significantly, Rosen argues, the professional norm of moral independence disserves the corporate client by permitting lawyers to ignore "organizational pathologies," such as managers who insist on their pet projects without regard to whether they are truly in the firm's best interest. Rosen argues that loyalty to the corporate client does not mean blind obedience to the corporate manager: "Loyalty to the client may require the lawyer to transcend the problem as set by the client [representative]" [p. 81]. Because the true client is the corporate entity, lawyers must "transcend the customer's definition of corporate interests and problems" and exercise some control over how corporate objectives are selected in the service of the collective enterprise. Rosen acknowledges that doing so isn't easy. However, he highlights that inside counsel, who have few explicit limits on their engagement [pp. 168-170] and are often tasked with overseeing compliance, are well positioned to influence corporate decision-making processes. Of course, many counsel would rather not rock the boat and prefer to take the path of least resistance. Rosen reminds us, however, that such a path may be morally deficient.

In 1984, Rosen wrote, "Although the profession prefers to avoid discussion of the influential lawyer, the growth of inside counsel has put it on the profession's agenda" [p. 169]. Twenty-six years later, it is still on the profession's agenda. But, thankfully, with the long-awaited publication of this manuscript, corporate lawyers will have something to guide them.

— Sung Hui Kim

School of Law
University of California at Los Angeles

Los Angeles, California
November, 2010

Preface to the 2010 Edition

The research reported in this book describes the choices that lawyers, managers and executives make about how lawyers are involved in companies' decisions. In the companies studied, beyond decisions regarding legal compliance, lawyers were involved in decisions ranging from finance to production to sales to returns to litigation. But the how, when and consequences of their involvements varied. This book analyzes these variations.

Relations between inside and outside counsel and the management of the corporate legal function are the principal subjects of this book. Since the early 1980s, corporate legal departments have become increasingly prominent and powerful. The corporate bar is increasingly subject to the politics of what I have called "the inside counsel movement": the demands by house counsel for professional respect and control. The "end of the hourly fee" and "outsourcing," the topics of today, reflect this politics. At one level, the inside counsel movement reflects corporations' desires to economize in the face of law firms' monopoly rents and minimize agency costs. Doing this requires managing outside counsel. And then it requires managing the inside counsel who substitute for outside counsel.

Managing corporate legal departments is different from the management of other staff functions: The multiple relations of law to business make it difficult to create procedures for when legal should be involved. Because legal risks are intermittently realized and usually settled on non-legal bases, they are not technical risks. Issues of public policy, legal compliance and business strategy, as well as professional identity, are at play. Managing corporate legal departments differs from the management of law firms: Inside counsel are captive and have captured a client. Their access to managers and intra-corporate power are not normally found in outside counsel.

This book's analytical framework derives from organization theory. It repeatedly calls on attorneys to understand the organizational context of their work. It repeatedly calls out attorneys who ill serve their clients because they failed as organizational analysts. In recent years there have been increasing calls for bringing business education into law schools. This book may have a place in an organizational behavior course for law students. It brings ideas normally associated with business education to analyze the choices that lawyers must make.

Drawing together the question of how lawyers serve corporations and organization theory drew me to the works of Philip Selznick and Robert Kagan. Their concerns with finding value in organization and attentiveness to the ways in which law may fail are found throughout this book. My discussion of the management of corporate legal services teases out their concerns with responsiveness and responsibility.

In addition to its subject matter and analytic framework, this book's methodology remains distinctive. I spoke with inside counsel, outside counsel and the managers with whom they worked. Researchers who do not study the corporate bar recognize that to understand legal services, one must understand clients' perspectives. Yet those who study the corporate bar generally only interview lawyers. Furthermore, those who study the corporate bar usually have adopted the posture of absorptive neutrals: They have let the lawyers speak and reported (and counted) the lawyers' speeches. They have ignored that lawyers, elite lawyers especially, are engaged in public relations exercises when they are interviewed, even when researchers promise confidentiality. Interviewing is a technique with limits: Most lawyers have an agenda and will run over interviewers who are merely absorptive neutrals. Interviewing the triad of inside counsel, outside counsel and managers who worked on a particular problem allowed me to check what each said. More important, because it triangulated how the legal problem was understood, I was able to see how the legal task had been structured. My methodology benefited from extended discussion with Laura Nader about how to "study up," and in particular how to study those who wield corporate power.

I still read many studies on the legal profession based *only* on lawyer interviews and *only* reporting what the lawyers have chosen to share. Although there are multiple instances in this book that reveal the dangers in basing findings solely on the responses of lawyers, let me give one example. One senior outside counsel whom I interviewed told me:

> The people I deal with happily listen to what I say. I've never confronted a situation where I say, 'This is the law and if you do x, you will wreak havoc on your company," and they don't listen. . . . My job is to tell people what the law is and by the force of my personality convince them that is the way to go. It works. [Quoted at page 145.]

A researcher who spoke only with lawyers might count this interviewee as someone who is concerned with ethics or who adopts the attitude of a "cop" or who provides evidence of the importance of personal relations in legal work. But, I also spoke with those who worked with him and who were inside the company. One such interviewee put it bluntly:

> He [the senior outside counsel quoted above] is used for nitpicking questions on regulations. And the manager leaves him saying, "He doesn't know the business." And the manager doesn't listen to him. [P. 146.]

No matter how many outside counsel I would have interviewed, I never would have been able to critically appraise their comments without the benefit of the perspectives of the managers and inside counsel with whom they worked. More important, without examining all three together, I would not have had access to the structuring of legal problems which enabled this outside counsel to believe that "It works." I would not have been able to develop one of the themes of this book: independence sometimes masks subservience.

This book also largely avoids categorizing legal departments or lawyers by their approaches and then counting them. I rejected the idea that inside counsel were "counselors," "cops," or "entrepreneurs," to borrow Nelson and Nielsen's terms. The lawyers with whom I spoke were cops in some matters, counselors on others and sometimes they thought that their job was to make legal a corporate profit center. My focus was to explore the sources of these variations. Nor did I attempt to count how often they were "ethical" and how often not. My focus, again, was to explore the possible sources that would push in one direction or the other. Similarly, except for some discussion of the processes as Drafter and as Educator, I did not categorize my findings by legal department. The organizational principles that I elaborate were found in some places but not others in the legal departments that I studied. Although my distrust of numeracy in a search to understand significant variation will be off-putting to some, I thank my dissertation chair, Robert Bellah, for supporting my acceptance of a complexity that escaped counting exercises, my search for the bases for civic good in corporate legal services.

The research on which this book is based was conducted between 1981 and 1983. That it retains relevance and poignancy is to be credited to its subject matter, analytical framework and methodology. I am very pleased to be asked so many years later to put this work into published form. Its continuing relevance is also attributable to the fact that I was a student at University of California-Berkeley, with access to firms in Northern California, including Silicon Valley. Four of the six companies that I studied were early carriers of the inside counsel movement.

Chapter One has not been previously published. Yet, its discussion of the "ideological devils" of "complexity, bigness and specialization" remains relevant. I still hear lawyers who pine for an ethical life they feel is foreclosed to them because, "[T]his is the city. It's big, inhuman and there is no going back" [p. 1]. The discussion of "differentiated specialization" today needs to be conjoined to the contrary development in some law firms of "client relations partners." For such a discussion, see my *"We're All Consultants Now": How Change in Client Organizational Strategies Influences Change in the Organization of Corporate Legal Services*, 44 ARIZ. L. REV. 637 (2002). The discussion of Daniel Webster was incorporated into *Rejecting the Culture of Independence: Corporate Lawyers as Committed to their Clients*, in Special Issue: LAW FIRMS, LEGAL CULTURE, AND LEGAL PRACTICE (Austin Sarat, ed.), 52 STUDIES IN LAW, POLITICS AND SOCIETY 31 (2010). The discussion of Brandeis identifies problems which plague all forms of holistic legal practice. Advocates for collaborative lawyering should consider the limits of Brandeisian advocacy.

Chapter Two has been revised from its form in the dissertation. Most of Chapter Two was further revised and published as *Problem-setting and Serving the Organizational Client: Legal Diagnosis and Professional Independence*, 56 U. MIAMI L. REV. 179 (2001). This chapter develops and extends organization theory to the analysis of legal problems.

Chapter Three has not been previously published. Its discussion of lawyers as decision consultants, however, has been cited in the literature. Its discussion of how lawyers and managers respond to legal risks has influenced my later writings, including *Risk Management and Organizational Governance: The Case of Enron*, 35 CONN. L. REV. 1157 (2003), and *Resistances to Reforming Corporate Governance: The Diffusion of QLCCs*, 74 FORDHAM L. REV. 1251 (2005). Its account of what happens inside an organization when legal risk management becomes understood as the task of lawyers is of relevance to those who develop compliance programs or create committees to oversee corporate risk management.

Chapter Four (although it includes the case that Professor Kim discusses in her foreword) is largely normative. Parts of it appear in *The Inside Counsel Movement, Professional Judgment and Organizational Representation*, 64 INDIANA L.J. 479 (1989). Its relevance is to those who are concerned with legal ethics or corporate governance.

When I began teaching at a law school, my Dean told me not to turn my dissertation into a book. He told me that my colleagues were already suspicious of my being a sociologist and that I needed to produce three "classic" law review articles. Being risk-averse, I listened and never did the hard work of creating a book that would be of general interest. Although I have done some work, each of the chapters could benefit greatly from much more sustained rewrites. And the reader will have to do more work than I would like. For example, she will have to put up with the use of masculine pronouns throughout the text. She also will have to deal with the fact that some of the discussion presumes background knowledge of law or sociology. That said, keeping this research buried is a disservice to its unique approach to the study of corporate lawyering.

I would like to express my deep thanks to Professor Sung Hui Kim for her kind introduction. I commend to you her writings on inside counsel and ethics that demonstrate a clarity of thought which I can only admire. I also thank Professor Alan Childress for pressing me to put this work "out there" and for the hard work to make this book look good.

— Robert Eli Rosen

Professor of Law
University of Miami

Miami, Florida
November, 2010

Preface

This study is based on a series of seventy interviews with inside counsel and upper and middle-managers in six major manufacturing corporations and with outside attorneys who represent these corporations. Access to the members of the corporation was secured through the corporation's chief legal officer, the General Counsel.[1] Outside counsel were individually contacted.

I chose to study only industrial corporations because of an interest in the role of lawyers in implementing corporate social responsibility. Industrial firms try and sometimes succeed in erecting buffers between their operations and the demands of the social and political environment. In comparison with financial and service companies, the other major employers of inside counsel, industrial companies are relatively insulated from the demands of customers, the public, and government regulators.[2] Industrial firms, then, should be least receptive to legal control and I expected to find their lawyers having the greatest problems in maintaining power and independence.

General Counsels were not given permission to choose the members of their departments to be interviewed. Instead, I selected inside counsel who, based upon their formal job descriptions, most closely resembled outside counsel.

It is crucial to compare lawyers who perform comparable functions.[3] To

---

[1] No General Counsel refused me initial access. While this is an indication that corporations accept that the public eye is on them, it is also an indication that the problems of this study are of great concern to corporate lawyers. In commenting on a failed study of lawyers, Douglas Rosenthal aptly described the situation: "To get the attention of lawyers and their cooperation in social research, the first critical step is to define an issue that is meaningful to lawyers; an issue they can understand; an issue they care about; one they feel merits some investment of their time." Rosenthal, "Comment on Obstacles to the Study of Lawyer-Client Interaction: The Biography of a Failure," 14 L. & Soc. Rev. 923, 923 (1980); see also Smigel, "Interviewing a Legal Elite: The Wall Street Lawyer," 64 Am. J. Soc. 159 (1958) (must maintain interest). Fortunately, today lawyers are interested in differences between inside and outside counsel, organizing corporate legal departments and maintaining smooth relations between inside and outside counsel.

[2] See J. Thompson, Organizations in Action 15-18 (1967) (distinguishing between the "long-linked technology" of industrial firms and the "mediating technology" of financial and service firms).

[3] O. Maru, Research on the Legal Profession: A Review of Work Done 4 (1972): "Students of the profession should recognize and affirm that there are many 'legal professions' in the sense that there are many kinds of law workers who do many kinds of legal work." Especially when professional autonomy is being analyzed, comparisons must take into account the level and kind of work being performed. See Lengermann, "Professional Autonomy in Organizations: The Case of CPA's," in Varieties of Work Experience 173, 177 (P. Stewart & M. Cantor eds. 1974) (reporting spurious effects due to not controlling for position levels in studies of CPA autonomy). For example, it is a common mistake of those who have previously examined both inside and outside counsel to compare inside business counsel with outside litigators. Slovack's study of the corporate bar concludes that outside

make a meaningful comparison between inside and outside counsel, I studied members of the corporate legal department whose work was the least routinized. Furthermore, I only interviewed lawyers attached to corporate headquarters who worked directly for the corporate legal department. Lawyers attached to other departments, such as tax, labor, oil and gas or real estate, were excluded.[4]

I interviewed inside counsel first. Based upon these interviews, I selected specific problems or cases for further analysis. I then contacted outside counsel and managers who had worked on these same problems. From these interviews with different participants, three versions of the same events emerged. I was thus able to reconstruct the problems to analyze the behavior of and the constraints facing the various actors.[5]

I also interviewed other managers and outside counsel for background and general information.

Interviews with inside counsel were relatively unstructured and did not rely on a set questionnaire. My main objective was to encourage them to freely discuss their work. Interviews with outside counsel and managers were also unstructured, except that I tried to direct them toward a discussion of the problems generated in the interviews with the inside counsel.

I rejected early on an interview format with formal questions. In the initial stages of this study, the interviewees berated me for my questions, claiming they couldn't deal with abstractions. Words like "ethics" proved to be loaded, producing defensiveness and generating stereotyped responses or evasion.[6] General questions about choices and policies produced a similar result.[7] To some extent, the lawyers seemed to avoid more abstract questions

---

counsel "tend to be specialists in legal combat." Slovack, "Working for Corporate Actors: Social Change and Elite Attorneys in Chicago," 1979 ABF Res. J. 468, 488. This conclusion, which is not inapposite to the conclusion reached here, however, derived from his over-sampling of litigators. At least 15 of his 23 outside counsel are litigators according to his specialization chart, *id.* at 488, where he puts 8 in civil litigation and 7 in defense antitrust work, which he fails to note is also a litigation specialty.

[4] Studying only industrial companies facilitated comparisons between the work of inside and outside counsel. Inside counsel at industrial companies most closely resemble outside counsel. At financial and service companies, the work of inside counsel tends to be routine. J. Donnell, The Corporate Counsel: A Role Study 17 (1971).

[5] I also was able to overcome some of the weaknesses of the interview method. While some have argued that organization studies demand interviewing as the methodology of choice, T. Mathiesen, Across the Boundaries of Organizations 23f (1971), Chris Argyris is correct in holding that "the interview...has serious limitations. The strongest limitation is related to the gap between how people say they behave and how they actually behave. This gap is especially crucial when studying the upper levels of managements." C. Argyris, Understanding Organizational Behavior 40 (1960). I attempted to avoid this problem by interviewing inside counsel, managers and outside counsel who had worked on one problem.

[6] Smigel found a similar result, E. Smigel, The Wall Street Lawyer 21 (1964).

[7] Smigel claimed that "[t]rained to make policy, to deal with general problems, the senior

because they were simply lazy. Because I was not a client paying them to think through complex problems, there wasn't enough incentive for them to respond. Also, they seemed frightened about the implications of being committed to a response to a set question. The problem in interviewing lawyers can be summed up as that of sailing "between the Scylla of tedious platitude and the Charybdis of professional inhibitions."[8]

I therefore abandoned a set formula with abstract questions and concentrated on tracing the ramifications of particular decisions. The lawyers, who are used to answering specific questions about a case, like those presented in a deposition, seemed grateful for this more concrete method. In addition to being encouraged to focus on specific decisions, the lawyers also were asked how other lawyers handled or would have handled the same issue. I used this projective technique to elicit data otherwise not directly obtainable. It prodded the lawyers to talk both about their action and about their reasons for acting.

The interview process required that I not be a passive participant, but instead voice my own views. Although I tried not to hinder the interviewees in expressing their ideas, I was not reluctant to disagree or ask why alternative courses were not taken. This approach is consistent with Lerner's finding that highly educated respondents would not talk to an absorptive neutral. Reciprocity and debate are demanded by such respondents.[9]

Despite all my attempts to create a useful interview situation, questions, of course, remain about the quality of the interview data. In some sense this is a hypothesis-generating study, not a hypothesis-testing study—as it should be given the lack of knowledge about the subject matter.[10] In another sense, this study stands on its own. Through these interviews, I collected ideas. Whether or not these ideas are appropriate to the reader's situation cannot be foreseen. Their limits are to some extent spelled out in the text. But, the reader will know whether or not they are useful.

— Robert Eli Rosen

Berkeley, California
November, 1984

---

members answered [Smigel's questions] broadly and boldly." *Id.* at 25. Perhaps Smigel's naive conclusions about the responsibility of the corporate bar can be traced to his acceptance of such responses at face value. My experience is that when facing general problems, lawyers give stereotyped responses. In the context of ethics, they repeat word for word the Code of Professional Responsibility.

[8] Charles Horsky, quoted in J. Goulden, The Super-Lawyers 1 (1971).

[9] Lerner, "Interviewing Frenchmen," 62 Am. J. Soc. 187 (1956).

[10] Although there have been some notable exceptions, as Richard Abel's summary of work on the legal profession concludes, "lawyers practicing in larger partnerships or employed by corporations and representing business interests have been largely ignored" by students of the law. Abel, "Redirecting Social Studies of Law," 14 L. & Soc. Rev. 805, 806 (1980).

Acknowledgments

During the time I was working on this project, I had the good fortune to be able to draw on many remarkable scholars and human beings: The Stanford Reading Group on the Legal Profession (especially Deborah Rhode, Robert Gordon, William Simon, Lawrence Friedman and Paul Brest) helped me believe that others were interested in the questions I was asking. Robert Bellah taught me that sociology and ethics were not disparate disciplines. Philip Selznick and Robert Kagan tried to teach me how to develop aspirations for legal service that were neither abstract nor without social groundings. Laura Nader tried to teach me how to read data. As I began writing these people all took the time to read and criticize my work, as did Robert Post, Richard Buxbaum, Harry Scheiber and Robert Cole, members of the Boalt Hall faculty, Philip Lewis at Oxford, and my fellow students Jane Rubin, Betty-Lou Bradshaw and Batya Friedman.

I am grateful that these teachers and friends gave me the freedom to attempt to be both critical and moralizing. The way in which the study combines these two elements may please none of them. My teachers taught me that social analysis must be sensitive to unintended consequences and experience's contradictions. But social analysis also has obligations to those who must live with the consequences and contradictions. Once I decided to write for not only students of the legal profession but also lawyers, I found that the level of my analysis changed. I could not rest with criticism. I needed to find a way to address practitioners. I settled on the concept of *mauvaise foi*. What are the choices corporate lawyers make that convince them their contradictions are necessary? Are there options for re-organizing their work so they overcome these contradictions? What could I tell them that would support their attempts to be moral men and women in an immoral society? Stressing the possibilities for change is what I learned from my teachers who understand sociology to be a moral science. But moralizing sociology often reads like flattery, teasing but upholding unjustifiable social relations. If this study can be so read, my teachers' grant of freedom to write a critical and moralizing study was a mistake. I hope the intensely serious nature of the problems described will not be forgotten by academic readers who long for the "big" contradictions and by practitioner readers who resist even minor changes.

I would not have had the liberty to engage in this enterprise without the support of the American Bar Foundation and the Thomasin and Abigail Bellah Foundation. I am in their debt.

— R.E.R.

Lawyers

in

Corporate

Decision-Making

Der Jurist, der nichts ist als ein Jurist,
ist ein armes Ding.

—Martin Luther

Chapter One

CHOICES IN CORPORATE LEGAL PRACTICE

INTRODUCTION

When lawyers compare their work to that of their predecessors, current legal practice comes up short. Both old and young attorneys deprecate their work in comparison to an idealized, but now foreclosed, type of practice. As one told me: "I would like to be like my father who practiced in a small town and could see a connection between his work and Lincoln's and between his ethics and the dispensation of justice by the old man who sat under the tree. But, this is the city. It's big, inhuman and there is no going back." Unlike that of his father's, the young attorney's practice is afflicted by the modern banes: complexity, bigness and specialization.

Comparisons between the past and present are notoriously inaccurate. Such reports do not provide materials for a ranking of the present against the past. They do, however, fulfill another function. We define ourselves, in part, through comparison. We apprehend ourselves not only in acting but also in reflecting on our differences and similarities to others. This forms the basis of the practical insight that we must carefully select our loves and hates. We become ourselves through these choices as much as we choose them because of who we are.

If our self-definitions are not to be arbitrary, the comparisons we invoke must be scrutinized. Historical and comparative analysis can belie the assumption that present social arrangements are necessary. Historical and comparative analysis also can reveal that moral choice is not solely self-regarding. Without such analyses, authority may be understood only as the arbitrary exercise of will and the choice of exemplars may be understood only as the result of unjustifiable charisma.

In this chapter, I will use comparative and historical analysis to examine the claimed fall of the legal profession, due to the rise of complexity, bigness and specialization. My object is to elucidate the choices lawyers can and do make in defining the character of their practice. To make repressed choices public, we must criticize ideology. Ideologies do not merely provide images of the desirable; they also provide figures of evil. Complexity, bigness and specialization are the devils of modern ideology.[1] By harping on the devils, we

---

[1] G. Simmel, "On the Concept and Tragedy of Culture," in The Conflict in Modern Culture and Other Essays 27 (1968). They do not only bedevil lawyers, of course. Big business and big government are also claimed to be disenabling.

avoid confronting the choices that seal our fate.[2]

By constantly pointing to the peculiarities of modern legal practice, lawyers also can cut themselves off from the demands of professionalism. Much of legal practice's integrity and moral strength derives from its tradition as one of the "learned professions." To retain continuing vitality, the aspirations of the legal profession require the unmasking of the modern ideological devils.

Organizational theorists discuss the ways organizations and roles within organizations can be so tightly tied to their environment and each other that there is little room left to maneuver.[3] In this situation, known as "tight coupling," leadership and strategic choice are not available. Because many people strive for high class and status in order to maximize their freedom of action, one would not expect to find, as I did, elite lawyers claiming that their positions are tightly coupled to the demands of the law and of their clients. Furthermore, outsiders often consider leadership opportunities to be one of the attractions of legal practice. In adversarial situations, with one winner and one loser, one would assume that leadership is necessary to win the day. Yet, lawyers argue that this confuses strategy with tactics. Lawyers, they say, only make tactical decisions about when and how to file motions and disclosure statements. Strategic decisions are made by the client, not the lawyer. The lawyer is merely a specialized process mover.

When lawyers attempt to specify the way in which opportunities for leadership have been limited, they tend to cite two social-historical processes. First, they point to the growth in the number of regulations. Second, they indicate the differentiation of leadership within the business sector. The expansion of the regulatory state has supposedly "tightly coupled" lawyers to legal requirements, forcing them to respond more to the demands of the law than to their own judgments. The state, not the private lawyer, is now the "architect of social structures," to use Fuller's famous description of the role of the legal profession.[4] Lawyers build according to the state's plans. Given the concentration required to master merely a portion of the regulatory state's plans, we are told, it would be sheer *hubris* for a lawyer to advise, let alone lead, when non-legal considerations enter the picture. To further explain their "tight coupling," lawyers will point to the growing

---

[2] Ideology is described in terms of "devils" in order to avoid making metaphysical claims about "false consciousness." At issue is *mauvaise foi*.

[3] See March & Olsen, "Choice Situations in Loosely Coupled Worlds," unpublished manuscript, Stanford University, 1975; Weick, "Educational Organizations in Loosely Coupled Systems," 21 Ad. Sci. Q. 1 (1976).

[4] K. Winston, ed., The Principles of Social Order: Selected Essays of Lon L. Fuller 264 (1981). See also H. M. Hart & A. Sacks, The Legal Process 200 (tent. ed. 1958). Others, in keeping with the differentiation of leadership generated by the second process, argue that economists, scientists and engineers are today the "architects of social structure." See, e.g., Miller, "Public Law and the Obsolescence of the Lawyer," 19 U. Fla. L. Rev. 514 (1966-67).

importance of other groups on whom their client rely: various types of consulting services outside the corporation and various planning and decision committees within the corporation. Our society, they argue, has witnessed the differentiation of leadership and it would be foolish to expect the elite lawyer to exert the same control as he once did. One of the ironies of this view is that the elite lawyer, who was a leader in the age of the entrepreneur, has forsaken his claim to that role in the age of the organization man.

We might accept that these two socio-historical processes have constrained the lawyer except that they are conjoined to two other movements, one in law and one in business. First, in the jurisprudence of our law-applying bodies, equity responsiveness is challenging rule-formalism.[5] Judges, unlike the lawyers appearing before them, are not specialists and do not ignore the substantive consequences of their decisions. It is not uncommon for major corporations and law firms to receive a worse decision than necessary because they relied on technical legal arguments.[6] Second, corporate clients are changing their decision-making modalities. As Daniel Bell tells us, in the post-industrial age corporations are moving from an "economizing" to a "sociologizing" mode of decision-making.[7] Whatever we might think of Bell's neologism which unduly flatters the sociologist, Bell correctly observes that corporations are introducing "non-economic" and "broader social values" into their decisions. Strategic choice in corporations

---

[5] See, e.g., Atiyah, "From Principles to Pragmatism: Changes in the Function of the Judicial Process and the Law," 65 Iowa L. Rev. 1201 (1980); Eisenberg & Yeazell, "The Ordinary and the Extraordinary in Institutional Litigation," 93 Harv. L. Rev. 4665 (1980); Fiss, "The Supreme Court, 1978 Term—Foreword: The Forms of Justice," 93 Harv. L. Rev. 1 (1979); Eisenberg, "Participation, Responsiveness, and the Consultative Process," 92 Harv. L. Rev. 410 (1978) (questioning the legitimacy of the shift); Chayes, "The Role of the Judge in Public Law Litigations," 89 Harv. L. Rev. 1281 (1976); Scott, "Two Models of the Civil Process," 27 Stan. L. Rev. 937 (1975).

[6] On judges as generalists, see D. Horowitz, The Courts and Social Policy 25-32 (1977) For discussions of poor results see various exposés in the American Lawyer and the National Law Journal. For the view of one judge, consider the comments of Judge Smith, of the U.S. Court of Custom and Patent Appeals, a court where you would expect specialization: "[T]hose of you who represent corporate interest whether in general or patent legal matters must find some ways to personalize and particularize the legal issues where justice to your client is in danger of being denied. A patent infringement suit by the XYZ Corporation against the ABC Corporation can easily degenerate into little more than a battle for a competitive advantage which can be measured in dollars and cents rather than in more human values. Perhaps this is one reason why patents have fared rather poorly in our courts.... Basically every corporate problem is a human problem which is hidden at times by the corporate entity. Wherever you can, tear off the corporate mask and state your legal problem in flesh and blood terms—the solution of a customer's pressing problem—an increase in employment, better working conditions and better earnings.... [Present] the personal element which you hope equals justice for your client [and] to which the judicial ear is particularly attuned." Smith, "Corporate Legal Philosophy," in Proceedings of Wisconsin's 10th Annual Corporate Lawyers Institute 151-52 (1965).

[7] D. Bell, The Coming of Post Industrial Society: A Venture in Social Forecasting 43 (1973).

is no longer merely economistic. Both in their organization and in their actions, the clients of elite lawyers deny the differentiation of leadership in society. They recognize that the business sector can generate political, cultural, and even legal innovations. Conversely, they recognize that laws do not create only contingencies to tactically negotiate. Laws often require strategic responses.

Yet, in an era in which equity reigns, lawyers have become rule-formalists. In an era in which businesses are becoming socially responsive, lawyers have forsaken their strategic role as advisors. Lawyers were not formalists and tacticians in the age of the robber barons.[8] Yet today, when courts and corporations seek responsiveness, if not responsibility, lawyers accept specialization and avoid leadership.

Doesn't the law provide its practitioners with the opportunity to integrate social needs and institutional forms and purposes? Yet, lawyers feel helpless and cry that they can't control their fate. Instead of blaming the devils of our time, I will argue that this fate results from choices about the structure of the legal profession and about what constitutes an ethical professional lawyer.

THE IDEOLOGICAL DEVILS: COMPLEXITY, BIGNESS AND SPECIALIZATION

SPECIALIZATION AND REPUTATION: ALTERNATE MARKETING DEVICES

If specialization is a devil, lawyers have certainly embraced it.[9] It is often argued that specialization is *the* fact of life of modern law practice. The argument here is that specialization is not in itself an evil. After all, the yearning for a generalist is often the yearning for a hero.[10] Specialization can take many forms. It is the form specialization takes in large corporate practice that is troubling. Although specialization in the large law firms has not led to routinization, it has engendered a retreat into technique, at the expense of power and leadership. Thus, it is "both a factor in and an

---

[8] J. W. Hurst, The Legitimacy of the Business Corporation in the Law of the United States 1780-1970, at 69 (1970); R. W. Gordon, Legal Thought and Legal Practice in the Age of American Enterprise, 1870-1920: Towards an "Ideological" Approach to Legal History (unpublished, dated Nov. 1980) [hereinafter cited as Gordon].

[9] See Laumann and Heinz, "Specialization and Prestige in the Legal Profession: The Structure of Deference," 1977 ABF Res. J. 155 (1977); Cal. St. Bar. Comm. on Spec., "Preliminary Report," 44 Cal. St. B. J. 140 (1969) (2/3 reported being de facto specialists); Ill. St. Bar Assn., "Economics of Legal Services in Illinois: A 1975 Special Bar Survey," 64 Ill. B. J. 73 (1975) (a little more than 1% of 2,000 respondents labeled themselves "general practitioners"). Writing on legal specialization is extensive; for a bibliography, see "Selected Checklist of Materials on Specialization," 34 Rcd. Assoc. Bar City N. Y. 441 (1979).

[10] V. Thompson, Modern Organization, 2d Ed., vii (1977): "Some people approach the problem of bringing knowledge and authority together [by urging] 'generalists' rather than specialists. A little thought will disclose all such proposals to be essentially regressive—a search for a hero or a magic helper."

expression of subordination."[11] Although specialization is a market asset to the lawyer and the law firm, it has brought on the malaise in the legal practice.

It is very hard to define what constitutes legal specialization.[12] There are various types of specialization. Lawyers may specialize by limiting the subject matters, clients or industries of their practice. Their specialties may also be defined by the forums in which they appear, the technical tools they employ, the side they prefer to take, and the willingness to invest time in particular matters.[13] The scope of specializations varies considerably. A federal litigation specialist may take on all types of cases handled by federal courts, while an antitrust lawyer may only litigate portions of the Sherman Act. Furthermore, the credentials to back up a claim of specialization vary greatly. A lawyer may claim to be a patent specialist because he holds an engineering B.S., advanced legal degree, attends seminars, is involved with a high-tech client, has handled one particularly involved case, or because he has a lifetime of practice in the patent field with a patent-law firm.

Specialization is best thought of as a marketing device. The ABA recognized this point when it defined a legal specialist as "a lawyer who develops and maintains an expertise in a field of legal doctrine, a legal skill or function, or a type of client *sufficient to distinguish himself from his fellow lawyers.*"[14] Except in those states which license a limited number of specialties, the lawyer chooses whether to distinguish himself in the marketplace by claiming a specialty. It is not surprising, given the pressures to attain a market position, the uncertainties of evaluating lawyer performance and the poor social control device of malpractice actions, that a survey of 2,000 Illinois attorneys found only a little over 1% labeled themselves "general practitioners."[15]

---

[11] M. Sarfatti Larson, The Rise of Professionalism: A Sociological Analysis, at 231 (1977). Contra, Laumann and Heinz, *supra*, at 207. Laumann and Heinz tell us that "[l]awyers who influence the expenditure of many millions of dollars, who determine whether corporate acquisitions or mergers will or will not take place, undeniably have an important sort of power." Yet, they also tell us that these lawyers have little autonomy. *Id.* at 210. The argument here helps explain this contradiction. Lawyers, "present at the creation" in important matters, forsake their power through choices they and their profession have made—choices summarized by the ideological devils.

[12] The courts have been faced with this task in determining the standard of care to be used in malpractice litigation. They have determined it "must be done on a case by case basis." R. Mallen & V. Levitt, Legal Malpractice, at 330 (2d ed. 1981). See also Note, "Regulation of Legal Specialization: Neglect by the Organized Bar," 56 Notre Dame Law. 293 (1980).

[13] Johnstone, "An Introduction to Specialization and Certification," ALI-ABA CLE Rev. # 15 (1973) (recognizing the matter, forum, skill, client and industry types), noted in Mindes, "Proliferation, Specialization and Certification: The Splitting of the Bar," 11 U. Tol. L. Rev 273, 279 (1980).

[14] A.B.A., Legal Specialization, Specialization Monograph #2, at 3 (1976) (emphasis added).

[15] Ill. St. Bar Assn., *supra*.

Specialization can be marketed either on the basis of its effectiveness or efficiency. Law firms have used it in their marketing primarily to stress their efficiency. As with other forms of rationalization, the claim to specialized efficiency emphasizes the technique, rather than its wielder. The office, not the official, becomes the focus.[16] Law firms' increased efficiency has not come through routinization. Although the use of form files and similar tools has expanded, elite lawyers' efficiency has increased because the breadth of their work has decreased. The efficiency of elite lawyers increases when their learning curve for new problems decreases. When lawyers need not customize their work for the client nor re-think the peculiar facts of the client's situation, then they are efficient from the lawyer's perspective. Such lawyers perform delimited and separable tasks. They are not "institutional actors" for the corporations they serve.[17] If lawyers were institutional actors for their corporate clients facing problems that require the exercise of discretionary judgments based on knowledge about the corporation as a whole, it would not be more efficient to act as a specialist than a generalist. Specialization is only efficient when there are delimited tasks requiring the mastery of limited information.[18]

Other studies of the corporate bar have recognized the relationship between the legal profession's increased specialization and lawyers' acceptance of not being institutional actors. These studies, however, have never been spelled out the consequences of this relationship for the quality of legal service's output. Heinz and Laumann found a correlation between specialization and "skills in handling highly technical procedures rather than skills in negotiating and advising clients."[19] In another article, they found a statistically significant correlation between prestige corporate specialties and a lack of freedom of action for the lawyer.[20] They explain these correlations by assuming that corporations are knowledgeable about their internal affairs and have decision-making structures to advise them.[21] Although Heinz and

---

[16] This result matches the needs of the large firm. Any law firm must convince the client to accept that his work will be handled mainly by associates. By selling legal work as specialized knowledge not dependent on the character of the "name" attorney, the large firm accomplishes this task.

[17] The term "institutional actor" is Philip Selznick's. This is in accord with Heinz and Laumann's treatment of specialization not as a function of legal expertise but as a function of the "characteristics of the clients and of their use of lawyers." Heinz & Laumann, "The Legal Profession: Client Interests, Professional Roles, and Social Hierarchies," 76 Mich. L. Rev. 1111, 1125 (1978).

[18] The fact that specialization tends to minimize the information required for a lawyer's work and results in diminished lawyer involvement with client choices is an example of what Thompson calls "buffering the technical core." By developing an inward-looking attitude, the law firm seeks "to seal off their core technologies from environmental influences." J. Thompson, Organizations in Action 19 (1967).

[19] Heinz & Laumann, *supra*, at 1123.

[20] Laumann & Heinz, *supra*, at 210.

[21] *Id.* at 168.

Laumann found, as we did here, that elite law firms are not institutional actors for the corporations they serve, their explanation is inadequate for two reasons. First, they take an overly formal view of corporate decision-making processes. The presence of structured decision paths does not preclude the exercise of influence by individuals outside those paths. Second, their explanation of the existing low demand for lawyers' discretionary judgments does not take into account the supply side of the equation. Due to the economics of large firm practice, specialized lawyers do not offer customized discretionary advice to their clients.

Historically, lawyers have been institutional actors in corporations. A distinctive feature of the American bar was that its elite members served as institutional actors for business. "In such men as Elihu Root and Louis D. Brandeis the bar developed a type of leader peculiarly its own," summarized legal historian Willard Hurst. "Such men mingled the roles of barrister, solicitor, business advisor, and statesman."[22] As a result of the growth of specialization, the legal role has changed. Where legal expertise once included and emphasized an understanding of business relationships, today legal practice's intellectual challenge is understood to be grasping the rapidly changing substantive and procedural law. This inward-looking legalism has had a profound impact on the role of the lawyer and on the lawyer-client relation.

His expertise can help the lawyer attain power. Because the client lacks the professional's specialized knowledge, the client must accept the professional's assessment of whether a problem exists, how it should be handled and what constitutes its adequate resolution. Both professionals' ethical conduct codes and socialization ideally function to prevent abuses of this power. When these fail to adequately protect the client, however, the monopolization of expertise normally serves the professional not the client or society. As Eliot Freidson studying the medical profession and Douglas Rosenthal examining parts of the legal profession,[23] among others, have uncovered, expertise can enable the professional to take the matter out of the client's hands and to substitute his interests for that of the client.

Elite lawyers' expertise, however, does not give them power. The specialization of the elite bar, which is inward-looking and legalistic, lessens rather than strengthens their influence. As Heinz and Laumann report, their evidence "suggests somewhat ironically that lawyers doing high-prestige work are less likely to define their clients' problems than are lawyers doing lower status work.... [T]he corporation planning a securities issue, an acquisition, or a merger will present a relatively specific set of issues to the lawyer."[24] Corporations employ a lawyer "to perform more or less well-

---

[22] J. W. Hurst, The Growth of American Law 310-11 (1950).

[23] E. Freidson, Professional Dominance: The Social Structure of Medical Care (1970); D. Rosenthal, Lawyer and Client: Who's In Charge? (1974).

[24] Heinz & Laumann, *supra*, at 1138.

defined services."[25] Lawyers' power is limited to determining legal tactics. Given the large corporation's potential for doing harm while complying with legal formalities, this limitation on elite lawyers' responsibilities and freedom of action is not merely ironic. It is also potentially tragic. Because formal compliance will not always prevent the equitable imposition of liability, this result may even be inefficient from the corporate client's perspective. As one lawyer summarized his frustration to me:

> The law firm used to really learn a lot about their clients: what marketing strategies they had, why if they needed more capital it should be debt vs. equity, or what kinds of problems they've had in issuing convertible securities and why they should go to private placement or to public equity.

> Today, we can't help with planning questions. Before a company, for example, decides to do an acquisition, there is discussion and planning of where they want to go, the nature of their business, where their markets are and where they are weak and we are not privy to that. Sure questions come up in the course of an acquisition, e.g. antitrust questions, and we get called up to give them advice on the dangers—Treaty of Rome or U.S. antitrust law questions—but you are given a question which is a defined task and you are hired as a hired gun to answer the question. They say "thank you" and you are through with that. They then put it into the hopper with advice they get from their accountants or maybe McKinsey. Since legal advice is so sensitive to facts, you don't know what use you've been when the final decision is made. But there is nothing we can do. We don't negotiate with clients about structuring their relation with us. We do what they want.

Although this lawyer's frustration accurately reflects the fate of modern practice, he seems oblivious to the fact that the marketing of specialization that made his 150+ person law firm possible might be partially responsible for the situation he deplores. If the sociology of the professions teaches us anything, it teaches us that professionals have great autonomy in determining the scope of their work. Professionals don't do just what clients want. They teach clients about what they offer. Consequently, instead of studying only clients' demand, I also have studied what lawyers choose to supply. In the face of court readiness to consider equity responsiveness and client readiness to engage in "sociologizing" decision-making, law firms have exercised control in choosing to supply technical specialists. What alternatives then exist to marketing specialized efficiency?

From the legal profession's perspective, the only alternative to marketing one's services based on specialized abilities is to claim superior character and judgment.[26] Traditionally, reputation in the community, which was understood as synonymous with character and judgment, was considered the proper manner for attracting clients.[27] In fact, the traditional ethical standards of the bar may be interpreted as attempts to insure that lawyers were chosen solely on the basis of their reputation for good character and judgment.[28]

To those who long for the days when clients chose as their lawyers gentlemen, not specialized technicians, three replies are usually made. First, lawyers who stake their market position on their reputation will lose out to specialists in a competitive market. Although it is commonly asserted that specialization is a means for broadening one's client base, this claim is not self-evident for at least two reasons. First, gentlemen lawyers never appeared to have had limited client pools. Second, specialization can limit one's client pool as well as broaden it. In certain geographical areas, experts in construction contracts, computer patent law, admiralty or airplane disaster litigation don't have many potential clients. Historically, specialists emerged not to increase a firm's competitive advantage in the market but to hold on to a client already in its stable. In these situations, specialization makes the firm more dependent on its clients rather than lessening it, as is generally argued. The second argument against reputation as a marketing device is that we are no longer a society in which the pattern of reputation referrals is possible. While this argument may be true for society as a whole,[29] it is not obviously relevant to the corporations who are the major clients of elite lawyers. One need not be an instrumental Marxist versed in the patterns of interlocking directorships and the uniformity of the power elite to recognize that reputation has a way of travelling in the dominant business community. The third argument against reputation as the marketing device of choice is more

---

[26] See H. Drinker, Legal Ethics xii-xiii (1953). Specialization and reputation are not the only techniques to attain a market position. Publicity and success records are alternate marketing devices, but both are proscribed by the profession. Until recently, lawyers were not allowed to advertise their services. Although elite lawyers sneered at the crass ways men like F. Lee Bailey used to garner publicity, they too found ways to publicize their services. Old-boy networks, attendance at meetings of the bar and commerce, as well as the appointment of famous men to the firm letterhead were among the ways the large law firms sought publicity. We only have anecdotal information about the importance of publicity to large law firm marketing. Sociologists have accepted the legal profession's position that publicity only works when it is backed by lawyers with satisfactory specializations and reputations. Regaling successes is another marketing approach. Professional ideology also condemns this approach, maintaining the justness of the cause, not the lawyer's talent, should predominantly determine success. Elite firms play on this argument when they contend that their success/lost ratio should not be examined because as a result of their superior abilities they get a disproportionate share of the tough and close (read: unjust and losing) cases.

[27] J. Auerbach, Unequal Justice: Lawyers and Social Change in Modern America 16-17 (1976).

[28] *Id.* at 40-53.

[29] Auerbach, *supra*, at 21 and passim.

to the point. Reputation can buttress parochialism. For example, the traditional ethical standards of the bar favored gentlemen, not gentlewomen or gentlepeople of color and ethnic heritage.[30]

This third argument reveals an inherent ambiguity in marketing one's reputation for character and judgment. As labeling theory has taught us, reputation may refer to a pre-existing predicate of the actor or it may refer to a label generated by interaction. Put another way, a gentleman may be a responsible leader or a gentleman may be a person who acts according to the prevailing standards of the situation. If the traditional ethical standards merely endorsed lawyers who could frictionlessly adapt themselves to their clients' requirements, the standards did not uphold the autonomy of the bar. In fact, the rather effortless transition to a specialized bar would support the theory that a lawyer's reputation merely implied an agreeableness on his part. Or as many young associates will tell you, learning to have "judgment" really means learning how not to make waves.

Reputation, then, failed to compete with specialization as a marketing device because it added nothing. Although it may have furthered the profession's ability to attain a monopoly and restrict entry, reputation offered nothing to the clients. Both lawyers with good reputations and lawyers with specialized skills can be agreeable. The profession never adequately spelled out the substantive values implied by a reputation for character and judgment. To discover alternatives to specialization, these values must be uncovered. I will explore the values, character traits and predispositions that might serve as the basis of an attorney's reputation in the following historical and the empirical results reported in Chapters 2 through 4.

SPECIALIZATION AND THE LEGITIMATION OF THE LEGAL PROFESSION

The nature of professional practice is determined not only by what is remunerative, but also by what the profession estimates to be "honorable, respectable, clean and prestige giving."[31] In this section, I will discuss specialization in terms of the legal profession's search for legitimacy, relating it to the three tasks of the legal profession's "professionalization project."[32] The tasks are the need to separating lawyering from politics, separating lawyers from the causes they expound, and depoliticizing inequalities in the distribution of legal services. The legitimacy of the legal profession, its capacity to generate honor, respect and prestige, depends on meeting these three tasks.

---

[30] See Auerbach, *supra.*

[31] E. C. Hughes, Men and Their Work 70 (1958), quoted in G. Greenwood & R. Frederickson, Specialization in the Legal and Medical Professions, at 52 (1964).

[32] The term is from M. S. Larson, The Rise of Professionalism: A Sociological Analysis (1977).

SEPARATING LAW FROM POLITICS

As Morton Horwitz tells us, "The desire to separate law and politics has always been a central aspiration of the American legal profession.... If law is simply a product of power or will, any special claims of the profession to determine the nature and scope of legal development is undermined. The special power of the legal profession in American society has always been grounded in some theory of the distinctively objective and autonomous nature of law."[33] When the legitimacy of business is under attack, it is not surprising that lawyers try to separate their work from business. In the late nineteenth century, legal reasoning's formality was enough to differentiate lawyers from businessmen. The revolt against formalism has gone too far, however, so that lawyers cannot help but be implicated when they extend the formal rights of predatory capitalism. In the twentieth century, lawyers stress their independence, their fidelity to objective law, and their inability to constrain their clients. Those not satisfied by those defenses are pointed to the political arena: "Make stronger laws and we will be more forceful in dealing with our clients."

In relations with their clients, lawyers also separate law from politics.[34] Having attained class and status perquisites during the entrepreneurial age, the legal profession hesitates to bet these perquisites against a promise of helping to maintain its client's capital generating abilities. Given the avowed purposes of the regulatory state and the uncertainties of the economy, lawyers now try to differentiate their tasks from the concerns of capital acquisition, generation and maintenance. They stress the complexities of mastering the law and prefer to leave lobbying to others.

Technical specialization thus functions to separate law from politics. In response to critics of the *status quo*, lawyers stress their lack of control over their big clients. In response to their client's demands, lawyers stress the complexity of the law and the necessity to specialize, so that their practice is relatively impermeable to non-legal considerations.

SEPARATING ADVOCACY FROM ESPOUSAL

As is true in all professions, the legal role's legitimacy depends on its affective-neutrality, to use Parsons' term. In their work, lawyers profess public knowledge. They do not join their clients' private missions. Given our cultural identification of voice and self, it's especially problematic for the legal profession to serve clients while being affectively-neutral. Lawyers often

---

[33] M. J. Horwitz, The Transformation of American Law, 1780-1860, at 256 (1977). See Howe, Book Review, 60 Harv. L. Rev. 839 (1947). See also M. J. Horwitz, *supra*, at 253-256; A. J. Paul, Conservative Crisis and the Rule of Law: Attitudes of Bar and Bench 1887-1895 (1960).

[34] Washington practice is an interesting exception to this argument.

have been criticized as "Men that hire out their Words and Anger."[35] As Judge Frankel states, that's an "old story"[36] which lawyers know how to counter. The lawyer is speaking "for" the client, not for himself. He represents clients; he doesn't espouse causes.

In a society without shared public discourse, beset by divisive conflicts, and where lawyers continually represent only one class of clients, the distinction between speaking for and with one's client is not easy maintain. Because the client "may even feel a need to have a lawyer sympathize with his position,"[37] it becomes especially difficult to deny that one espouses the client's position. In practice, the lawyer's ability to be affectively-neutral is constrained by the absence of shared public discourse. Clients believe that "[i]t is important that the lawyer, in discussing a client's problems, speak the client's language, both literally and symbolically...that the lawyer and client share a range of discourse."[38]

Although the legitimacy of the lawyer's role depends on his being affectively-neutral, practice requires that the lawyer be the client's friend. Given the conditions of modern practice, the lawyer must become Charles Fried's "special purpose friend"[39]—a concept Aristotle would have considered oxymoronic. To create such a relationship, and at the same time maintain that the criticisms of legal advocacy are merely the "old story," lawyers must insure that problems are amenable to a "checklist of symptoms" and make their actions "follow a standard format."[40] The lawyer serves a "special purpose." His service is different from other services. His service is unrelated to many of his client's needs and is concerned with only a limited number of consequences. In short, legal specialization creates a defined and delimited discourse so that we can distinguish advocacy from espousal.

DEPOLITICIZING THE DISTRIBUTION OF LEGAL SERVICES

Inequality in the distribution of legal resources is one of the forces de-legitimating the law and the legal profession. The government acknowledged this problem when it introduced neighborhood legal services programs: "By giving the poor ready access to lawyers when needed, a sense of respect for

---

[35] The Spectator, #21, quoted in M. E. Frankel, Partisan Justice, at 29 (1978).

[36] M. E. Frankel, *ibid.*

[37] Heinz & Laumann, *supra*, at 1139.

[38] *Ibid.*

[39] Fried, "The Lawyer as Friend: The Moral Foundations of the Lawyer-Client Relationship," 85 Yale L. J. 1060 (1976).

[40] Heinz and Laumann, *supra*, at 1130. This is in accord with scientism's attempt to systematically deny personality as a condition of events. William James thought that this systematic denial was science's most serious defect. See W. James, The Philosophy of William James 203 (Modern Library Edition).

law...would begin to replace a general cynicism in the low income communities where legal institutions and processes seem alien and hostile."[41] Legal specialization both maintains inequalities in the provision of legal services and depoliticizes these inequalities. The "haves" who can afford specialists come out ahead and they do so, it appears, because they have better lawyers.[42]

Because legal practice is an exercise in the competitive handling of information, merely extending the availability of legal services will not reconcile diverse interests. Specialization provides the lawyer with a capital fund of information and restricts successful entry by outsiders. Specialists

> in any arena of practice develop numerous "understandings" among themselves and with the institutional personnel who operate the arena. These understandings provide the software by which the formal system is able to work, determining the procedural and substantive applicability of the formal rules of the system.[43]

These "understandings" discriminate against nonspecialized lawyers and their clients. Single shot players have difficulty competing with repeat players not only because the law is vast and complicated, but also because these understandings are informal and overriding. But, these understandings appear to be politically neutral.

Specialists and their clients have little to fear from the extension of legal services. Legal processes will continue to discriminate against clients who do not have the social or economic resources to obtain the specialist's services while simultaneously restricting the material relevant for consideration by legal institutions. The poor will get lawyers and the rich will get specialists. Extension of legal services thereby legitimates the legal system without affecting outcomes, except that specialists' services become ever more precious.

COMPLEX DECISIONS: THE IMPERMEABILITY OF DIFFERENTIATED SPECIALIZATION

The type of specialization we have been describing can be called "differentiated specialization."[44] Its essential feature is that legal norms are

---

[41] U.S. Dept. Health, Educ. and Welfare, Neighborhood Legal Services—New Dimensions in the Law 4 (1966), quoted in Lefcourt, "Lawyers for the Poor Can't Win," in Law Against the People 134 (R. Lefcourt ed. 1971).

[42] Galanter, "Why the 'Haves' Come Out Ahead: Speculations on the Limits of Legal Change," 9 L. & Soc. Rev. 95 (1974).

[43] Mindes, *supra*, at 278.

[44] The proper term, following Weber, would be "rational specialization." To avoid misleading those who do not follow Weber's special use of rationality, I have not used that

distinguished from norms governing in other arenas. Legal reason is a thing wholly apart.[45] Even its greatest advocates, for example, do not argue a good businessman or parent should think like a lawyer.

The differentiated specialist's hallmark is an insensitivity to pragmatic considerations. To maintain his competitive advantage, the differentiated specialist must shroud the law and build institutional mazes. Although the legislature and the judiciary have generally contributed to these developments in the law, differentiated specialists have advanced them. All specialists become "fixated on their own special techniques and subject matter."[46] They tend to perceive evidence and materials outside the tunnel vision of their specialties as criticisms[47] and seek to eliminate competition by others who "organize the problems differently."[48] Although they recognize means and ends interact, their focus is never on the ends and they use anti-competitive devices to prevent consideration of the ends. If the legal system will not accomplish the client ends, the issues become a matter for administrative reform and client choice, not lawyerly concern.[49]

---

term. Instead, I follow Parsons', speaking of differentiation. As in Parsons, the rub here is the lack of integrative mechanisms to transform this differentiation into an adaptive upgrading.

[45] It is esoteric and artificial. As Blackstone pointed out, in the law a bastard has no ancestors. 1 W. Blackstone, Commentaries on the Laws of England 290 (std. pagination).

[46] Mindes, *supra*, at 276. See also Laski, "The Limitations of the Expert," Senate Comm. on Gov't Operations, Specialists and Generalists (1968). Chief Justice Warren expressed the point as follows: "There are thousands of lawyers... As a result...we find that ordinarily lawyers specialize [which]...tends to segmentize the law and, to some extent, emphasizes the mechanics of the law as distinguished from a broad sense of justice acquired from familiarity with the legal problems of people of different walks of life in a variety of situations." Warren, "Law, Lawyers and Ethics," 23 DePaul L. Rev. 633, 635 (1974). The point is not to attack specialization. That is an essential in our society. The point is to attack a type of specialization in which the profession develops as a craft, rather than as an instrument of justice.

[47] See Leff, "Injury, Ignorance and Spite—The Dynamics of Coercive Collection," 80 Yale L.J. 1 (1970), and other sources cited in Mindes, *supra*, at 281.

[48] Mindes, *supra*, at 280.

[49] To demonstrate that differentiated specialization is not the only possible type of specialization, consider the classic legal specialty, admiralty law. Admiralty law did not emerge as a specialty in this century. In this century, however, it moved from being an undifferentiated specialty to being a differentiated one. Specialization in admiralty cases has always been required because of the special norms that apply to them. Admiralty law differs from common law; admiralty procedure, based on civil not common law, differs from procedures in other areas; and admiralty has its separate forums. (See G. Greenwood & R. Frederickson, *supra*, at 79, and sources cited therein.) To be a "proctor in admiralty" required special expertise. But, proctors in admiralty were not the differentiated specialists who now characterize the bar. As one admiralty lawyer stated at the ABA hearings on specialization: "I do want to make one point wherein we differ from the patent people. We do not think we are specialists. We think *we* are the most general generalists at the bar. We get into the bankruptcy field, the taxation field, general and state, with and without juries. Our clients are in every kind of legal hot water that can be imagined. We think we are

To comprehend the consequences of differentiated specialization, consider just one type of legal work, litigation. Whether to settle a case is a central decision in any litigation process. In fact, over 90% of filed cases are disposed of through settlement. One increasingly popular technique for deciding when to settle is litigation risk analysis. This method is a technique of differentiated specialization. Briefly, litigation risk analysis means the lawyer advises the client on whether to settle based on the his measurements of the chances for victory and of the various exposures the client faces in any later settlement or decision on the merits. In a simple case, if a $100,000 settlement offer is offered and the exposure is $200,000, then the client should settle assuming the chance of losing is greater than 50%. Clearly the risks of various legal outcomes are the key parameters in this analysis. The differentiated specialist attorney, who is privy to the implicit understandings of the legal process, is best able to make such judgments.

Knowledge of the client's business will not make the attorney more competent to engage in litigation risk analysis. Competency in litigation risk analysis requires an inward-looking legalistic perspective. Yet, the lawyer who is familiar with his client's business may recognize other litigation costs beyond the exposures amounts. He may know how the settlement would affect the company's employees and shareholders. He might better assess its effect on the chances for further disputes later on. He might be able to forecast future events in the industry. Due to his knowledge of the client, he might be better able to predict the facts that will emerge at trial than the differentiated specialist and thus produce a different risk estimate of the various legal outcomes. He might be better able to judge both his client's and opponent's management flexibility. And, finally, he might be better able to determine the practices his client should implement to future litigious situations.

The differentiated specialist would not deny the importance of any of these factors. All this information is useful, he would respond, but it is

---

exceedingly general, not a specialty." (*Id.* at 88.) Admiralty lawyers were general counsel to their clients. They functioned as institutional actors, assuming business leadership roles. Admiralty law, despite its special rituals, did not look inward, instead it focused on the practicalities of commerce and the shifting common notions of equity. Although admiralty law had its special procedures and esoteric language, its practitioners did not develop the legalistic tunnel vision of the differentiated specialist. Pragmatic considerations were at the heart of the admiralty specialty. It was not uncommon for firms to require that "new employees must have had sailing experience or must be willing to work a short time on lake vessels...a certain amount of technical knowledge of vessels and knowledge of seamen's duties and prejudices is deemed important." (Testimony of one practitioner quoted in *id.* at 17.) In part this was due to the fact that the market which supported this type of admiralty practice was particularly stable and noncompetitive. It has been estimated that a dozen firms handled at least 75% of all U.S. admiralty business. Client loyalty was strong. Firms functioned as general counsel and at least one steamship company maintained its connection to one law firm for over a century. (*Id.* at 81. The century long relation is from *id.* at 87.) For the firm, the investment in having one's lawyers learn about one's client's business could thus be expected to be repaid over time.

information that the corporate client should possess. Because the knowledge is not distinctively legal, the lawyer's task is not to uncover it. Given the turbulence and complexity of the legal environment, a division of labor is necessary. These issues are the client's business, not the lawyer's.[50]

I will deal with issues of what is and is not the lawyer's business, what is a legal concern, throughout this work.[51] At this point, let us examine two consequences of the choice between a differentiated and an undifferentiated approach to specialization that are suggested by comparative data. The first consequence affects the status of the legal profession and the second affects the nature of legal institutions.

In England and the Commonwealth, differentiated specialization has progressed further than in the United States. In England, for example, accountants and labor specialists deal with problems we would normally assign to lawyers.[52] Differentiated specialization enables other professions to supplant the legal profession. Of course, lawyers may desire this result, especially if it means turning over repetitive and routine work. It is doubtful that the elite commercial bar would mourn the loss of collections, residential real estate transactions, foreclosures and the like to other professions.

The choice of transactions to be performed by lawyers, however, was not well thought out in England and the Commonwealth. An Attorney General of Australia, in introducing a new antitrust law, took it upon himself "to remind lawyers of the functions lost in the past to other professionals by refusal to widen their knowledge and skills, and the stultification of new fields which must yet follow if they persisted in this refusal."[53] To the English businessmen "the emphasis has changed from lawyer's law to accountants' law and bankers' law,"[54] as a result of differentiated specialization. Consequently, in England "[t]he lawyer's status in business circles" is one of "diminishing prestige and prosperity."[55] And status is not the only thing on the decline.

---

[50] See also Miller, "Public Law and the Obsolescence of the Lawyer," 19 U. Fla. L. Rev. 514, 529 (1966-67) (discussing dependence of lawyers to economists and engineers in developing impact statements); "Board 'Outsiders' Win Favor," N.Y. Times 3/30/83 (Directors claiming lawyers take narrow, legalistic viewpoint and misserve their clients).

[51] Cf. V. Aubert, The Sociology of Law 174 (1964): "Bentham once said that 'jurisprudence can be defined as the art of being methodologically ignorant of what everybody knows. And Veblen coined the phrase trained incapacity'... To learn a specialty means to adopt a differential attention to the environment, whereby that which forms the nucleus of the specialty pushes aside that which is professionally irrelevant. Let it suffice to say that a systematic mapping of the *irrelevancies* of the various professions is a sociological task of the first order. It is one of the important ways in which the sociological description of a profession differs from the description which the profession gives of itself."

[52] J. Stone, Social Dimensions of Law and Justice 58 (1966).

[53] *Ibid.*

[54] L. C. B. Gower, "Business," in Law and Opinion in England in the 20th Century 143, 169 (M. Ginsberg ed. 1959).

[55] *Ibid.*

Fees are also being reduced.[56]

Although it is easier to measure the negative effects of differentiated specialization on the legal profession, it has also been argued that the law itself suffers from unplanned differentiated specialization. In England, where the legal profession "allowed the law to become so out of touch with realities that the customer has lost interest in our [the legal profession's] wares...[t]he law lost contact with business. Mercantile custom has ceased to be a reviving source of the common law.[57] English law now develops as a result of legalistic conflicts. Commercial interests are left to the business client, resulting in the law and the lawyer manifesting a "growing remoteness from commercial realities."[58]

Of course, it could be argued that the results of differentiated specialization are all for the better. Lawyers' status is too high and they are overused. The law works best when it is interstitial. Individuals should create their own frameworks and choose their own directions without the interference of the state and the state's law.

By examining the effect of differentiated specialization on legal control, we can effectively respond to this argument. We begin by reiterating the paradoxical fact that differentiated specialization arises just when legal institutions start to advance communitarian, not libertarian, values. Whatever its history, the law today is not interstitial. The regulatory process is inherently opposed to differentiated specialization. Effective regulation "presupposes the availability of knowledge and insights from several social sciences, and of the lawyer's receptiveness to these."[59] Lawyers and the corporations they serve are part of the regulatory process. When lawyers fail to be receptive to extra-legal considerations, and blind themselves to regulatory purpose by legalistically looking inward to a differentiated body of law, it only maximizes regulatory unreasonableness and increases regulatory costs to clients and society.

As Julius Stone argues, differentiated specialization prevents the lawyer from having "a balanced perspective over the contemporary social order and its problems."[60] Today's lawyers do not "earn such titles as 'architect' or designer,' 'founder' or 'father' " of collaborative structures because they do not engage in "finding common ground between antagonists, in articulation and persuasive expression, in mediating conflicts and formulating terms of compromise."[61] To the differentiated specialist, the law is not a "seamless

---

[56] *Ibid.*

[57] *Id.* at 168, 171.

[58] *Id.* at 172.

[59] J. Stone, *supra*, at 59.

[60] *Id.* at 60.

[61] *Ibid.*

web." "[I]f human life and knowledge were divided up into water-tight compartments, and it were possible to deal with each compartments by itself" then the differentiated specialists' approach would not be dysfunctional, argues Lord Macmillan. "But we cannot isolate any one factor in the social organism. The interrelations of the parts with each other and with the whole are infinitely complex."[62]

Stone goes too far in arguing that specialists do not recognize that they work on only a piece of the pie. Law firms contain a range of specializations and colleagues often consult one another. When a firm handles a corporate reorganization, for example, tax, labor, antitrust and other experts are brought together to assist the partner dealing with the case. Under the banner of differentiated specialization, however, this multidisciplinary approach often fails in two distinct ways. I have already touched on the first type of failure. Because these specialties are already differentiated, the experts may overlook commercial realities. The second type of failure results from differentiated specialization's affinity for a reactive stance. When various specialists are brought together in conference, they offer suggestions largely based on their specialties' substantive law. The law is the motivator and determiner of cross-fertilization. Each of the specialists has "an in-looking attitude."[63] They adopt their frame of reference from the law and fail to "initiate basic policies."[64] Differentiated specialization can make these lawyers "insensitive to influences which require change" and their approach "may be too far removed from the needs and desires of the public."[65]

If these conclusions derived from comparative research are supported by this study's data, then differentiated specialization serves neither the client nor the public. Lawyers respond to the legal environment rather than shaping it. Multi-specialty conferences develop issues, not architectonics. Specialists converge to identify the parameters that will increase their client's negotiating power. They are not brought together to create structures for collaboration. What they create are insurance arrangements. And insurance becomes ever more necessary where lawyers fail to respond to undifferentiated concerns.

LAWYERS AND "BIG" CLIENTS: THE BETRAYAL OF LEADERSHIP

An unintended consequence of differentiated specialization is that the lawyer has no defense against his clients' shifting their work to other

---

[62] Lord Macmillan, The Professional Mind (1934), quoted in G. Greenwood & R. Frederickson, *supra*, at 132 n.2.

[63] Gallagher, Proc. Nat. Conf. of Bar Presidents, Aug. 3-5, 1962, at 108 (1962), quoted in G. Greenwood & R. Frederickson, *supra*, at 132 n.2.

[64] G. Greenwood & R. Frederickson, *supra*, at 133.

[65] *Ibid.*

specialists in the same area of law. In other words, because differentiated specialization provides no basis for client loyalty, it is difficult for the lawyer to develop a stable pool of clients whom he represents on an on-going basis. Work that is based on an inward-looking legalistic orientation can be reproduced by another specialist after a very short learning curve.

In order to prevent fractious competition within the subgroup of specialists, lawyers use two tools to maintain client loyalty. First, attorneys develop personal relationships with the people in the organization supplying the information that is to be translated into legal forms. Second, law firms adapt themselves to fit their client's organization, thereby reducing transaction costs in the exchange of information between the client and the lawyer. This second tool is a standard of interorganizational linkages, termed "mapping" by organizational theorists. Through these devices, the law firm gains a position of competitive advantage over other specialists.

These tools have their cost. Law firms serve neither the corporate agents nor corporate sub-units. They represent "the corporation as an entity."[66] Furthermore, basing loyalty around frictionless transaction mechanisms hinders lawyers when they might need to exercise leadership.

An example can best reveal these costs. Consider a recent case that attracted a great deal of attention but which is in fact rather typical: O.P.M. Leasing Co. and the Singer Hutner law firm.[67] O.P.M.'s business was computer-leasing and it used the Singer Hutner firm to produce loan instruments, among other services. These loan instruments were implicated in a massive fraud, stemming from inaccurate data given to lenders by O.P.M. in these documents. The documents inflated the value of collateral, and the same collateral was used for different loans. Forged lease agreements also backed up the loans. Singer Hutner drafted the loan agreements and supplied opinions to the lenders about the legal status of O.P.M.'s title and lease agreements.

Although there is some controversy about the lawyers' knowledge of the fraud, at least two issues are incontrovertible. First, the lawyers' loyalty flowed to the O.P.M. agents who supplied them with the information that was the basis for their work. Second, the law firm limited its auditing of the client. Given that Singer Hutner rejected any leadership role during its representation of O.P.M., it is little wonder that the most that can be said in its defense is that they "were the instruments, the unwitting instruments, of

---

[66] ABA, Model Code of Professional Responsibility, EC 5-18 (1969); cf. ABA, Model Rules of Professional Conduct, Rule 1.13 (Proposed Final Draft, 1981) ("...represents the organization as distinct from its directors, employees, members, shareholders or other constituents").

[67] The account of this representation is drawn from Taylor, "Ethics and the Law: A Case History," N.Y. Times Magazine 31 (9 Jan. 1983).

the fraud."[68]

When informed that its contact man at O.P.M. had committed past frauds, Singer Hunter reacted at if its duties were owed to this agent of the corporation. The lawyers did not inform others at O.P.M. of the fraud, let alone defrauded third-parties, and they counseled their contact man that the attorney-client privilege covered past wrong-doing. The lawyers also informed the contact man that they could not be silent about future wrong-doing. When the contact man replied that he would defraud no more, the lawyers assumed that loyalty required them to believe him. During this period, they tried to convince their contact man "to try to be rational."[69]

This part of the story reveals not only the problem arising from loyalty to an agent, it also demonstrates the weakness of differentiated specialization. The agent certified that he would not engage in future frauds and the lawyers accepted that certification. The client, however, was engaged in a pyramid scheme. Even the most elementary economic analysis would indicate that the agent could not stop the frauds. That intelligent lawyers could testify that they did not recognize the economic implications of the scheme attests to the distortions engendered by differentiated specialization.

Singer Hutner's response also was partly determined by its "mapping" onto the client. They did not seek information from either O.P.M.'s internal or outside accountants. Because O.P.M.'s inside lawyer was not involved with the loan agreements, he was not contacted. In fact, Singer Hutner kept the inside lawyer in the dark about the instruments' problems even after the inside lawyer told them, "if something is wrong with these deals, then I want to know it today."[70] Absent some understanding of the organizational links engendered by differentiated specialization, it is particularly puzzling that Singer Hutner allowed the defrauding contact man to edit the memo it sent to the inside counsel on due diligence verification procedures. As a result the corporation was prevented from effectively auditing its organizational sub-units.

This case attracted national attention in part because it is a morality play. All involved paid for the continuing fraud. Where no one led, all fell. Although at this point, I will not prescribe what Singer Hutner should have done, I do stress that any recommendation should be mindful of the relation between Singer Hunter's professional stance and the organization of O.P.M. This situation arose because of Singer Hunter's loyalties to certain corporate agents against others and against the corporation "as an entity." It also developed because the lawyers' professional expertise was captured by the

---

[68] *Id.* at 48.
[69] *Id.* at 50.
[70] *Id.* at 49.

process of "mapping" which insulated organizational sub-units from other ones. The claim that the nature of the lawyer-client relation is relevant for ethical analysis therefore may appear self-evident. Yet, the legal ethics consultant Singer Hutner relied on throughout this episode asserts that one need not know anything about "the mechanics" of the relation.[71] This opinion, in fact, is the dominant one. Legal ethics are not based on empirical analysis. Perhaps empirical analysis can fuel moral action. Its absence does not impede costly morality plays, such as this one.

SPECIALIZATION AND THE RECONCILABILITY OF INTERESTS:
THE PSYCHOLOGICAL REDUCTION

At a minimum, all professional relationships are educative processes. As we have already seen, even as the legal profession strives to limit itself to a representative function, it is forced to admit that lawyers are friends.[72] The lawyer as friend to his client is "of counsel." The nature and extent of a lawyer's involvement with his client is a central choice in legal practice.

That lawyers not only represent clients but also counsel them appears to contradict the concept of differentiated specialization presented here. The current form of lawyers' counseling, however, does not refute but in fact advances the argument being developed. Even in counseling, the profession today separates the public and private aspects of the lawyer's role. Counseling is a private affair. Counseling does not mean merging the public and private, law and business, or law and moral choice. When the profession today talks about counseling, it does not speak of reconciling diverging interests, it speaks of psychological sensitivity.[73]

Consider, for example, the West Casebook on counseling by Harrop Freeman.[74] Its premise is that lawyers are counselors and not only representatives. As the author explains on the first page: "I recently heard the senior partner of perhaps New York City's largest law firm opine that 90% of his work was counseling in not strictly legal matters."[75] The student, perhaps preparing for that esteemed position, immerses himself in the text. The casebook covers marital-family, criminal and psycho-neurotic problems as well as business-financial problems. Certainly, the senior partner spends no more than a negligible amount of his counseling time on the first three. When the casebook moves from counseling in personal to business matters, however, it changes names and facts but not the nature of its analysis.

---

[71] *Id.* at 50.

[72] See discussion of Fried, *supra*.

[73] See sources cited in Simon, "Homo Psychologicus: Notes on a New Legal Formalism," 32 Stan. L. Rev. 487 (1980).

[74] H. Freeman, Legal Interviewing and Counseling: Cases and Materials (1964).

[75] *Id.* at 1.

Reading the casebook, one would conclude that divorcing marriage partners and fractious business partners pose identical problems for the lawyer. The analysis is totally devoid of the teachings of social psychology, organizational sociology and, one can only suspect, common sense. Business-financial dealings require counseling because businessmen are "frustrated"[76] or have "clammy hands"[77] and have difficulty facing business realities. The lawyer's counsel helps the beleaguered businessman bear up. Social reality finally intrudes into this bizarre scenario with a comment by David Riesman: "It seems to be that people can practice in either a huge Wall Street firm or alone on State Street and never face any of the kinds of experiences described in these reports."[78]

One might respond to this kind of book by claiming it does no harm, except in misrepresenting its usefulness to the student seeking to become a Wall Street partner. It might even be possible to justify the introduction of human relations into law school curriculums as an attempt to humanize law students and make them better human beings, if not better lawyers.[79]

In his analysis of this vision of the counseling function, William Simon criticizes it for conceptualizing the lawyer-client relation as a psychiatric "community of two,"[80] thereby denying the public responsibilities of the lawyer. The lawyer's goal is not to mediate between public values and private interest but to support the expression of private feelings and to help the client reconcile those feelings to the structures he faces. The lawyer's task becomes to "tune into feelings, his own and his client's."[81] His orientation is not to "justice in general" but to "the satisfaction of the parties."[82] Drawing on the well known critiques of existential psychology,[83] Simon analyzes how the seemingly humane attention of the lawyer to his client's "whole person" transforms legal practice into an apolitical, privatizing and alienated enterprise:

> By emphasizing the immediate and the personal aspects of the lawyer-client relation, the Psychological Vision obscures the consequences to those outside the relation which lawyering produces.

---

[76] *Id.* at 171.

[77] *Id.* at 186.

[78] *Id.* at 70.

[79] See Pincus, "The Clinical Component in University Professional Education," 32 Ohio St. B. J. 283 (1971).

[80] Simon, *supra*, at 492, 496-505. The term is Philip Rieff's, see The Triumph of the Therapeutic: Uses of Faith after Freud 52 (1966).

[81] Goodpaster, "The Human Arts of Lawyering: Interviewing and Counseling," 27 J. Legal Educ. 5, 5 (1975), quoted in *id.* at 506.

[82] C. Curtis, It's Your Law 3 (1954), quoted in *id.* at 507.

[83] See sources cited in *id.* at 490 n.7.

By celebrating the relation as an end in itself, it subverts the comparatively impersonal legal, social, and ethical considerations in terms of which consequences might be identified and the actions which produced them justified or condemned.[84]

By equating legal counseling with the techniques of existential psychology, the lawyer is oriented toward safeguarding the personal norms of trust and loyalty and focuses his attention away from the consequences of his actions. A single example can clearly illustrate this point. Freeman claims that Dean Griswold's argument for the importance of psychological understanding in labor law was one of the initial impetuses for "training the lawyer in human relations so that he may fill his role as counselor."[85] Griswold based his argument on the claim that labor "problems are often human rather than monetary."[86] The labor lawyer only exacerbated difficulties when he treated labor problems as legal problems, not as human ones.[87] A good labor lawyer would be sensitive to psychological dynamics and counsel management that "what the workers wanted most of all was to be someone, to *be* accepted as important, as belonging...."[88] The labor lawyer would help solve labor problems by assisting his client in recognizing the need for good public relations in the workplace. According to Griswold, a good labor lawyer knows that there are concerns beyond the questions of "liberty, due process, governmental power."[89]

Recognizing problems' psychological dimensions can be a move away from differentiated specialization. But casting the psychological dimension as an alternative to the law only intensifies differentiated specialization. As Simon describes the vision implicit in Griswold's approach:

> Here ... [s]atisfaction does not depend on the material world; it is merely a function of how people feel. Individuals do not need money as much as they need to be "accepted" as "people." To treat individuals as "people" means to ignore the distinctions of class, of wealth and power, which separate them and to emphasize the abstract affective needs they share. It means to flatter them, to encourage them to retreat from the social and material world to passive self-love. The price of being treated as "human" is acquiescence in the prevailing social and material inequalities....

---

[84] Simon, *supra*, at 502.

[85] H. Freeman, *supra*, at 1.

[86] Griswold, "Law Schools and Human Relations," 37 Chi. B. Rcd. 199, 206 (1956) [hereinafter Griswold], quoted in Simon, *supra*, at 521. See also Griswold, "Educating Lawyers for a Changing World," 37 A.B.A.J. 805 (1951).

[87] Griswold, "Law Schools and Human Relations," at 204.

[88] Griswold at 206, quoted in Simon, *supra*, at 521.

[89] Griswold at 199, quoted in Simon, *supra*, at 555.

[It is also] the anguish and terror [that arise when] claims of reason and justice evoke only a personal response.[90]

Dean Griswold's approach not only fails at the level of social analysis, it fails from the profession's point of view. As we have already seen, differentiated specialization allows other professions to encroach upon lawyers' territory. In the labor law area, human relations managers, industrial relations experts, and public relations staffs, rather than lawyers, today speak to managers about getting workers to "belong." Because Dean Griswold's vision did not link the affective needs of workers to industrial justice, lawyers could not compete with other experts. In accord with the logic of differentiated specialization, lawyers were relegated to handling the legal procedures involved in labor conflicts.

The problem is not merely that Dean Griswold's vision results in limiting the market for legal services. By failing to connect public and private realms, the psychological reduction of counseling restricts the law's domain in a manner which is neither efficient nor equitable. Ironically, organization theorists now analyze the ways public norms penetrate the organization. Unlike Dean Griswold, management theorists are convinced that concepts of liberty and due process must be incorporated into effective management of the workplace. As David Riesman long ago noted, the human relations movement—like the psychological reduction of counseling—was flawed by its failure to include the concept of justice in its conflict resolution process. It believed resolving conflict required "only the commodities interpersonal effort and tolerance—that the other directed person is already prepared to furnish."[91] Business schools now reject this approach. Strangely enough, law schools still accept it.

BALANCED CHOICES AND IMBALANCING SOCIAL CHANGES

In the previous sections, I argued that the triumph of differentiated specialization did not result from historical necessity. Its origins and growth are, instead, problems for research. I outlined how, at the level of legitimation processes, differentiated specialization appears to meet the legal profession's professionalization needs. Then, I described how in practice differentiated specialization fails to provide a coherent response to three basic dilemmas of any legal practice: the permeability of legal expertise, the leadership capabilities of the lawyer and the priority of client needs over other interests. Client needs for effective service and public needs for an equitable legal system require us to understand the potentials for transforming differentiated specialized legal practice.

---

[90] Simon, *supra*, at 521.

[91] D. Reisman, The Lonely Crowd, at 153 (1961).

In this section, I will present three alternative models of legal practice. The next section examines the careers of four exemplary lawyers and demonstrates the working out of these models in practice. These two sections begin a sketch of the social dependence of the lawyer's role.

Three models of legal practice have co-existed in America.[92] First, there is a republican model, advocated by such disparate figures as Whig-Federalists and Louis Brandeis. Second, there is the democratic model, also advocated by very different individuals, such as Jacksonians and so-called "strict constructionists." Third, there is the liberal model, advocated by progressives and the corporate elite.

The republican model understands law as a structure of rights and obligations mediating between the self and the public, between the elite and the masses. Law, in this model, is a variety of political and ethical argument. The lawyer is seen as a trustee, whose expertise is used in the service of society. Just as minors need trustees to curb their uneducated appetites, so society requires trustees to restrain the tyranny of the majority. The fiduciary relation he develops with his client and his training in public discourse enable the lawyer to function as society's trustee. Guarding his client's moneys, secrets and safety teaches the lawyer virtue. But the lawyer's fiduciary capacities are primarily acquired by his immersion in legal classics.

In the democratic model, society is ruled best by fraternal justice based on the conscience of everyman not on the arcane reason of the law. The law must be permeable, accommodating common morality. Rights should be defined not by the laws of the past, but by individuals within institutions and by legislatures based on "natural reason, universal justice, and present convenience."[93] The common man who is in touch with everyday and commercial realities and who can study and comprehend the law should exercise leadership. Because the conscience of everyman is the best guarantor of liberty, a lawyer is used strictly for instrumental reasons. He is only the client's agent.

The liberal model is an amalgam of the two previous models. Like the republican, it fears the tyranny of the majority. Stripping the embodied law of its function as *paideia*, the liberal model assumes the legal system is institutionally competent to accept but restrain common morality. To preserve this institutional competence, the liberal model must separate law from politics. In the liberal model, leadership resides not in everyman, but in the legislature. The liberal lawyer's allegiance is neither to his client nor to the commonweal. It is to the craft of the law.

---

[92] This account of the three models is drawn from Gordon.

[93] Sampson's Discourse, and Correspondence with Various Learned Jurists, upon the History of the Law, with the Addition of Several Essays, Tracts, and Documents, Relating to the Subject (P. Thompson, ed.) 32 (1826), quoted in M. Bloomfield, American Lawyers in a Changing Society, 1776-1876, at 76 (1976).

In the republican model, the lawyer attains status in proportion to the virtue he possesses. The democratic model challenges the elite status of the legal profession. In the liberal model, the lawyer is entitled to the status he can garner in the marketplace. To the liberal, the lawyer may have virtues, but they are the virtues of other craftsmen: "To the mass of practitioners, the law is not, except on rare occasions an intellectual pursuit.... We are clever men of business...and no more. It is our BUSINESS TALENTS, our PROMPTNESS, ACCURACY, and DILIGENCE, that commands success, respect and influence."[94] The liberal lawyer must learn, not leadership, but "[s]elf-control and a heightened consciousness of one's personal limitations and dependence on others."[95]

Before we examine these models in action, we should understand the appeal of the liberal model. Certainly it has been the dominant model in America. Its appeal does not depend on the importance of liberalism as a political philosophy. The liberal model's attractiveness results from its ability to render nugatory the second and third choices described above. In the liberal model, the lawyer is neither leader nor follower; he is a craftsman. In the liberal model, the lawyer need not choose between competing interests; the law chooses. The liberal lawyer's function is entirely different from that of either the republican lawyer or the democratic (pro se) attorney. In the republican and democratic models, the lawyer speaks about "how people should behave toward one another in a wide range of social situations where neither they themselves nor the legislature had prescribed express obligations."[96] The liberal lawyer does not prescribe behavior. His task is to ascertain whether an action can be sanctioned by the law. Where the law is silent, so is he. His is not an art or a science of conduct. His is a mechanical craft.

The lawyer can escape these choices only if the rule of law, the centerpiece of liberal political philosophy, is not only the basis for the social contract but also the motivator of all social action. The rule of law's interstitial character is one of the primary reasons the liberal model has never been the only model of lawyering in society. Because, as Weber long ago noted,[97] the rule of law does not guarantee the security of transactions, unplanned conflicts of interest need to be resolved. Because the rule of law tells people they are free to exercise discretion within protected spheres and does not guide discretionary judgments, leadership is required. To summarize two hundred years of jurisprudence in one sentence, neither an expansive economic sector nor deprived underclasses have limited their conduct to the juristic equality of the rule of law. At various times, deviating in various ways from the rule of

---

[94] From "Office Duties," Am. Law Reg. 4, 193 (1856) (emphasis in original), quoted in M. Bloomfield, *supra*, at 150-51.

[95] M. Bloomfield, *supra*, at 162-63.

[96] Gordon at 29.

[97] M. Weber, On Law and Economy in Society 308 (M. Rheinstein, ed., 1954).

law, they have sought lawyers who adopt the republican and democratic models. In the next section, I examine these models in practice, describing how all three persist in modern society and how in the face of social forces none has found an equilibrium position.

EXEMPLARY LAWYERS

In this section, the careers of four exemplary lawyers are examined. These men are not "representative." They are great lawyers. The tragedies of their practice should alert us that it is far too simple to reject the troubles of the modern corporate practitioner as the petty travails of Babbitts.

The four lawyers are Rufus Choate, Daniel Webster, John W. Davis and Louis D. Brandeis. In different ways, Choate, Webster and Brandeis spring from the republican model and Davis from the liberal model.[98] All had successful but troubled careers as lawyers. All re-shaped the models. Webster and Brandeis were more successful than Choate and Davis because they did not limit themselves to the lawyer's social role as prescribed by the model. Although the republican model idealizes public rhetoric, Webster found the model worked best in counseling in an office practice rather than oratorizing in a litigation practice. Although the republican model idealizes the classic arts as the inculcator of the legal spirit, Brandeis found the model operated best in the researcher and implementer of social science.

Rufus Choate

Rufus Choate experienced a tension all lawyers feel to some extent, the tension between being a businessman, "a specialized professional in a world of other specialized professionals,"[99] and being a guardian of civic virtue. For him, as for other republicans, this tension could be resolved through education and oratory. Although Choate recognized that legal education often appeared as a "sort of Ishmael...with its hand raised against all sorts of knowledge, that are liberal and refined but happen not to fall immediately within its own dominion,"[100] he thought the practicing lawyer could use liberal education. He advised those studying for the bar to remain in college because "no diligence in a profession can ever meet the want that liberality, breadth, comprehension and elegance of mind, taste and aims, which it is the specific function of university education to impart. One may grow dexterous, sharp, clever; but he will be an *artisan* only—narrow, illiberal, undeveloped,

---

[98] No example of the democratic model is discussed. For elite lawyers, the democratic model was a challenge. To retain their status, they had to demonstrate their superiority to the democratic model. Hence, to elite lawyers, the democratic model was the "background" against which they painted themselves.

[99] J. V. Matthews, Rufus Choate, The Law and Civic Virtue 28 (1980).

[100] H. S. Legare, quoted in *id.* at 18.

subordinate."[101]

Unlike other republicans, Choate did not believe that serving one's clients in itself taught virtue. Virtue came only through education and oratory. His idol was Cicero.[102] He read aloud daily a page from a noble author[103] to escape "those more specific, defined and limited attainments and accomplishments which ought to bound the aims of a man of business."[104] He absorbed classics to develop his skills as an orator. Choate saw three audiences for his oratory: his fellow lawyers, the public and the court.[105] Absent from this list were his clients. Surprisingly, perhaps, he did not consider it his duty to engage his clients in speech.

Choate spoke to his fellow lawyers. In the first half of the nineteenth century, the members of the bar spoke to one another in the most refined terms, as a way not only to continue their education in the law, but also to instill "a strong morale and an exalted conception of their function among lawyers themselves."[106] In oratory, the profession met the challenge of Jacksonian democracy. To maintain the republican image even when the client determined a lawyer's actions, the bar spoke to each other,[107] so much so that the bar was described by Perry Miller as a "speaking aristocracy."[108]

Choate also lectured to the public. His usual topics were the patriotic duties of a free citizenry and liberal learning. "[A] lecture by Choate on English poets could draw an audience of four thousand."[109]

In both forms of oratory, Choate's aim was to inculcate virtue.[110] In our psychological society, we often overlook the teaching power of words. Antebellum America, however, praised oratory for its ability to shape good habits and prompt correct action. Colleges trained students in rhetoric. Both in schools and in society, education was seen as merely the prerequisite to eloquence.[111] And, "careers were made and reputations established by the power to speak."[112]

---

[101] *Id.* at 26 (emphasis in original).

[102] *Id.* at 45.

[103] *Id.* at 44.

[104] *Id.* at 28 (emphases omitted).

[105] *Id.* at 43-49.

[106] *Id.* at 26.

[107] Matthews, *supra*, at 26.

[108] See P. Miller, The Life of the Mind in America: From the Revolution to the Civil War, Book Two (1965).

[109] *Id.* at 43.

[110] See, generally, *id.* at 82-103.

[111] See sources cited in *id.* at 42-43.

[112] *Id.* at 43.

Oratory can only inculcate virtue—as Choate put it, "induce the people ...teach them to prefer, to desire"[113]—when the orator and the listener share values, when there is "a deeply emotional...communion between speaker and audience."[114] As Edward Parker stated, "The capital of the orator is in the bank of the highest sentimentalities and the purest enthusiasms.... If these are not stored away in the hearts of the people, so that whenever he speaks he can draw on them, his drafts will be dishonored, and his speech will not rise above a shopkeeper's oratory."[115] Choate was a master in this economy. In fact, he was criticized by a contemporary because "[h]e seemed to use words not exactly to *convey* ideas to his hearers, but rather to assist and guide their minds in the work of constructing the same ideas that were his own."[116]

As Choate spoke, however, the bank on which oratory drew was being undermined. The developing capitalist economy shattered shared values and images. Although Choate realized that business did not teach virtue, he never recognized that capitalism destroyed the basis for oratory. His attitude can be called an Anglican response, accepting the duplicity of personal nature while exalting the social order.[117] He stuck to the belief "that in a developing economy the interests of all men were essentially the same."[118] He saw industry as the guarantor of the commonwealth[119] and never saw poverty as destructive of social harmony, thinking it made people "become curious, flexible, quick, progressive."[120] These qualities could be combined with virtue to restrain self-interest. They could be channeled into public debate to advance the commonwealth. Choate believed that private and public learning alone could insure the self-restraint and conservatism essential to social improvements.

To counter the individualism that preferred private to public interests and to mend the divisions manufacturing created, Choate called for "a *psychology* of virtue."[121] He argued that the disruption of the economy and society could be handled by "feeling right" and by "the proper emotional attachments."[122] As he expressed it, "the dying of a nation begins in the heart."[123] Psychology was necessary so the heart could become what Haw-

---

[113] *Ibid.*

[114] *Id.* at 44.

[115] *Ibid.*

[116] *Id.* at 46 (emphasis in original).

[117] I am indebted to Robert Gordon for pointing this out to me.

[118] Matthews, *supra*, at 75.

[119] *Id.* at 77.

[120] *Id.* at 80.

[121] *Id.* at 85 (emphasis in original).

[122] *Ibid.*

[123] *Id.* at 89.

thorne called it, "the great conservative."[124] To this end, Choate called for the creation of romantic fictions about America's founding in the Revolution,[125] in order to "kindle and feed the moral imagination."[126] Such literature "corrects the cold selfishness which would regard ourselves, our day, and our generations, as a separate and insulated portion of man and time."[127] Choate also repeatedly spoke on public occasions, like the Fourth of July, and at public places, like Plymouth Rock, to commemorate the sacred founding of a republic with liberty and legitimacy.[128]

Choate did not extend this psychology of virtue to dealings with clients. In these interactions, he replaced concern for virtue and myths about the republic's founding with what he called "the idle business of law and life."[129] Although he lectured lawyers that the legal profession was "almost an order of chivalry in the service of the state,"[130] he saw his individual practice as consisting of "litigious terms, fast contention, and the dreams of 'flowing fees.' "[131] Like other republicans, he saw the law as "one mighty and continuous stream of experience and reason, accumulated, ancestral, widening and deepening and washing itself cleaner as it runs on, the grand agent of civilization, the builder of a thousand cities, the guardian angel of a hundred generations."[132] Yet, in his office, the law was a continuous stream of "facts sometimes without interest, and rules sometimes without sense."[133]

In comprehending the disjunction between law and lawyering, Choate did not differ from other republicans:

> On one level, as they encountered law in their daily lives as businessmen or professional lawyers, they regarded it instrumentally: the courts were the day-to-day arena in which the adjustments necessary to the development of a dynamic economy were being worked out. But overlaying this pragmatic attitude there developed an increasing tendency towards a mystical reverence of the law, not as an instrument of policy, but as an overarching guarantee of that order and unity [which was the

---

[124] *Ibid.*

[125] *Id.* at 90.

[126] *Id.* at 97.

[127] *Id.* at 92.

[128] *Id.* at 48. Cf. R. N. Bellah, The Broken Covenant: American Civil Religion in a Time of Trial (1976).

[129] 1 Works of Rufus Choate with a Memoir of His Life by Samuel Gilman Brown 415 (1862) [hereinafter Choate].

[130] Matthews, *supra*, at 179.

[131] Choate at 415.

[132] Matthews, *supra*, at 178.

[133] Choate at 415.

Union].[134]

This attitude toward the law was not mystification. Reverence was an essential ingredient in nation-building. The law, and the men who practiced in its courts, enunciated a "symbolic framework in terms of which to formulate, think about and react to political problems."[135] The Union was being created. The great preserver of the American Union, Abraham Lincoln, was engaged in this project of nation-building when he declared in 1838: "Let reverence for the laws become the *political religion* of the nation."[136]

The irony of the republicans is that for all their understanding of culture (their theories of psychological and political education are being rediscovered today), they failed to understand the relation of law to society. They saw law as the cultural form *par excellence* but failed to examine law's functioning in society. Their balancings of the choices in lawyering are therefore untenable.

To the republicans, the law was open to all influences; economics, politics, and morals should transform the law. This openness created no serious problems because all conflicts, such as those between capital and labor, were reconcilable.[137] Whenever a court pronounced its legal decision the character of law guaranteed that "equality of right, of burthens, of duty, of privileges and of chances, which is the very mystery of our social being—to the Jews, a stumbling block; to the Greeks, foolishness—our strength, our glory."[138] The republicans never understood that this permeability would drag the law into the irresolvable clash of interests in political and economic markets where conclusions are judged by their substance, not their form. They saw law as above civil society, not in it.

In the republican model, the lawyer is a leader, but not a leader of his client. To Choate, the legal profession was a branch of statesmanship.[139] In a lawyer's briefs, "law, logic, eloquence, must be studied and blended together" so that the court might declare a "new truth, or old truth" as law.[140] The lawyer's task was to engage the court not his client in discourse. It was the function of the courts and "the divine and nature and immortal reason of law"[141] to develop the "sentiments and opinions"[142] necessary to maintain the republic. Although he recognized the republic could not survive unless a

---

[134] Matthews, *supra*, at 174.

[135] *Id.* at 49.

[136] *Id.* at 180 (emphasis in original).

[137] *Id.* at 74, 175. See also Gordon at 20.

[138] Choate at 420.

[139] *Id.* at 416.

[140] *Id.* at 87.

[141] *Id.* at 418.

[142] *Id.* at 423.

leader's attention was directed to "the reformation of our individual selves, the bettering of our personal nature,"[143] he did not believe that could be done in interaction with one's clients. This was a task of culture. In the office, the business of being a lawyer "is not more than to be a good carpenter...it's a knack, simply moving a machine."[144] Leadership comes from serving the courts, not helping clients see their true interests and improving their capacities for virtuous action.

Choate might never have experienced a conflict between his reverence for the law and his pragmatic attitude toward client interests had he been an appellate advocate arguing great constitutional cases. Choate's practice, however, was in the lower courts, especially the criminal courts where he spent a great deal of time "saving the seemingly guilty."[145] As one of his contemporaries accusingly noted, Choate was said to be the lawyer "who made it safe to murder, and of whose health thieves asked before they began to steal."[146]

Taking a pragmatic attitude toward his service to his clients, Choate represented individuals regardless of their cases' virtues. As one of his clerks reported, once a trial began, "the Client's interest was Choate's religion."[147] A contemporary attorney relates the result: "No one who has not been frequently his antagonist in intricate and balanced cases can have adequate conception of his wonderful powers and resources; and especially in desperate emergencies, when his seemingly assured defeat has terminated in victory."[148] Choate described the legal profession as possessing "a cunning logic, a gilded rhetoric, and an ambitious learning, wearing the purple robe of the sophists, and letting itself to hire" and he developed these pragmatic talents to win in court even "when law and facts and argument were against him."[149] His sophistry was applauded by his fellows at the bar who noted "his wonderfully methodic arrangement, where method would serve him best, and no less wonderful power of dislocation and confusion of forces, when method would not serve him."[150]

Unlike modern lawyers, Choate did not justify zealous representation on the basis of the client's right to have his interests defended at law.[151] Nor did he, like the democrats, justify it by claiming that the law should be

---

[143] *Id.* at 421.

[144] Matthews, *supra*, at 179.

[145] C. Fuess, Rufus Choate, The Wizard of the Law 56-57 (1928, 1970).

[146] Wendell Phillips, quoted in *id.* at 141.

[147] *Id.* at 175.

[148] Charles G. Loring, in Choate at 251.

[149] *Ibid.*

[150] *Ibid.*

[151] C. Fuess, *supra*, at 141-42.

representative of the diverse interests in society. Like other republicans, he recognized that the processing of rights and interests did not build a stable society. He recognized that individualism did not sustain a republic. Instead of justifying the legal profession by the process of law, he justified it by the educative effect of law. When courts decided cases on the basis of eloquent presentations by counsel, they "helped to keep alive the sacred sentiments of obedience and reverence and justice, of the supremacy of the calm and grand reason of the law over the fit full will of the individual and the crowd."[152] He was not concerned by the decision's consequences. He thought courts sullied themselves by attempting to direct society. In words that sound naive to the modern era—except to those Marxists who have studied the power of hegemony—he said all that we needed was "a more diffused, profound, and graceful, popular, and higher culture; it is a wider development of the love and discernment of the beautiful in form, in color, in speech, and in the soul of man,—that is what we need,—personal, moral, mental reform—not civil— not political!"[153]

This vision's weakness is that it was never applied in civil society. Choate never engaged himself with the culture of his clients, feeling that he did not serve them, but used his profession *"to serve the State."*[154] He applied an ideology fit for great constitutional adjudication to the representation of narrow interests. Like other republicans, Choate set out to develop the grandeur of the republic while neglecting the civil base that made the republic possible. The result was the ironies of the American system that Tocqueville reported and the indifference of Choate's clients to his displays of eloquence—except, of course, in so far as it served their interests.

Daniel Webster

There are two aspects to Webster's legal career. Like Choate, he was a great orator. Unlike Choate, Webster was also a legal counselor to business. In both branches of his legal career, Webster struggled with the republican model.

Webster, even more than Choate, won fame for his courtroom orations. Webster had the good fortune that evaded Choate, to appear often before the U.S. Supreme Court. He did not need criminal cases to demonstrate his eloquence, he had important commercial ones. Yet, even in that more rarified atmosphere, he perceived the contradictions to which Choate was blind. Or perhaps, because he argued great commercial cases, Webster could not view the law as merely the constitution-making device Choate loved. Webster saw that the State did not merely establish webs of fiduciary relationships but also was an active participant in economic expansion. He

---

[152] Choate at 417.

[153] *Id.* at 421.

[154] *Id.* at 416 (emphasis in original).

was often called upon, both as a lobbyist and as an advocate, to move the government from a laissez-faire stance to an interventionist one.[155] Although a Whig in philosophy, he acted as a Federalist, using the government to aid his clients, the men of commerce and manufacture.[156] In addition to being a litigator, he also was the general counsel to banks, insurance companies and factories around Boston.[157] He later became "their" Representative and then Senator in Washington.[158] From his experience in Congress, Webster certainly learned the law not only was the protector and inculcator of virtue, but also fulfilled the more mundane task of creating enforceable patent and bankruptcy legislation to encourage the flow of commerce.[159] Through the introduction of carefully crafted legislation and "by means of his influence, contacts, and energy, [Webster] helped to divert public money in large sums...at a critical time in the expansion of the Bostonians' industrial empire."[160] Although evincing the republican belief that "[c]ustom and deference permitted all men to assume a basic harmony of interests and enabled the mute majority to trust its leaders to seek and serve the common good,"[161] Webster led the Congress and the courts to favor his clients' special interests.

We are not concerned here with Webster's possible hypocrisy. Let the psycho-historians inquire into the conflicts in Webster's character.[162] We are not interested in the tragedy that the man idolized by the public for honesty and character saw himself as "Black Dan" and did not trust himself.[163]

---

[155] See Prince & Taylor, "Daniel Webster, The Boston Associates, and the U.S. Government's Role in the Industrializing Process, 1815-1830," in Essays from the Lowell Conference on Industrial History 1980 and 1981, at 114 (R. Weible ed. 1981). For a description of Webster as a republican, see S. Nathans, Daniel Webster and Jacksonian Democracy (1973).

[156] *Id.* at 117.

[157] *Id.* at 117.

[158] Konefsky, "Introduction," The Papers of Daniel Webster: Legal Papers, Volume 1: The New Hampshire Practice (A. S. Konefsky, et al., eds.) xxxvi-xxxvii (1982).

[159] Prince & Taylor, *supra*, at 120.

[160] *Id.* at 123.

[161] S. Nathans, *supra*, at 6.

[162] At least one psycho-biography has been published on Webster: I. Bartlett, Daniel Webster (1978). For a different approach to the problem of hypocrisy, see Goodman, "Ethics and Enterprise: The Values of the Postwar Elite, 1800-1860," 18 Am. Q. 437 (1966).

[163] I. Bartlett, *supra*, at 7. This is not to deny that there is a link between sociology and psychology. An introduction to the link may be gleaned from C. Wright Mills' description of the nineteenth century lawyer: "Before the ascendancy of the large corporation, skill and eloquence in advocacy selected nineteenth-century leaders of the bar; reputations and wealth were created and maintained in the courts, of which the lawyer was an officer.... An opinion leader, a man whose recommendations to the community counted, who handled obligations and rights of intimate family and life problems, the liberty and property of all who had them, the lawyer personally pointed out the course of the law and counseled his client against the pitfalls of illegality. Deferred to by his client, he carefully displayed the dignity he claimed to embody. Rewarded for apparent honesty, carrying an ethical halo,

Instead, we will discuss Webster's innovations in his legal practice. Unlike Choate who was content to accept the split between the law and lawyering, Webster attempted to create a republican office practice.

Both Webster's early and late practices were office practices. Before he entered the worlds of Washington and Boston, Webster was a lawyer in rural New Hampshire. His practice, which consisted largely of debt collection, depended on the existence of republican virtue embodied in community belief both in the sanctity of contract and in the protection of debtors. The state was the enforcer of last resort. "[T]he enforcement mechanisms for credit transactions were, for the most part, informal."[164]

In practice Webster had to be aware of his actions' substantive effects upon the community and could not be content with the hegemonic function of the law. Alfred Konefsky describes such a rural practice as follows:

> [T]he lawyer was free to formulate informal mechanisms and strategies that conformed to community norms of appropriate and necessary economic conduct. The lawyer's creative role and service to the social group, then, was a synthetic outgrowth of the need to be flexible within the formal demands of the anti-communal nature of the legal system and the communal influence of his social environment.[165]

In arguing on his client's behalf, the lawyer "had to balance the interests within the community in order to limit the harshness of any purely legal outcome."[166] Serving his own interests in the development of his practice, Webster had to help maintain the economic and social community of which he was part. Webster had to lead his clients away from pure self-interest to an appreciation of the community's shared values.

Although Webster achieved fame as an orator after leaving New Hampshire, "he seemed to feel more comfortable in the office dispensing advice."[167] Webster performed as much office work as possible. In Boston, Webster "developed an early version of an office practice as counselor to individuals attempting to avoid litigation or plan legal transactions."[168]

Practice in the big city, Webster soon learned, differed substantially from

---

held to be fit material for high statesmanship, the lawyer upheld public service and was professionally above business motives." C. W. Mills, White Collar: The American Middle Classes 121 (1951), quoted in Laumann and Heinz, *supra*, at 205.

[164] Konefsky, *supra*, at xxxii.

[165] *Id.* at xxxiii.

[166] *Ibid.*

[167] *Id.* at xxxviii.

[168] *Ibid.*

lawyering in New Hampshire. Shared community values offered little protection from the anti-communal effects of the legal system. Debtors were forced to meet the standards of the law, not the needs of the community. The market and the formal mechanisms of the law governed their fate, not their fellows and informal methods of conciliation.

While working for the manufacturing and commercial classes, Webster longed for the community of New Hampshire. To reduce this conflict, he switched from litigation to business planning. In the commercial society he had placed himself, he knew it made a significant difference whether the lawyer was handling an issue before or after the problem arose. If he got a problem after it arose, he could not use informal methods of control but had to resort to the formals mechanism of the law. He saw law as "increasingly technical and intellectual"[169] and knew its anti-communal impact. Unlike Choate, Webster was at the center of commerce and saw how court decisions affected the community. Webster preferred to meet his clients before problems arose and interests had solidified. Although Boston was not New Hampshire, Webster could at least try to use his republican conception of community to lead his clients and reconcile interests. "The movement toward an office practice, then, was an attempt through planning to reassert control over the capriciousness of the marketplace."[170]

Webster preferred office practice to oratory because he felt it offered more freedom of action. Although in speech he could choose his words and rhetorical tactics, Webster knew that as orator he was merely a dependent extension of his clients. His words enabled clients to pursue *their* aims. By tackling problems before they arose, he could pursue republican ideals. "As he rationally ordered, planned, and advised, he...distanced himself from his dependency."[171] Drawing on the permeability of law in the republican model, Webster tried to exercise a non-republican form of leadership.

Although Webster could lead his clients from unnecessary differences with others, conflicts still remained. Even the great Webster could no longer devise compromises and solutions acceptable to all parties. It simply was not possible in Boston. His office practice was a "refuge"[172] from the worst dilemmas of an expanding economy. As Konefsky succinctly states the case: "It was too much to expect in this environment that anyone, particularly a legal representative, could somehow assume responsibility for the whole."[173] Furthermore, in New Hampshire Webster served both creditor and debtor, while in Boston he only served business interests. He did not move between conflicting interests shoring up each side's ability to compromise and defend

---

[169] *Ibid.*

[170] *Id.* at xxxv.

[171] *Id.* at xxxviii.

[172] *Ibid.*

[173] *Id.* at xxxv.

itself.

Where Choate had a republican conception of the State and a pragmatic attitude toward civil society, Webster had a pragmatic attitude toward the State and a republican conception of civil society. Both were unable to translate their republican ideals into a meaningful practice. Their attempts to inculcate virtue neither restrained representative government nor commercial transactions. Although they both hoped, in different ways, that their lawyering would stem individualism, their practice inevitably supported individualism. Webster, at least, recognized that fine words alone would not work. If his office practice was a failure, it at least points toward lawyering's proper response to the emergence of a capitalistic social structure.

John W. Davis

John W. Davis is the archetypical modern lawyer. He is "the lawyer's lawyer."[174] He argued more cases before the United States Supreme Court than anyone since Webster, served on many corporate boards and developed a great law firm.

Davis exemplifies both the liberal model of lawyering and differentiated specialization. For Davis, law was a set of unchanging principles and clearly drawn statutes which could be mechanically applied by lawyers and judges to resolve cases. He opposed his day's anti-formalist movements, legal realism and sociological jurisprudence. Roscoe Pound succinctly enunciated the antithesis to Davis' position:

> Law is not scientific for the sake of science.... It must be judged by the results it achieves, not by the niceties of its internal structure; it must be valued by the extent to which it meets its end, not by the beauty of its logical processes or the strictness with which its rules proceed from the dogmas it takes for its foundation.[175]

Law was not a species of ethics or political science to Davis, nor the watchman of the economy. He opposed most of the legal changes of the twentieth century, claiming to be a witness to the degeneration of the law into "a perpetual flux of speculative ideas," responsive not to precedent but to "the circumambient atmosphere or the social urge."[176] His opposition to anti-formalism did not prevent him from being a successful advocate; when needed to win the case for his client "he readily invoked semantics, legislative history, or public policy."[177]

---

[174] In the phrase of his biographer. See W. H. Harbaugh, Lawyer's Lawyer: The Life of John W. Davis (1973).

[175] Quoted in *id.* at 415.

[176] *Id.* at 418.

[177] *Id.* at 91.

Davis' animosity to the great legal changes of the time was not only, or even primarily, theoretical. As he admitted, "I've never had any interest in the philosophy of law."[178] His animosity stemmed from his belief that the challenge to formalism undermined the legal profession. He condemned administrative law because "no lawyer can keep pace with" it.[179] He condemned judge-made law for similar reasons, if more humorously:

> Here comes a client...he may be willing to pay a modest fee for the lawyer's opinion. The lawyer reads the decisions of the Supreme Court of the United States and says that the law has been settled so and so.... The next week the Court says the law...is exactly to the contrary. This is hard on the lawyer and may be even harder on the client.... He ceases to employ lawyers and goes down and throws dice with the cop on the corner.[180]

Instead of recognizing that uncertainty can make the lawyer's advice even more valuable, Davis viewed it as cheapening the lawyer's value. Davis' view is rooted in the conception that a lawyer merely expounds the formal law, neither guiding his client to new trends, bringing background values to bear, nor fashioning formal and informal mechanisms through which the client can act. To Davis, the lawyer's task was to read the law objectively and that requires static law.

What is puzzling is that Davis held these views while building a firm that capitalized on the law's uncertainties in the administrative state. Davis maintained this position in theory even though in practice he used policy arguments to defend his clients. One can solve this puzzle, however, if one recognizes that the theoretical framework enabled Davis to believe he was independent and objective when, in fact, he was subordinate and partisan.

Davis is usually seen as a leader of business. He sat on many corporate boards, including U.S. Rubber, the Atchison, Topeka & Santa Fe R.R. and the National Bank of Commerce. For a man who knew that corporate laws placed the board in charge of the corporation, he narrowly interpreted his function:

> Davis usually avoided comment on the strictly economic elements of a problem, and even at directors' meetings he remained silent until a legal issue was raised and his opinion solicited. He could tell his corporate clients what they could or could not do within existing interpretations of the law, but he never devised novel or ingenious ways to circumvent the law.[181]

---

[178] *Id.* at 413.

[179] *Id.* at 417.

[180] *Id.* at 416.

[181] *Id.* at 263.

Davis conceived that his job on the board was to render advice on an objective law. Instead of directing the business, he prided himself on telling clients what they did not want to hear: the law prevents such and such actions. But where the law was silent, so was he. "Davis privately...deplored child labor. He disapproved the abuse of the injunction. He discountenanced monopoly in the abstract."[182] Yet, he served on boards of corporations that engaged in all of these practices, often in an outrageous manner, and he simply helped them to pursue these activities legally.[183] He was not a leader of his clients, he was a legal specialist:

> It was my duty to find out what the law was, and to tell my client what rule to follow. That was my job. If the rules changed, well and good.... [The lawyer] does not create. All he does is lubricate the wheels of society.... The lawyer must steel himself...to think only of the subject before him & not of the pain his knife may cause.[184]

Davis did not bring his social and political views to the boards on which he served because he thought a lawyer's prize virtue was his independence. Yet, critics often attacked Davis for not being independent from his clients. "There is nothing I resent more," he responded, "than the idea that a lawyer sells himself body & soul to his clients.... No one in all this list of clients has ever controlled or even fancied that he could control my personal or my political conscience."[185] He was a differentiated specialist, "just a law lawyer,"[186] and, as he put it, "[I] always kept my clients' business and my political views in two separate compartments."[187]

Some challenged his independence arguing it was not possible to maintain that distinction. Yale philosopher W. E. Hocking said that "[a]ssociations alter interpretations."[188] Felix Frankfurter, in a series of unsigned *New*

---

[182] *Id.* at 203.

[183] *Id.* at 202.

[184] *Id.* at 46, 23, 46.

[185] *Id.* at 199.

[186] *Id.* at 263. Davis' partner, who propounded this description, elaborated: "He knows little or nothing about reorganizations, etc." *Ibid.*

[187] *Id.* at 197.

[188] Quoted in *id.* at 201. Karl Llewellyn made a similar argument in a general criticism of the corporate bar: "[A]ny man's interests, any man's outlook, are shaped in greatest part by what he does.... His sympathies and ethical judgments are determined essentially by the things and people he works on and for and with.... Hence the practice of corporation law not only works for business men toward business ends, but develops within itself a business point of view—toward the work to be done, toward the values of the work to the community, indeed, toward the way in which to do the work." Quoted in Laumann and Heinz, *supra*, at 204-05. Compare this problem with what I call "the sociological problem" of being counsel to the situation, *infra*. The argument as phrased by Llewellyn, Hocking and Frankfurter goes too far. It denies the possibility of leadership.

Republic pieces, argued: "Like the rest of us..., [Davis] is mastered by the material with which he works.... Of course...[n]o man could possibly 'control' Mr. Davis,"[189] but control need not be overt and explicit.

I, like others, think that this differentiation is possible but argue that this "professional tunnel vision was designed to obliterate those disturbing substantive issues that Davis preferred to ignore."[190] Davis concentrated on purely legal issues and knew little or nothing about the non-legal aspects of the problems he handled.[191] The "main aim," he said, "is simply to answer the problems brought to you. That's all."[192] His approach combined a "dedication to the case at hand"[193] with a "compulsion for technical perfection."[194] Although doing something very well is certainly laudable, it is sad when a leader of American bar and business considers his own accomplishments and concludes, "I seem to have caught at the skirt of great events without really influencing them."[195] Similarly, his biographer Harbaugh concludes that Davis' "indifference to management and corporate policy strengthened Davis' conviction that he was a free moral agent, that his legal counsel had no relation to his social and political conscience."[196] This is freedom without responsibility, subservience masquerading as independence.

Without questioning Davis' objectivity from a psychological point of view as Hocking and Frankfurter did, we may conclude that Davis' lauded objectivity was nothing but partisanship. Only a non-lawyer would be shocked by Davis, after agreeing to dedicate himself to a client's cause, beginning the meeting by jestingly asking his client, "Just how guilty are you?" Or later quoting John G. Milburn's quip: "Who is going to tell the lies when they start asking the questions?"[197] A practicing lawyer would recognize that these are simply techniques to create an illusion of disengagement from the client. What few lawyers would claim is that in this partisan atmosphere they were able to maintain their objectivity.

One example should suffice to reveal the limits of Davis' objectivity. Davis defended a Morgan partner accused of tax evasion on the sale and re-sale of securities between the partner and his wife that led to the claim of a capital loss. Both in court and before a congressional committee, Davis strongly defended the partner, presenting excellent documentation of the transaction

---

[189] *Ibid.*

[190] Auerbach, Review, 87 Harv. L. Rev. 1100, 1110 (1974).

[191] W. H. Harbaugh, *supra*, at 253, 263.

[192] *Id.* at 253.

[193] *Id.* at 321.

[194] *Id.* at 45.

[195] *Id.* at 523.

[196] *Id.* at 264.

[197] *Id.* at 266-67.

prepared by his firm. The government successfully prosecuted the partner, arguing that the issue was "the *bona fides* of the transaction, not the mere form."[198] Differentiated specialization poorly serves the client when intent can be seriously questioned. Anyone who practices law like Davis will find he can only restate his client's declaration of intent not objectively inquire into its *bona fides*.

Three lessons can be drawn from the Davis example. In the lawyering model Davis exemplifies, lawyers in their practice and rhetoric do not shirk from undermining the legitimacy of the administrative state that makes lawyers' existence necessary and guarantees their status. Although these lawyers attain high status, they do not exercise power, assuming subservience to be a condition of their station. Finally, they retreat into an alienated technical role to insulate themselves from the consequences of the power they in fact exercise but have delegitimated.

Louis D. Brandeis

Although Brandeis is most famous for his Supreme Court service, it is his law practice that concerns us here. In his practice, Brandeis attempted to remodel the republican view along democratic lines. The result was that his law partner, Sam Warren, considered this Jew from Kentucky to be "more brahmin than the brahmins."[199]

Brandeis viewed legal practice as an opportunity to reform society. Like the republicans, he considered reform to be a conservative force building on collective traditions: "true conservatism involves progress."[200] Brandeis stands in the line of American moral reformers who attempted to link individual opportunity with individual responsibility so the institutions of civil society would not "lose their foundations."[201] He rejected the modern equation of virtue with the individual pursuit of interest and returned to the republican image of fiduciary webs. Like Choate, his concern was for *paideia* in civil society. Brandeis approached this task with a philosophical pragmatism, believing that "the method of morals and the method of science are one."[202]

His approach infuriated the legal and political establishment of his day. At his confirmation hearings for the United States Supreme Court, *six* former

---

[198] *Id.* at 330.

[199] M. I. Urofsky, A Mind of One Piece: Brandeis and American Reform 3 (1971) [hereinafter Urofsky]. See also Katz, "Henry Lee Higginson v. Louis Dembitz Brandeis: A Collision between Tradition and Reform," 61 N. Eng. Q. 72 (1968).

[200] Urofsky at 6.

[201] *Ibid.*

[202] *Id.* at 6-7. See also Schudson, "Public, Private and Professional Lives: The Correspondence of David Dudley Field and Samuel Bowles," 21 Am. J. Legal Hist. 191, 210-11 (1977).

presidents of the American Bar Association certified that he was "not a fit person to be a member of the" high court.[203] The brahmins A. Lawrence Lowell and Charles Francis Adams also protested his appointment.[204] After studying Brandeis' legal practice, Elihu Root concluded that Brandeis was "intellectually acute and morally blind."[205] Although these comments may be understood best as political assessments masquerading as character judgments, they do testify to a gulf between Brandeis' choices about the constitution of his legal practice and the conception of professional responsibility dominant then, as well as now.

Unlike Choate, Brandeis believed that legal education was moral education. As he told a group of Harvard undergraduates: "[N]othing can better fit you for taking part in the solution of these [social] problems than the study and preeminently the practice of law."[206] The study of legal rules, logic, research skills and the application of these skills to practical problems "leads to the development of judgment."[207] A difference between Choate and Brandeis is that Brandeis did not believe that to study of law was to learn an illiberal specialty. Properly understood, legal study was an education in all the social sciences. It could not be otherwise, "for out of the facts grows the law," as Brandeis often repeated both in practice and on the bench.[208] He criticized practicing lawyers because they were merely "solvers of legal conundrums," not masters of fact. As he told one young lawyer: "You are prone in legal investigation to be controlled by logic and to underestimate the logic of facts. Knowledge of the decided cases and rules of logic cannot alone make a great lawyer. He must know, must feel 'in his bones' the facts to which they apply—and must know, too, that if they do not stand the test of such application the logical result will somehow or other be avoided."[209]

"Counsel to the situation" summarizes Brandeis' approach to practice. The distance between Brandeis' position and the accepted modern framework has led some to claim that Brandeis never actually held these views.[210] These attempts to reinterpret Brandeis are mere sanitizing jobs. Brandeis tried to lead his clients. He, like Frankfurter, criticized lawyers who "instead

---

[203] Frank, "The Legal Ethics of Louis D. Brandeis," 17 Stan. L. Rev. 683 685 (1965). For a full account of the appointment controversy, see A. L. Todd, Justice on Trial: The Case of Louis D. Brandeis (1964).

[204] A. L. Todd, *supra*, at 106.

[205] *Id.* at 128.

[206] Quoted in Levy, "The Lawyer as Judge: Brandeis' View of the Legal Profession," 22 Okla. L. Rev. 374, 383 (1969).

[207] *Id.* at 389.

[208] Urofsky at 31-33, 158.

[209] *Id.* at 27.

[210] E.g., Frank, *supra*.

of being advisers...were collaborators in their client's short term interests."[211] He criticized lawyers who merely did their clients' bidding, rather than helping their clients understand the forces with which they were dealing. Instead of clients who would ask "Tell me the best way to reach my ends," Brandeis sought clients who would inquire "What should I do?" He saw the possibilities for both power and responsibility in the lawyer's role. "I would rather have clients than be somebody's lawyer,"[212] was the phrase he used to equate lawyering with leadership.

A "counsel to the situation" is a mediator, an "honest broker to all sides and parties to an issue."[213] One of the charges raised against Brandeis at his confirmation hearings was that he had to be convinced of the justness of the clients' position before accepting a case.[214] Brandeis became infamous for informing a family, whose breadwinner had become bankrupt and committed suicide, that he would not help them resolve the ensuing financial difficulties until they promised to pay the creditors first. To Brandeis, being a lawyer meant looking "for a harmony larger than either side had conceived when they called on their lawyers."[215]

Two examples best depict Brandeis' approach. The head of a large shoe manufacturing company, beset by labor problems with his workforce, called on Brandeis for assistance. The client wanted to cut employee wages. The client argued that in lean times he could no longer afford to pay the rate to which he had previously agreed. Brandeis discovered the workers were subject to long layoff periods so that although their hourly rates were high, their annual wages were low. After studying the economics of the shoe industry, Brandeis proposed that the client revamp his operations, accepting orders long before proposed delivery and then rescheduling operations to eliminate the layoff periods. Both the client and the employees profited from Brandeis' advice.

Brandeis took a different approach to the labor problems of E.A. Filene's department store. He recommended establishing the Filene Cooperative Association. This association, helped to institute democratic reforms in the workplace, establish joint worker-management committees and reduce labor problems.

In these cases, Brandeis did not act as "just a law lawyer." He used econ-

---

[211] Urofsky at 21. Cf. Brennan, "The Responsibilities of the Legal Profession," in The Path of the Law, 1967, at 90 (A. Sutherland ed. 1968): "[The lawyer is] an agent, and as such can afford, emotionally and intellectually, to take a broader long-term view of his client's needs—whether the client be a private corporation, an individual or a government agency—than can the client himself."

[212] M. I. Urofsky, Louis D. Brandeis and the Progressive Tradition 12 (1981).

[213] Urofsky at 36.

[214] Levy, *supra*, at 393-95.

[215] Urofsky at 230.

omics and industrial psychology to resolve potential legal problems. He did not practice law as a differentiated specialist. He led his clients to reconceive their interests so that he could, then, comfortably espouse them. Furthermore, he sought solutions that satisfied, to a degree, the interests of potentially opposing parties.

The contrast between the Brandeis notion of "counsel to the situation" and the modern conception of professional responsibility could not be sharper. The modern conception enshrines principles of both neutrality and partisanship. As neutral, the lawyer is detached from the client's ends and does not judge their justness. As a partisan, the lawyer works aggressively to advance these ends.

The modern conception is based on a particular theory of morality, knowledge and professionalism. In the modern view, demand alone determines value and moral judgments are individual, subjective and arbitrary. Brandeis rejected this concept of morality. He believed we have a moral duty to ease pain[216] and moral judgments must be responsive to lived experience and scientific inquiry.[217] The modern conception of knowledge is that it is amoral and specialized. To Brandeis, knowledge is moral and always responsively inquiring across boundaries.[218] Modern professionalism enshrines an amoral morality in professional-client relationships. Brandeis responded that amoral morality is appropriate only in certain types of professional relations. A public defender perhaps should be neutral and partisan toward the criminal defendant but the lawyer in other circumstances should be counsel to the situation.[219]

Brandeis was certainly correct in recognizing the modern conception is not the only way of ordering the professional-client relation. On one hand, the doctor-patient relation is neutral but not partisan. If the client's interest is something other than health, the doctor will not pursue it. On the other hand, the politician-constituent relation is partisan but not neutral. The politician is engaged to pursue his constituent's ends but he also judges them. In the republican model, the lawyer-client relation is determined by the law. In Brandeis' revision of this model, it is determined by the advice needed.

---

[216] Urofsky at 155.

[217] See Freund, "Mr. Justice Brandeis," in Mr. Justice (A. Dunham & P. Kurland, eds.) 97 (1956). "Professor Paul A. Freund of Harvard Law School has pointed out to me that the Brandeis brief was originally designed to show than an impressive body of opinion could be mustered to support the judgment of a legislature against constitutional attack; its aim was to resist the play-it-by-ear tendency of cavalier judgments, but not to set itself up as a scientific arbiter beyond that." Riesman, "Law and Sociology: Recruitment, Training and Colleagueship," in Law and Sociology: Exploratory Essays 28 n.20 (W. Evan. ed. 1962).

[218] Urofsky at 30-31.

[219] The inability to be counsel to the situation may be a reason why Brandeis avoided criminal defense work, see Urofsky at 33.

APPRAISING "COUNSEL TO THE SITUATION"

This chapter raises three problems with the notion of counsel to the situation. The problems are educational, sociological and political in nature. Adequately resolving them is still of vital concern to the profession. These three problems confronted not only Brandeis but also the lawyers interviewed for this study.[220]

The Educational Problem. An advantage of differentiated specialization is that it limits what the lawyer has to learn. Being counsel to the situation may require the lawyer to know more than we can reasonably expect him to know. For "the logic of words" to "yield to the logic of reality,"[221] those trained in the law must grasp the relevant facts in whatever situation they encounter. If not, as Brandeis used to say, quoting Charles Henderson: "One can hardly escape the conclusion that a lawyer who has not studied economics and sociology is very apt to become a public enemy."[222] Can we educate lawyers to be counsel

---

[220] The problems with the counsel to the situation notion are not those commonly stated. It has been charged that Brandeis practiced law in a paternalistic fashion and that his reading of morality in facts was determined by his pre-existing biases. Kate Millett in *Sexual Politics* attacked Brandeis' supposed paternalism in connection with his work on *Muller v. Oregon*, 208 U.S. 412 (1908). In *Muller*, the Supreme Court upheld an Oregon statute limiting the number of hours women could work in bakeries. The court distinguished the case from *Lochner v. New York*, 198 U.S. 45 (1905), drawing on the statistics contained in Brandeis' "Oregon Brief." Millett condemns Brandeis for maintaining and advocating "the smug assumption that 'women are fundamentally weaker than men'" K. Millett, *Sexual Politics* 125 (1969, 1971), quoting in part from *Muller v. Oregon*, 208 U.S. 412, 421-22 (1908). Urofsky defends Brandeis stating "it is inane to condemn men of good will because they were not prophetic enough six decades ago to realize that women's lib might come along." Urofsky at 180. Urofsky's defense is inadequate. We should avoid paternalism precisely because of our limited prophetic abilities. Urofsky should have pointed out that Brandeis' work in this case was part of a women's movement. Women in the Consumers League collected the statistics contained in his brief. Millett's attack, then, should be against this movement. If Brandeis was part of an anti-progressive movement, so be it. That, however, is a different charge than claiming he used his knowledge paternalistically. The second charge often levied against Brandeis, that he merely used science to cover his own moral beliefs, can be levied against anyone who doesn't subscribe to the "is-ought" disjunction. The reason this argument does not work on Brandeis does not depend, however, on a philosophical argument. Brandeis tried to create a relationship with his clients in which he was their equal and where they both set out to uncover the moral meaning in facts. His biases and moral presuppositions were thus exposed and subject to refutation. For all his sympathy with brahmin morality, Brandeis did not set himself out as steward for society. He had no new answer to Plato's question, "How can the good govern?" Rather, he joined and created social movements and engaged in dialogue with his clients to discover the situational good.

[221] Urofsky at 32, quoting from Brandeis' dissent in *DiSanto v. Pennsylvania*, 273 U.S. 34, 37, at 43 (1927).

[222] Brandeis, "The Living Law," 10 Ill. L. Rev. 461, 464 (1916), quoted in A. T. Mason, Brandeis: Lawyer and Judge in the Modern State 21 (1933). Brandeis recognized that lawyers were going to specialize in an area of law, but argued that their specialization need not be a "differentiated" one. Yes, specialize but "correct its distorting effects by broader education—by study undertaken preparatory to practice and continued by lawyer and judge

to the situation? If creating an army of Brandeises seems impossible, let us not be overly sanguine about education in the model of differentiated specialization. As Brandeis believed, and as the brahmin Henry Adams demonstrated, miseducation can be both an individual and a collective failure.

The Sociological Problem. How can we expect lawyers to lead their clients? How can we expect lawyers to avoid being captured by their clients? Consider another portion of Brandeis' advice to the young lawyer beyond his injunction to become master of the facts:

> Cultivate the society of men—particularly men of affairs. This is essential to your professional success. Pursue that study as heretofore you have devoted yourself to books. Lose no opportunity of becoming acquainted with men, of learning to feel instinctively their inclinations, of familiarizing yourself with their personal and business habits.... The knowledge of men, the ability to handle, to impress them is needed by you...most important of all is the impressing of clients and satisfying them.[223]

Constraints on the lawyer-client relation as well as the client's control over fees force the lawyer into the role of the courtier not the grand vizier. To assess the possibilities for lawyers to lead their clients and not merely be led by them, we must understand constraints on the lawyer-client relation.

The movement from entrepreneurial to organizational capitalism has made the model of counsel to the situation more problematic. Both the shoe factory and the department store Brandeis represented were entrepreneurial firms. Brandeis advised a client who could singlehandedly follow his recommendations. Is it possible to be counsel to the situation in an age of organizations? Isn't there an affinity between bureaucracy and differentiated specialization? Yet, are we to deny lawyers the opportunities and responsibilities Brandeis had merely because of organizational inertia? To understand the opportunities and responsibilities of leadership, the professional relation in the organizational context must be understood.

Brandeis must have recognized the difficulties of leadership. He understood the loyalties and predispositions created by working for organizations. In attacking interlocking directorships, he said, "The principle that no man can serve two masters...is fundamental, and when a man undertakes to serve two corporations that are dealing with one another there is always the danger that the unethical relation may result in loss."[224] He also understood the

---

throughout life: study of economics and sociology and politics which embody the facts and present the problems of today." Brandeis, *id.* at 470, quoted by Mason, *ibid.*

[223] Urofsky at 27.

[224] Urofsky at 84.

psychic worth of commitment and the principle-sustaining qualities of split loyalties. In defending himself from attacks that his Zionism watered down his Americanism, Brandeis said: "Multiple loyalties are objectionable only if they are inconsistent.... A man is a better citizen of the United States for being loyal to his family, and to his profession or trade; for being loyal to his college or lodge."[225] The dictum, "to be in it, but not of it" may puzzle us, while it directs us to further inquiry. In studying corporate counsel, perhaps especially inside counsel who are both employees and professionals, we will need to explore this puzzle.

The Political Problem. Are not private ends less reconcilable than allowed for by the model of counsel to the situation? To Brandeis, the conflict between labor and capital was a "sign of man's failure to regulate their affairs rationally."[226] Many would argue, however, that this is not a failure of reason but a recognition of insurmountable political conflict. How generalizable are the shoe company and Filene examples? In these two cases, Brandeis managed to enlarge "the pie" so conflicting interests were resolved to everyone's satisfaction. It's a nice trick if you can do it. But if you can't, how do you resolve conflicting interests? In fact, the two cases, do not really challenge the ethic of defending client interests. Both the shoe factory owner and Filene got richer. The more difficult issue is: how are choices between conflicting interests resolved in zero-sum situations?

Brandeis had three responses to this political problem. First, it is precisely when interest can't be easily reconciled that the lawyer's choice of whom to represent is most important and not neutral. Like Webster, and unlike Choate and Davis, Brandeis recognized that the choice of a particular clientele is a moral choice, that is not eliminated by the principle of everyone's right to representation. When interests can't be reconciled, it matters which side you are on. Second, the lawyer need not act only when interests are fixed and irreconcilable. Webster's office practice is one example of attempting to influence the formation of interests. Political action is another way to alter the terms of social conflict. Brandeis, for example, worked with the People's Lobby, the National Civil Federation, the Good Government Association, among others. Third, and most important, a lawyer can contribute to the Administrative state's attempts to integrate society. Brandeis appeared repeatedly before congressional committees and administrative hearings, advocating the improvement of institutions.

In working with movements, Congress, and administrative agencies, Brandeis was an educator. His model of lawyering, whose applicability to the modern lawyer will concern us in later chapters, combines the republican and democratic models. For all his belief in the educative power of correctly

---

[225] *Id.* at 95.

[226] A. L. Todd, *supra*, at 45.

practiced law and lawyering, he was a "serenely implacable democrat":[227]

> Refuse to accept as inevitable any evil.... But do not believe you can find a universal remedy for evil conditions.... And do not pin too much faith in legislation. Remedial institutions are apt to fall under the control of the enemy and to become instruments of oppression.

> Seek for betterment within the broad lines of existing institutions. Do so by attacking evil *in situ*.... Remember that progress is necessarily slow...that because of varying conditions there must be much and constant enquiry into facts...and much experimentation; and that always and everywhere the intellectual, moral, and spiritual development of those concerned will remain an essential—and the main factor—in real betterment.

> This development of the individual is thus both a necessary means and the end sought. For our objective is the making of men and women who shall be free self-respecting members of a democrary and who shall be worthy of respect.

> The great developer is responsibility. Hence no remedy can be hopeful which does not devolve upon the workers participation in, responsibility for, the conduct of business....

> But democracy in any sphere is a serious undertaking.... It is more difficult to maintain than achieve.... Success in any democratic undertaking must proceed from the individual. It is possible only where the process of perfecting the individual is pursued. His development is attained mainly in the processes of common living.

To Brandeis, the real meaning of the political problem is that it highlights the importance of the lawyer's choices about whom to serve, in what sorts of situations, and toward what ends. Thus we must be concerned with the market for legal services, its structural setting, and the educative impact of lawyering. As Brandeis would tell us, we must therefore become "masters of the facts" about lawyers and the services they provide.

CONCLUSION: EXORCISING THE IDEOLOGICAL DEVILS

As I noted in this chapter's introductory section, the comparisons a speaker draws not only delineate objective differences between situations, they illuminate the moral choices through which the speaker defines himself. In comparing their practice to that of their predecessors, lawyers point to the

---

[227] This was the judgment of Alvin Johnson. Urofsky at 156. The quote from Brandeis, to follow in text, is from *id.* at 155-56.

complexity, bigness and specialization of modern legal practice. I termed these three features "ideological devils." By using this term, I do mean to deny that these three features objectively describe features of practice. I simply mean that they often mystify the moral choices in practice. Because of these ideological devils, the character of lawyers appears to be a matter of necessity, not a matter of choice.

There are at least three choices any lawyer must make. First, he must establish how open his expert knowledge will be to other forms of knowledge. Second, he must determine how much influence he wishes to exert in his relations with clients. And third, he must declare allegiance in the face of the conflicting interests associated with his work.

When lawyers complain about the complexity of law, they argue that, given the limits of time and intelligence, a lawyer can only master the law, and a limited portion of the law at that. Consequently, it would be *hubris* for the lawyer to advise on the basis of non-legal knowledge. Complexity requires the lawyer's law to be impermeable to other forms of social knowledge. As both Choate and Brandeis demonstrate, what a lawyer chooses to master need not be determined by the legal complexity of his clients' problems. Complexity is an ideological devil because it obscures the lawyer's choice. When lawyers speak of the complexity of the law, they are choosing to believe there is no non-legal basis for making moral judgments and that there is no non-legal basis for criticizing the present system. They reject the republican notion that a virtuous trustee can prescribe behavior and the democratic notion that everyday morality must guide behavior.

The complaint of "complexity" is a choice to accept that all moral judgment collapses into the question of whether or not an action is sanctioned by law. Moral values in complex decisions, however, transcend the abilities of differentiated specialists. Modern lawyers are not prepared to make moral judgments in complex situations. Since modern ideology presumes the lawyer has no justification for such judgment, is it any wonder that modern lawyers wish to believe they are not making moral judgments nor marketing their characters?

When lawyers complain about the bigness of modern society, they argue that they are tightly controlled by their role and environment. In organizational society, lawyers either speak to the "great men," who have other advisors, or they speak to ineffectual underlings. It, therefore, is naive to expect lawyers to assume leadership roles. As both Webster and Brandeis demonstrate, if the modern lawyer's claim that they cannot be leaders is true, it is true only because they have chosen a particular type of practice. Bigness is another ideological devil because it mystifies the lawyer's choice to practice in a particular setting in organizational society. When lawyers speak of the bigness of modern society, they are choosing to ignore the openings for leadership in corporate life. They are prematurely accepting limitations on their influence, just as Davis did when he sat on corporate boards and chose subservience. They reject the republican notion of the cultural leadership of law and the democratic notion that institutions contain principles of natural justice.

The complaint of "bigness" is a choice to decline leadership. Bigness implies that lawyers have little influence. The alternate models reveal that this claim is conclusory. Lawyers who argue that bigness limits their options have adopted a tunnel vision focused on the formality of corporate organization and the impersonality of corporate authority. As the examples of Griswold and O.P.M and Singer Hutner demonstrate, corporations have informal organizations and personal authority relations. Those not at the top can and do exercise leadership.

Without the necessary information and analysis, lawyers are properly hesitant to trade on their clients' loyalty in order to exercise influence. Instead of engaging in analysis to understand the contours of responsible leadership, however, lawyers shirk influence. Since modern ideology assumes our relations with each other are arbitrary—merely dependent on the affects we choose to share—is it any wonder that modern lawyers choose to decline the responsibility to influence rather than accepting the challenge of solidarity?

When lawyers point to the specialization of the law, they argue that they are not responsible for the consequences of their actions. In modern society, professionals speak in their own language and deal only with their profession's concerns. It is therefore naive to expect a lawyer to be concerned with any problem's diverse interests. Specialization is another ideological devil because it obscures the fact that lawyers can be proficient if they immerse themselves in a problem. When lawyers blame specialization, they are choosing to evade an analysis of law in society, adopting the position that a gap exists between lawyering and life and lawyering and politics. In their lives, Webster and Davis "displayed persistent symptoms of discomfort, avoidance, and repression" as a consequence of such "debilitating divisions."[228]

Their tragedies are tied to the malaise of the modern lawyer. Brandeis' career demonstrates that the modern choice is not necessary, that it's possible to be proficient through an alternative type of specialization and to reconcile interests through the recognition of the potentialities for social change. Since modern ideology claims interests are subjective and intelligence is always an esoteric enterprise, is it any wonder that modern lawyers choose not to confront the possibility that interests can be reconciled and that integrating intelligence can be applied in the modern world?

The ideological devils of complexity, bigness and specialization mystify moral choices. As we have seen, the choices they support are not necessary

---

[228] This judgment was made not about Webster but about Davis and Charles Evans Hughes in Auerbach, Review, 87 Harv. L. Rev. 1100, 1110 (1974). But see the psycho-histories of Webster.

ones. Yet, alternatives to the modern choices must be carefully examined. We cannot simply reject the choices institutionalized in modern legal practice. There are dangers to be avoided. Rejecting the law as a technical specialty may result in a disintegrating personalistic culture. Making lawyers leaders may result in abuses of power. Brokering interests may result in the tyranny of the majority. As Brandeis warned, our approach must be that of "attacking evil *in situ*,"[229] remembering "that progress is necessarily slow; that remedies are necessarily tentative; that because of varying conditions there must be much and constant enquiry into facts...and much experimentation."[230] I, therefore, will turn in the next chapters to an examination of modern legal practice attentive to variations, exploring possibilities.

---

[229] Urofsky at 155.

[230] *Ibid.*

Chapter Two

SERVING THE CORPORATE CLIENT: THE PROBLEM OF PROBLEM-SETTING

FOUR CASES WHERE LEGAL ADVICE FAILED

(1) DIVISION WORLD

Three lawyers in one firm were outside tax counsel to Division World. They would receive work from Division World's inside lawyers who, in turn, were responding to questions from corporate and divisional finance departments. "We [outside counsel] would be asked whether a particular tax code provision has been interpreted in one way or another. We would research the question and report back to the inside counsel." The inside counsel then would communicate the information to "the client."

Eventually, a securities class action suit was brought against the company for overstating its financial position. Although any of the entries in the corporate books arguably could be justified, in sum they constituted misrepresentation. The company did not survive this suit.

(2) HYPERTECH

Hypertech produces sophisticated electronic products. Their staff of research engineers is serviced by a prominent outside patent law firm. These attorneys are available and responsive to Hypertech's engineers. Whenever an engineer asks for a patent, the law firm processes it. Hypertech now possesses a ream of patents, of undetermined value. No inquiry has ever been made for any patent about its desirability to the company. Hypertech has yet to enforce any of its patents, yet it annually spends at least one million dollars on this process.

(3) INTERNATIONAL CHEMICALS

An International Chemicals salesman contacted one of the company's inside counsel to draw up a contract for a sale to Beauty, Inc., a major manufacturer of personal products. Beauty planned to use the chemical it was buying in its perfumes. Chemicals previously had sold the chemical only for use in making steel. The salesman was delighted, but concerned. He saw a new market opening up, but was worried because the chemical's medical effects were unknown. He explained the problem to the inside counsel. The lawyer responded by drawing up a contract with a disclaimer of warranties of fitness for the proposed use and with an indemnification clause in the event of third-party suits against Chemicals. The salesman, satisfied his company was insured against liability, proceeded not only to deal with Beauty but also to aggressively market the chemical to the beauty industry.

After International Chemicals became a major supplier to the beauty industry, the chemical's adverse medical consequences were uncovered. Although largely protected by the indemnification clause, the company, in response to public pressure, made efforts to compensate those harmed. The efforts may have been token, but nonetheless they were costly to International Chemicals. The company also increased its public relations expenditures, trying to restore its good name. Eventually, the government intervened and imposed costly regulations on the chemical's manufacture and distribution.

(4) GOOD LABS

Good Labs contacted a Washington outside counsel, inquiring about whether a certain vitamin supplement could be marketed in the United States. The lawyer researched the law and wrote a memo, correctly stating that it could be marketed. Through personal contacts, the outside counsel discovered the FDA was concerned about the product because it was being hailed spuriously as a "wonder drug." He also reported these concerns.

The lawyer's advice did not surprise Good Lab managers. An internal dispute about whether to market the vitamin supplement, dividing corporate management, had motivated the inquiry. One management coalition said: "It's probably legal but it's going to be bought as a 'wonder drug' and our company shouldn't be identified with it. Anyway, the FDA will eventually limit its use." Another coalition argued: "Let the customers decide. We won't violate any laws, but until they come into effect, we can make good money."

The vitamin supplement was marketed. The sales exceeded projections, mostly due to the "wonder drug" claim. The FDA publicized the product's lack of proven effect, condemning the company for profiting from a patent medicine. When regulations restricting the product's sale were enacted, Good Labs withdrew it. The company never measured the degree to which marketing this product tarnished its public image. The FDA, however, viewed the marketing of this product as a sign of Good Labs' mercenary management and began an investigation of the company's major product to determine whether it was being overprescribed. Publicity stemming from that investigation reduced the sales of what had been the company's major profit center. Good Labs' profits declined in just the subsequent four months by the amount they had increased due to the sales of the vitamin supplement.

PROFESSIONAL ROLES AND CLIENT CONTROL:
PROBLEM-SETTING AS A PROBLEM

In one sense, none of these lawyers can be faulted for their work. The information they provided was accurate. In one sense, they served their clients. They followed instructions. In one sense, these cases do not illustrate the failure of legal advice. When confronted with the consequences to their clients and the public, the involved lawyers replied with variants of what has been called the lawyer's "kiss-off": "That's not my job."[243]

What is a lawyer's job? The answer to this question is basic to three related inquiries: (1) What is the lawyer's social function? It is hardly surprising that a lawyer involved in one of the above cases concluded: "A lawyer is essentially a nonproductive drag on society. I have a completely parasitic function;" (2) How do lawyers serve clients? A manager involved in one of the cases said, "I want the lawyer to make me feel comfortable in my job." He wanted the lawyer to assume responsibility for more than solving the "legal" problem. Each of the four cases demonstrates the potential gap between serving clients and solving legal problems; and (3) What are the ethics of legal practice? As the interviewed lawyers demonstrate, "It's not my job" is the classic attorney response to ethical inquiry.

How a job comes to be constituted is what organizational sociologists call "the problem of job-definition."[244] This problem has special poignancy for lawyers. A distinctive trait of professionals is that they control their work. The lawyer, like any professional, should be expected to define his job. He is not a worker who must take the task given to him. "The [professional's] client, unlike the customer, is not always right:" "A profession proceeds on the assumption that...the individual does not know what is good for him. The client...is often ignorant. Authority passes to the professional, who must give him what he needs, rather than what he wants."[245] No matter how surprising it is that anyone in the second half of the twentieth century can react to normative challenges by responding that the problem lies outside his job-

---

[243] Simon, "Ideology of Advocacy: Procedural Justice and Professional Ethics," 1978 Wisc. L. Rev. 29, 74 n.100 (1978).

[244] Most discussions of job definition distinguish two dimensions—control over product and control over procedure—which separate ends and means. In discussing "problem-setting," I reject this distinction, following the proclaimed neutrality of professionals, which collapses ends into means. (For example, there is supposedly no difference between representing the guilty and the innocent.) I chose to reject this distinction because my concern is with how professional judgment influences outcomes. Because of the choice not to separate means and ends, this discussion is close to what may be called, "the construction of legal problems." See P. Berger & T. Luckmann, The Social Construction of Reality (1966).

[245] Marshall, "The Recent History of Professionalism in Relation to Social Structure and Social Policy," in Class, Citizenship, and Social Development: Essays of T.H. Marshall 158, 164 (1965). The consequence of letting the client, like the customer, be always right is that the professional prematurely retreats to technology. See P. Selznick, Leadership in Administration 75 n.9 (1957).

definition, it is even more surprising that a professional would make such a claim.

Work can be controlled by various means. Control may be exercised through command, through selection of who is to be employed, through manipulating the psychology of those employed, and through structuring the incentives facing those doing the work. Current discussion of the autonomy of lawyers in their work deals with only these methods of control. For example, inside counsels' supposed lack of autonomy is said to stem from their greater attention to the commands of businessmen, weak background, loyalty to the corporation and dependence on long-term employment with the corporation.

There is, however, another method of control. The task of this chapter is to bring it to the center of discussions of lawyer autonomy. That method is problem-setting. To control the lawyer's work agenda, the topics and programme of his research, is to control the lawyer's autonomy. It may be a "roundabout" method of control,[246] but it is a primary one. If what a lawyer takes as his problem is restricted, his ability to exert independent judgment is, from the beginning, sharply constrained.[247]

The following discussion explores three aspects of problem-setting in corporate legal work. First, I analyze the cases introducing this chapter in terms of recurrent features of organizational life, bureaucratic and political pathologies. By ignoring these organizational pathologies, the lawyers involved in the above cases misserved their clients. If the function of legal service is not to exacerbate these pathologies, lawyers must be sensitive to them, recasting their problems when necessary. Second, I consider recurrent features of corporate legal work, timing and fragmentation. Their presence in the above cases should have alerted the involved lawyers to the need to confront how their problems were set. Failing to recast the problem in response to these signals will misserve the client. Finally, I consider problem-setting in terms of the legal profession's ideology and ethics.

---

[246] R. Dahl & C. Lindblom, Politics, Economics, and Welfare 110 (1953).

[247] One of the principal findings of Heinz and Laumann is that corporate clients control problem-setting, restricting the lawyer's autonomy. Heinz .& Laumann, "Client Interests, Professional Roles, and Social Hierarchies," 76 Mich. L. Rev. 1111, 1125 (1977). The importance of problem-setting in other professions also has been recognized. See Moore's summary of the literature, W. E. Moore, The Profession' Roles and Rules 88 (1970). As E. C. Hughes notes: "It is characteristic of many occupations that the people in them, although convinced that they themselves are the best judges, not merely of their own competence but also of what is best for the people for whom they perform services, are required in some measure to yield judgment of what is wanted to those amateurs who receive the services." E. C. Hughes, Men and Their Work 54 (1958).

PROFESSIONAL AUTONOMY AND ORGANIZATIONAL GOALS: POLITICAL AND BUREAUCRATIC PATHOLOGIES

As Durkheim emphasized, much can be learned from negative cases. To explore how problem-setting affects the service lawyers' tender to their corporate clients, I will develop the brief horror stories that introduced this chapter.

The Division World case would seem to be an inappropriate one for discussing controls on lawyer problem-setting. It deals with tax practice, which is frequently hailed as the area where lawyers have greatest control. In tax, the open secret is that lawyers are setting the problem, if not inventing purposes, when they argue that "clients often need help in thinking out and articulating their own real objectives."[248] Yet, lawyer control in tax practice has a single groundnorm: minimizing client tax liability. Applying this norm at Division World wreaked havoc. Why?

The outside firm applied the norm of minimizing tax liability to each discrete inquiry. The different divisions sought and obtained advice favoring their own balance sheets. In this case, as an involved lawyer later realized, someone was needed to play a supervisory role, telling management: "We did this here, but this is happening over there. And if this is true, you have got problems and you better handle them now."

The outside counsel didn't assume that role, exercising control over how the problems were set, for at least two reasons. First, several partners at the firm "represented" Division World. The partner who initially obtained the representation, who had been a golfing buddy of the company's starting entrepreneur, had retired and passed the reins to three lawyers he had trained. These lawyers did not communicate with each other, perhaps because of intra-firm competition or personality differences. Second, the outside counsel thought Division World's inside counsel were "purchasing agents" for their services. They thought the inside counsel analyzed the problems before they were set and sent to outside counsel. In fact, the inside counsel merely forwarded to outside counsel requests from Division World's different divisions.

The divisional manager, the inside counsel and the outside attorney formed a triangle. Each did his own work "without seeing the bigger problem." Everyone only grasped a piece of the structure. Each legal problem was seen as a discrete project and the outside counsel felt, as one explained, "no encouragement or inducement to go that further step." They relied on the inside counsel, while the inside counsel relied on them. No one asserted that quality legal service required seeing the larger picture. No one performed the necessary coordination and the company did not survive the securities class

---

[248] Darrell, "Conscience and Propriety in Tax Practice," in The Lawyer in Modern Society, 2d Ed., at 361, 363 (V. Countryman, et al., eds. 1976).

action suit.

The outside counsel blamed the client. They blamed Division World's inside counsel and managers for failing to explain that they didn't want the norm of minimizing tax liability to be applied to each of their transactions, but rather to the entire corporate balance sheet. It was Division World's responsibility, outside counsel claimed, to set up a relationship where the lawyers did not exacerbate the tension between the goals of individual managers and the corporation. Outside counsel's denial of responsibility, however, is too easy. Legal clients, like the clients of any professional, take cues from their lawyers to determine how to act as clients.[249] Lawyers are obligated to help their clients obtain professional service.

The Hypertech case reveals another way that the disjunction between the goals of corporate personnel and the goals of the corporation can affect the usefulness of legal advice. The outside patent attorneys were satisfied to satisfy the engineers. They did not question the engineers' goals. They did not ask, "Why should the corporation want this patent?" Yet, without an answer to that question, the lawyer only can be a conduit—a mover of the legal process. He can have no strategy to guide his actions, and thus, regardless of the costs incurred, he cannot assess the utility of his work to the corporate client. The corporation perforce will find itself both "over-serviced and under-serviced."[250]

The Hypertech lawyers also blamed the corporation. Hypertech should have established standards for patent work, they argued.[251] Yet, the company did have standards. The Vice-President of Research and Development blamed outside counsel for overriding these standards in processing the claims for their "customers," the engineers:

> [Outside counsel] have less reason to be circumspect about the breadth of the claims they file and the usefulness to the company of their time and effort. With inside counsel, the corporation is the client, not the technical people. As manager of R & D, I don't have the time to police technical people. When we used outside counsel, I saw that the filings and the extent of the claims were often not in the best interest of the company. We needed to intercept that process so we hired inside counsel. I am not suggesting dishonesty or lack of integrity. Outside counsel were satisfying the customer. But the technical people don't have the company's long-term perspective. They have a personal interest in filing a case on which they have been involved. We try to educate them about commercial

---

[249] P. Elliott, The Sociology of the Professions 104 (1972).

[250] Fitch, "The Role of the Outside Patent Law Firm," in Proceedings of Wisconsin's 10th Annual Corporate Lawyers Institute, 1964, at 127, 129 (1965).

[251] Fitch analyzes a similar problem in this manner: "Management doesn't know why it is taking out patents...the Outside Patent Counsel is left floundering....," *ibid.*

considerations, but... Outside counsel were satisfying the customer. For our patent filings to serve the company, there can't be a lawyer-client relation. There has to be a duality of interests between the lawyer and the client.

The Hypertech case involves more than inattentiveness to corporate goals. The lawyers undermined hierarchical control within the corporation. The lawyers neither understood the effect of their work on intra-corporate processes, nor did they work through these processes: "We need the lawyer to force the clients to document their work well. The attorney has to rake the bench chemist over the coals and make sure he has done all the right things. We have instituted forms but the lawyer must insist that these forms are filled out well. If a sloppy form triggers a patent process then the clients [the engineers] know they can get attention quickly." In forsaking control over problem-setting, the lawyer is assuming that his work is either the end-product of corporate decision-making or a datum that will be unproblematically ingested by corporate decision-makers. Having made this assumption, Hypertech's outside counsel misserved their clients.

Hypertech ended the lawyer-client relationship described in the case. They took their patent work from outside counsel and assigned it to the corporate legal department. They turned to inside counsel to insure that the interests of technical people and the interest of the company would be conjoined. They also expected inside counsel would set the legal problem so that it would be more consistent with corporate controls. They did not think outside counsel could move beyond the engineers' expressed interests to perceive the goals of the entire company.

In both the Division World and Hypertech cases, outside counsel did not "go that further step" to recognize a standard feature of corporate life: bureaucratic pathologies. Bureaucratic pathologies are displacements of corporate goals.[252] Goals are displaced when (1) instrumental values become terminal values,[253] (2) corporate goals conflict and contradictions are resolved by selective attention to a sub-set of the goals in particular operations,[254] or (3) goals of sub-units diverge from the goals of the organization as a whole.[255]

As the two cases demonstrate, bureaucratic pathologies are commonplace in corporate legal practice. Lawyers know that managers may want their "pet

---

[252] Merton, "Bureaucratic Structure and Personality," in Social Theory and Social Structure, 1968 Enlarged Edition 249 (1968).

[253] *Ibid.*

[254] R. Cyert & J. March, A Behavioral Theory of the Firm, 28, 35-36 (1963).

[255] Warner & Havens, "Goal Displacement and the Intangibility of Organizational Goals," 12 Ad. Sci. Q. 545 (1968); Perrow, "The Analysis of Goals in Complex Organizations," 26 Am. Soc. Rev. 854 (1961); Selznick, "An Approach to a Theory of Bureaucracy," 8 Am. Soc. Rev. 49 (1943).

project" to go through, no matter what. They know managers might be tempted to favor the instant customer at corporate expense. They know divisions will often be concerned with their immediate balance sheet and therefore avoid spending money now, even if it will cost them much more later.[256]

Lawyers, however, frequently ignore these facts. An obvious indication of the problem is that lawyers, both inside and outside, will frequently call corporate sub-units, and the managers employed by them, "my clients," even though they know the corporation "as an entity" is the client. And lawyers prize having these sub-units and their managers call them "my lawyer." The solution to this problem is that lawyers must exercise more control over how problems are set for them by their "clients"—corporate employees.

Hypertech's decision to internally hire patent lawyers illustrates the most common response to bureaucratic pathologies: create a staff function.[257] But, because of both their relation to Hypertech's organization and the profession's concept of its role, outside counsel should have been able to recognize and resolve bureaucratic pathologies. Outside counsel engage in "communication out of channels," are "marginal men" to the corporation and engage in "boundary spanning." The organizational literature suggests that such characteristics enable one to detect and respond to bureaucratic pathologies.[258] Lawyers are loyal to the corporation "as an entity," and the professional literature has long recognized this service may depend on counteracting bureaucratic pathologies by "communication out of channels."[259] Why weren't the lawyers in the first two cases sensitive and

---

[256] Of course, these are not the only reasons for bureaucratic pathologies. Bureaucratic pathologies also stem from "excessive efforts on the part of persons in leadership positions to maintain aloofness from their subordinates; ritualistic attachments to formal procedures; petty insistence on the rights of one's status within the organization; insensitivity to the needs of subordinates or clients; resistance to conflict within an organization; and resistance to change." I. Sharkansky, Public Administration: Policy Administration in Government Agencies 52 (1972).

[257] On the use of staff to reduce bureaucratic pathologies, see Wilensky, "Intelligence in Industry: The Uses and Abuses of Experts," 38 Annals of the Am. Acad. of Pol. Soc. Sci. 46, 51-53 (1970).

[258] See, e.g., H. Wilensky, Organizational Intelligence 47 (1967).

[259] E.g., "One of the great handicaps the American corporation has...lies in the clogging up of lines of communication. Though communication 'through channels' is not the fetish it is in the military, there is a strong tendency to insist on it, and the result is an inevitable distortion.... Here is a significant opportunity for real service by the lawyer. Without any threat to corporate morale, he can cut through the hierarchic lines of communication...." Fuller, "The Role of the Lawyer in Labor Relations," 41 A.B.A.J. 342, 344 (1955); "Free and open discussions are possible and usual between the executive personnel and inside counsel...In other words the inside counsel can have a kind of amalgamating effect between the divisions and units of the company and he can thus be a very positive influence far beyond his professional job." Ruder, "A Suggestion for Increased Use of Corporate Legal Departments in Modern Corporations," L'Juriste de Enterprise 281 (Comm. droit et view des affaires 1968).

responsive to the presence of bureaucratic pathologies?

In the International Chemicals and Good Labs cases there was not a split between management goals and corporate goals, as there was in the first two cases. They are not cases of bureaucratic pathologies. At International Chemicals and Good Labs, corporate goals were not fixed. But, as in the first two cases, because the lawyers failed to analyze the corporate organization and control how their problems were set, they misserved their clients. The last two cases reflect lawyer insensitivity to, what I term, "political pathologies."

At International Chemicals, salesmen are allowed, even encouraged, to discover new markets. For the company to succeed, it must grant discretion to its sales' force. In sales, in particular, International Chemicals is a modern, flexible corporation. To label it a "bureaucracy," would be inaccurate. Many managers have the power to mobilize corporate resources and contribute to defining corporate policies.

The absence of hierarchical checks and balances is part of this flexibility. In particular, the International Chemicals salesman in the case did not have to convince his line-supervisors that the chemical was not defective in its proposed use. Initially, the salesman said he "didn't think the profits on this minor sale justified gearing up the whole process [of testing for defects]." After the beauty industry recognized the chemical's advantages, testing no longer seemed necessary. The salesman substituted the test of the market for medical tests.

It is worth emphasizing that no one at International Chemicals wanted to sell harmful products. Instead, the company lacked organizational systems that combined the desired flexibility at the sales level with adequate safety procedures. An objective of products liability law is to induce companies to develop such organizational systems.

International Chemicals did require the salesman to contact a lawyer. The lawyer, even after being told of the manager's concerns, set the problem as a contracts case. Unconcerned about International Chemical's organizational weaknesses, the lawyer defined the problem as one of insuring the company through contractual clauses.

Unlike International Chemicals, which involves the problematic exercise of discretion at rather low levels, the Good Labs case deals with discretion at the top of the company. In asking its Washington counsel to determine whether the vitamin supplement could be marketed, Good Labs was asking its lawyer to assist it in choosing its character in the marketplace. The Washington counsel defined the problem as one of information gathering. The information conveyed, in one sense, was neutral with respect to the battle within the company. The sides had been formed assuming the information the lawyer tendered. Yet, the lawyer unwittingly commanded one coalition's charge.

While the Washington counsel blithely ignored the divisions within corporate management, he was being drafted. His authoritative presentation of his findings, which was scrupulously neutral with respect to the ultimate business judgment, was a powerful weapon in the "let the customers decide" coalition's campaign. The timing of his report and its concentration on regulatory liability empowered the more "legalistic" coalition.

The battle within management demonstrates that corporations pay homage to values other than avoiding liability and consumer sovereignty. Corporate reputation concerned at least some of the managers. Why did it not concern the lawyer?

As in the International Chemicals case, we might have expected the Good Labs' attorney to have set the problem differently. To put it grossly, *caveat emptor* and the FDA assume and depend upon corporate concern for reputation. The legal regime relies on corporations to strive to maintain good will and voluntarily refuse to sell useless products even though a customer might buy them.

As he set the problem, the Washington counsel misunderstood the client's question. This misunderstanding is understandable, if unfortunately it is also commonplace. Businessmen want to be professionals, but they also don't want to appear weak. They sometimes ask their lawyers to translate their moral ideas into legal norms so that they can say, "The reason for this is supported in the law." But, to avoid appearing weak, businessmen may ask this only implicitly. If the lawyer is insensitive to this implicit request, he is doing a disservice to his client. The client is asking for more than information gathering.

In these last two cases, the lawyer saw the choice of corporate policy as a "business judgment." He claimed to be only a resource-person. He emphasized his expertise's neutrality with respect to goals. Yet in both cases, the expertise helped shape the goals. The lawyers never considered either the vast discretion the corporation delegated or the inadequacies of the corporate organization supposedly supporting the delegation.[260] Both corporations had decision-making structures whose inadequacies legal service exacerbated.

Lawyers confront the problem of inadequate decision-making structures in other contexts. A litigator, for example, reported:

It often happens in litigation that you can't find out what hap-

---

[260] Regulators, unlike lawyers, as the Good Labs case demonstrates, are concerned about company's organizational weaknesses. According to Bardach and Kagan: "[I]nspectors...treat business corporations as monolithic legal entities, with a single will and an internally consistent attitude toward social and legal responsibilities. To corporate managers, on the other hand, the corporation is a loose conglomeration of separate departments and managers, each with distinct problems." Bardach & Kagan, *supra*, at 81. Bureaucratic and political pathologies, consequently, may be very costly to the company.

pened. No one knows. We kid ourselves that when you take a deposition in a Japanese organization you can't find anyone who made the decision because it was made by consensus. But, at times in American companies, you also can't find this out. Decisions grow up like topsy. Sales are off doing this and others are over there, but all of a sudden you have a corporate decision.

This litigator also failed to confront the dilemma of corporate discretion: "I told the client I would quit unless they put in a litigation support team." The team helped the lawyer process the instant case, but it did not help the corporation make future decisions. The client continues to find itself in avoidable litigation.

I call these problems, "political pathologies." They arise because corporations continuously choose goals and policies. Clients do not always bring set goals to their lawyers.[261] The lawyer may be part of the corporate goal-creating process.[262] Where bureaucratic pathologies displace goals, political pathologies distort goal creation and implementation.[263]

Managers implicitly understand Marx. If they were to blindly pursue profit, crises would result. To avoid these crises, managers choose goals and policies that take into account both the internal needs of the corporation and the external demands of the environment.[264] An organic metaphor fits. The

---

[261] See Perrow, "The Analysis of Goals in Complex Organizations," 26 Am. Soc. Rev 854 (1961); Selznick, "Foundation of a Theory of Organization," 13 Am. Soc. Rev. 25 (1948).

[262] For the centrality of the staff's political contribution to the organization, see, e.g., D. Katz & R. Kahn, The Social Psychology of Organizations (1966).

[263] Distinguishing bureaucratic and political pathologies is consistent with Samuel Huntington's distinction between "executive" and "legislative" processes. Bureaucratic pathologies plague "executive" processes. (In an executive process: "(1) [T]he participating units differ in power (i.e., are hierarchically arranged); (2) fundamental goals and values are not at issue; and (3) the range of possible choice is limited.") Political pathologies plague "legislative" processes. (In a legislative process: "(1) [T]he units participating in the process are relatively equal in power (and consequently must bargain with each other); (2) important disagreements exist concerning the goals of policy; and (3) there are many possible alternatives.") S. Huntington, The Common Defense 146 (1961), quoted in G. Allison, Essence of Decision 156 (1971). This approach reveals a weakness in Cyert and March's definition of bureaucratic pathologies as including action in the face of inconsistent goals. They claim that in such a situation, it is proper to speak of the displacement of goals. Cyert & March, *supra*, at 35-36. In some instances, that may be true, such as when a minor policy displaces a major goal. But, in some instances, the supposedly inconsistent goals actually indicate the corporation has failed to agree on a goal. In such cases, a poorly-functioning bureaucracy may not be at fault. Rather, the openness of goals attests to the presence of political choice, which may or may not be adequately organized.

[264] McGuire is accurate, if exceedingly vehement, in seeing that "one obtains from Selznick the picture of the firm in a sort of organizational bathysphere, moving through the water-like environment which presses on it from without, and filled with air-like pressures which tend to explode or collapse its organization, or at least alter its symmetrical shape." McGuire, "The Concept of the Firm," in Readings in Organizational Theory: A Behavioral Approach 18 (W. Hill & D. Evan eds. 1966).

corporate body cannot set goals on its own terms. Setting a maximum bodily temperature is appropriate for a crematorium, but not for a body that must make peace with its internal organs and its environment.[265] Today, even economists recognize corporate goals are not just profit maximization and any theory of the firm must describe the corporation setting goals to reach equilibrium with the systems with which it interchanges.[266]

Organizations are systems in which goals are dynamic, structures are multifunctional and power is a shifting resource.[267] Instead of defining a corporation only as a bureaucracy, consequently, one must also define it "as a coalition of interest groups, sharing a common resource base, paying homage to a common mission, and depending upon a larger context for its legitimacy and development."[268] The corporation is both a bureaucracy and a political body.[269] Students of organizational behavior, therefore, seek to understand not only the frailties of command, but also the organization's political system.[270]

Corporate actions are conditioned by both dependence and independence. Organizations provide bases for both cooperation and conflict. Many corporate decisions are best understood as "political resultants": *"Resultants in the sense that what happens is not chosen as a solution to a problem but rather results from compromise, conflict and unequal influence. Political in the sense that the activity from which decisions and actions emerge is best*

---

[265] The metaphor is from Byrom, "Business in the Society of the Future," in The Changing Role of Business in Society 41 (G. Steiner ed. 1976).

[266] See I. Horowitz, Decision-Making and the Theory of the Firm (1970); O. Williamson, Corporate Control and Business Behavior (1970) (In imperfectly competitive markets, the internal structure of the firm cannot be overlooked because competition does not ensure that only efficiently organized firms will survive).

[267] On dynamic goals, see R. Cyert & J. March, A Behavioral Theory of the Firm 346 (1963); Mohr, "The Concept of Organizational Goal," 67 Am. Pol. Sci. Rev. 470 (1973). On multifunctional structures, see H. Koontz & C. O'Donell, Management: A Systems and Contingency Analysis of the Managerial Function (1976); Yuchtman & Seashore, "A System Resource Approach to Managerial Effectiveness," 32 Am. Soc. Rev. 891 (1967). On shifting power, see G. Allison, Essence of Decision (1971); P. Selznick, Leadership in Administration (1957).

[268] Miles, "Introduction," in Resourcebook in Micro-Organizational Behavior 1, 5 (R. Miles ed. 1980).

[269] "[T]he experts who deal with external interests and clienteles on behalf of their corporate employers... must perforce represent their clients within the corporation...The large corporation has moved very far toward a 'pluralist government,' representative of many constituencies, without ever really intending to. That government is not precisely democratic, but neither is it automatic or monolithic. The experts are heard—and sometimes believed after suitable deflation." W. E. Moore, The Conduct of the Corporation 186 (1962).

[270] The literature is reviewed in Roger Noll, "Government Administrative Behavior: A Multidisciplinary Survey," in The Changing Role of Business in Society 97 (G. Steiner ed. 1976).

characterized as bargaining among regularized channels among individual members."[271]

Corporate decisions are subject to all the distortions of political behavior. Constitution-writing is a precarious task. Responsibility must be divided and consequent coordination is fragile, subject both to unforeseen demands on the system and territorial battles between groups. In other words, corporations may allocate discretion without insuring that its exercise is accountable.[272] Consequently, to serve a corporation as an entity, as the International Chemicals case demonstrates, the lawyer cannot stop his inquiry after learning that the manager with whom he deals is authorized to make the decision.

Political systems depend not only on control, but also on leadership. When leadership is not properly exercised in its internal politics, corporations will have distorted decisions. Corporations will drift from political battle to political battle. Individual strivings for power will become the imperative of decision-making. Decisions will be the result of the sheer play of power, unconnected to the corporate mission. Political pathologies, not adaptive flexibility, will result.[273] But, leadership is a challenge and can be easily subverted. As Philip Selznick explains, guiding discretion is always

---

[271] G. Allison, Essence of Decision 162 (1971) (emphasis in original). For organizations as coalitions of groups with divergent claims and interests united in a continuous process of bargaining, see Cyert & March, *supra*, at 27; F. Kast & J. Rosenzweig, Organization and Management: System Approach, 2d Ed., 42 (1971). For the emphasis on decision processes, as opposed to individual choice, see H. Simon, Administrative Behavior, 1st Ed., 220-22 (1947); O. Williamson, Corporate Control and Business Behavior, Chapter 3 (1970); M. Crozier, The Bureaucratic Phenomenon (1964); J. K. Galbraith, The New Industrial State, Chapter 8 (1967); Lazarsfeld & Menzel, "On the Relationship between Individual and Collective Properties," in A Sociological Reader on Complex Organizations 499 (A. Etzioni ed. 1969).

[272] R Miles, et al., *supra*, at 20-21. Mark, Planning on Uncertainty: Decision Making in Business and Government Administration 130 (1971); Cohn, "Bureaucratic Flexibility: Some Comments on Robert Merton's 'Bureaucratic Structure and Personality,'" 21 Br. J. Soc. 390 (1970).

[273] P. Selznick, Leadership in Administration 25ff (1957). Of course, this is not a complete list of the causes of political pathologies. In a political system, mobilization is a problem: Issues may not be on the agenda; involvement may be unstable; the buck may be passed; or slack may be used as side-payments to demobilize challenges. In a political system, decision-making is also problematic: Actors may be obstreperous; they may make non-negotiable demands; demands may escalate, be stalemated, or be resolved by unjustified mutual adjustment issues may not meet because of the conflict of incompatible expertises; or issues may be resolved not on their merits, but because of rivalries, coalitions, large majorities or small minorities. Samuel P. Huntington summarizes the pathologies of political decision-making as: (1) "avoiding controversial issues, delaying decisions on them, referring them to other bodies for resolution"; (2) "compromise and logrolling, that is, trading off subordinate interests for major interests"; (3) "expressing policies in vague generalities, representing the upon assumptions which may or may not be realistic." S. Huntington, The Common Defense, 162, 163, 164, 165 (1961), quoted in G. Allison, Essence of Decision 157 (1971).

problematic: "In exercising control, leadership has a dual task. It must win the consent of constituent units, in order to maximize voluntary cooperation, and therefore must permit emergent interest blocks a wide degree of representation. At the same time, in order to hold the helm, it must see that a balance of power appropriate to the fulfillment of key commitments will be maintained."[274] Consequently, to serve the corporate client as an entity, as the Good Labs case demonstrates, the lawyer must understand how leadership is being exercised within the corporation. A lawyer seeking neutrally to supply information must understand distortions in the corporation's processing of that information.[275] A lawyer who understands that corporate decisions are political resultants will consider how his service affects the functioning of the corporate political system and the control of employee discretion by the corporate mission.

To serve the client "as an entity," the corporate lawyer perforce must engage the corporation's decision-making processes. "Mending information nets,"[276] is important, but will only correct bureaucratic pathologies. To be effective, a lawyer also must be able to mend intra-corporate political processes.[277] As the horror stories in this chapter illustrate, the lawyer must be concerned with "the special requirements for authority concentrations and distributions within the corporate structure."[278] He must evaluate power and discretion within the corporation guided by what Herbert Simon has called the "third basis for decision-making": "[T]he social value of the organizational structure may be determined by noting the degree of coincidence between the organizationally correct and the socially correct decisions."[279]

---

[274] P. Selznick, Leadership in Administration 63-64 (1957). This also implies, as is well known, corporate boards by themselves cannot govern. For the relationship of this fact to implementing corporate social responsibility, see Coffee, "Beyond the Shut-Eyed Sentry: Toward a Theoretical View of Corporate Misconduct and an Effective Legal Response," 63 Va. L. Rev. 1099 (1977).

[275] Cf. J. Pfeffer & G. Salancik, The External Control of Organizations 1978. "If organizations are constrained by their context, it is important to assess how the context becomes known, what important dimensions of the environment affect organizations, and how organizations may be managed to avoid making mistakes in attending to the environment." Id. at 88. "[T]he organization responds to what it perceives and believes about the world...[which] is largely determined by the existing organizational and informational structure of the organization." Id. at 89.

[276] C. Stone, Where the Law Ends: The Social Control of Corporate Behavior, Ch. 18 (1975).

[277] Compare the approach here with L. Sherman, Scandal and Reform: Controlling Police Corruption (1978). See also J. Thompson, Organizations in Action 128ff (1967).

[278] R. Eells, The Government of Corporations 10-11, quoted in D. Vogel, Lobbying the Corporation 5 (1981). Such a goal, of course, is the goal of much of corporate law. The Model Rules of Professional Conduct appears to partially recognize this in requiring the lawyer to consider "the responsibility in the organization and the apparent motivation of the person involved." Model Rules, Rule. 1.13(b). The Model Rules, however, don't help the lawyer in making this judgment. Such a judgment requires organizational analysis.

[279] H. Simon, Administrative Behavior, 2d Ed., 200 (1957). Bureaucratic and political

The lawyer therefore must evaluate corporate decision-making processes,[280] as well as the corporate legal environment. In short, the lawyer must engage in political analysis and political work.[281] He must affect and, if necessary, change corporate organizational arrangements. He must, when appropriate, guide the way managers exercise their discretion. This argument clarifies the question of professional autonomy and client control. The question is not whether lawyers give corporations goals, but what goals do lawyers advance?[282]

Since bureaucratic and political pathologies are endemic in corporate life, serving the corporation as an entity requires the lawyer to consider the setting of legal problems. In the face of known adverse consequences to the

---

pathologies not only hurt the corporation, they prevent the operationalization of corporate social responsibility. Responsible policies "are likely to founder at the operational level if the intent of top management is not made clear and if operating level management cannot or will not identify their personal goals with those of the corporation." Sethi & Votaw, "How should we develop a new corporate response to a changing social environment," in The Corporate Dilemma: Traditional Values versus Contemporary Problems 210 (D. Votaw & S. Sethi eds. 1973). Or, as Bardach and Kagan conclude: "Despite internal preventive rules, irresponsibility and dangerous actions, continue to occur, stemming from the drift of managerial attention, conflicting goals and pressures, inadequate supervisory and supporting systems, and insufficient power on the part of internal regulators, such as safety and environmental engineers." Bardach & Kagan, *supra*, at 224. To their list of internal regulators, lawyers can be added.

[280] Harold Williams, in passing, claims that the lawyer "should also be concerned with the process by which the company evaluates" its environment. From a speech by Harold Williams, then SEC Chairman, "The Role of Inside Counsel in Corporate Accountability" (10/4/79), quoted in Coombe, "Multinational Codes of Conduct and Corporate Accountability: New Opportunities for Corporate Counsel," 36 Bus. L. 11, 28 (1980). In another context, Harold Williams stated: "[L]awyers along with their more mundane responsibilities must be architects of the accountability process which provides the corporate structure with the discipline necessary for effective decision making." Speech before the ABA, 8/5/80, reprinted in The Legal Times 23, 25 (Aug. 11, 1980).

[281] Compare this conclusion about the nature of the lawyer's representative function to Hannah Pitkin's general conclusion about representation: "Thus the development and improvement of representative institutions, the cultivation of persons capable of looking after the interests of others in a responsive manner, are essential if the fine vision that constitutes the idea of representation is to have any effect on our actual lives." H. Pitkin, The Concept of Representation 239 (1967).

[282] As already noted, organization theory requires this perspective. Organization theorists dwell at length on the mistaken conception of organizational goals embodied in the traditional notion of professional autonomy. Casting lawyers as only conduits of established corporate goals is based on a misunderstanding of corporate processes. "It seems to me perfectly obvious that a description that assumes goals come first and action comes later is frequently radically wrong. Human choice behavior is at least as much a process for discovering goals as for acting on them." March, "The Technology of Foolishness," 69, 72 in Ambiguity and Choice in Organizations (J. G. March & J. Olsen 1971). Hence, lawyers must follow organizational theorists and take the position that "[i]nstead of asking Do organizations have goals? we will ask the questions, Who sets organizational goals, and How are organizational goals set?" W. R. Scott, Organizations: Rational, Natural and Open Systems 264 (1981).

corporation, the lawyer has an ethical duty to move beyond the initial definition of the problem. These four cases and organizational analysis demonstrate this duty must be expanded if lawyers are to serve their corporate clients. The corporate agent's setting of the problem is only the beginning of inquiry.[283] To serve the client as an entity, the lawyer must be sensitive to the corporate client's organization. Otherwise, his service may exacerbate bureaucratic and political pathologies. The lawyer must confront how his problems have been set.

Prescribing this expanded duty is difficult for at least two reasons. First, it requires lawyers to engage in organizational analysis, a discipline in which they may not have been trained. I suspect, however, that training is not a serious obstacle. Lawyers are "quick readers" and can understand the organization of their clients. The obstacle rather is professional ideology and ethics which seek to make lawyers independent from the organization they serve. I analyze professional ideology and ethics in the final section of this chapter.

Second, lawyers may not be able to meet an expanded duty of loyalty. As the four cases reveal, the problems lawyers face can be set so the lawyer in unaware of the pathologies or is not in a position to deal with them. In the next section, I explain what features of their problems should both alert lawyers to the organizational dilemmas of their clients and signal to them that they must confront how their problems have been set.

THE CORRELATES OF PROBLEM-SETTING

To understand the setting of legal problems, talking to the involved actors might seem a logical first step. But, in interviews, the actors claim they are not involved in problem-setting.

Top management says the lawyer determines his engagement. For example, a Chief Financial Officer, when asked about his corporation's production and financial controls over outside counsel, responded, "We can't do it." When asked, "Why not? You control the work and budgets of other specialized technical services," he responded, "We can't. Lawyers are special." Middle management says someone else has made the determination. Middle-level managers claim they use lawyers "as we are organized to use them." Going to a lawyer is simply "part of the job."

Lawyers say the client is in charge: "We are not asked about structuring our relation with the client.... It is given to us and we have to deal with it as it

---

[283] This does not deny that agent definition of the problem are entitled to presumptive validity. Accord, Model Rules, Rule 1.13 Comment "The Entity as the Client": "[T]he decisions [of corporate agents] ordinarily must be accepted by the lawyer even if their utility or prudence is doubtful." *Id.* at 50. But, as the next section reveals, there are indicators that rebut this presumption.

is given to us." A senior member of a large firm explained: "Many general counsel give outside counsel too much of a narrow charge. You don't get good information that way. *That's a problem for the corporate law department and the corporation not for the outside law firm.*" To many lawyers, client control over problem-setting is inherent in the notion of representation: "You are hired by your client for what they see fit." Yet, loyalty demands more.

The buck passing these interviews describe may account for the cases introducing this chapter. No one appears to want to assume responsibility for organizing legal service so that it best serves the client. In the previous section, I explained the frailties of corporate organization that legal service may exacerbate. Given the variation in types of services lawyers perform and client organizations, I cannot give a complete account of the determinants of problem-setting. Yet, it is possible to give a general account of situations whose presence should alert lawyers and clients to the need to confront the setting of legal problems.

THE FRAGMENTATION OF WORK

The Division World case best exemplifies the fragmentation of legal advice. Legal work may become piece-work. A client need not hire just one lawyer or firm. A client need not ask his attorney to be a counselor. A client need not make it easy for the attorney to have access to necessary information. A client may see the occurrence of legal work as unpredictable, unnecessary and unimportant. A lawyer may handle "a case" as "a case." A lawyer may view his work as specialized. A lawyer may see his role as a purely formal one. A lawyer may be hesitant about expanding his task.

Given such forces at work, it is not uncommon for legal work to appear to be a fragment, unconnected to the corporate background. The work appears as a fragment both to the client, who sees it as being removed from his purposes, and the lawyer, who sees it as a limited call on his time. In sum, today, corporate legal service is provided by a changing cast of characters who administer to complex organizations increasingly specialized and impersonal technical services which parse the organization and its legal problems.

Because of the fragmentation of legal work, the problem as set for the lawyer may be more or less co-extensive with the problem it purports to resolve. Furthermore, the actions lawyers take may be unrelated to actions taken by corporate managers and other lawyers. As at Division World, unintended consequences may follow.

What is the lawyer to do? Lawyers cannot and should not demand to take control of the client's problem. Lawyers are not required to wrest the problem from others and take the helm. But, lawyers, like managers, are demanded by their loyalty to the corporation to be both sensitive to how their work may misserve the corporation and alert to signals which indicate such a result. The fragmentation of legal work is such a signal. Lawyers must understand the lessons of fragmentation, develop judgment about what its appearance entails and respond to it, helping the client receive good service.

One lesson of fragmented legal service is a commonplace. Lawyers must know the law. Fragmentation challenges lawyers who seek to provide prudent work. Lawyers must be careful not to mischaracterize the technical legal problem at stake. Examples could be easily multiplied of the adverse consequences of that peculiar lawyerly ability to see a legal problem without seeing to what else it is connected.

I wish to focus on another lesson of fragmentation. Lawyers must know organizational dynamics. Providing service to corporate clients requires lawyers to consider information and responsibility networks within the client organization and their own. Obviously, lawyers would not often give the sole copy of their report to the valet at their client's office building. Less obvious are other ways in which organizational dynamics may frustrate the delivery of their services. When delivering fragmented legal service, lawyers should be alert to at least four ways in which their work interacts with organizational dynamics:

(1) *Fragmentation and Undermining Corporate Controls*. As already explained, at Hypertech, legal services unwittingly impeded the functioning of corporate hierarchical controls. When a lawyer receives a fragmented problem, loyalty demands that he consider its impact on corporate controls.

Hypertech is not a unique case: An inside counsel at Foodstuffs was contacted because of concern that the company was violating the antitrust laws by selling a product below cost. What should be included in costs is a legal question with possible alternative answers. Foodstuffs' inside counsel called an outside counsel who was put in touch with the manager in charge of the product. The outside attorney found a way to defend the manager's position, satisfying the manager who wanted to push his product.

Inside counsel refused to accept the outside counsel's conclusion. Although the inside lawyers knew the conclusion was legally defensible, they felt it did not resolve the pricing decision. Inside counsel conceptualized this decision as one in a series of pricing decisions made by different product managers throughout the company. To inside counsel, this problem involved the maintenance of corporate procedures for the determination of costs. Defending the manager's choice, as outside counsel concluded was possible, would undermine corporate controls. To avoid such a result, the corporate legal department favored a different method for computing costs.

A conflict ensued between the manager, supported by outside counsel, and the corporate legal department. The manager argued that if he didn't use the method supported by outside counsel his product would get killed in the marketplace. Inside counsel admitted there was enough slippage in the law to justify the marketer's action. Inside counsel argued the real problem was whether the corporation would be run according to "common sense"—not because common sense was just but because internal controls required a common sense response. Inside counsel, who had a less fragmented view of the problem, recognized its connection to problems in Foodstuffs' decision-making procedures. It's not known whether the anticipated benefits from marketing the product at the manager's price outweighed the incident internal costs to the company. What is known is that outside counsel never weighed the costs.

(2) *Fragmentation and Increasing Communication Failures.* Although general counsel claim, "a lawyer who is asked to give an opinion in respect to one aspect of a transaction is entitled to look at anything and everything he wants to that might possibly bear on that transaction,"[284] this often doesn't happen. The more fragmented his work, the less the lawyer knows about the information he actually has or needs to have. As one lawyer put it, "The system is set up to keep really knowledgeable people from getting together."

Furthermore, when legal work is fragmented managers may give lawyers only enough information for the lawyer to do a piecemeal job. Managers restrict the flow of information out of both ignorance and insecurity. When it affects the lawyer's work, restricted information is in actuality a corporate decision, which is perhaps being made at an inappropriate level.

Fragmented work also affects a lawyer's ability to verify the information he receives: "Many managers paint the rosiest possible picture. Because I am inside, I can identify such people and deal more carefully with them. You know how much credit to give them and can take steps not to let them push things through. If you were outside, you would give him an opinion letter with a very limited opinion." When a lawyer hedges his bets in response to uncertain information, of course, he only increases the likelihood that his advice will be miscommunicated. Fragmentation challenges lawyers to control the information they receive and communicate.

(3) *Fragmentation and the Fragmentation of Responsibility.* The fragmentation of legal work is based on the assumption that responsibility may be divided unproblematically: there are legal questions and there are other types of questions. In certain cases, however, responsibility is difficult to divide.

Consider what happens when a union files for arbitration of a grievance. The plant manager asks the lawyer whether he acted "properly." The lawyer has the labor-management contract and the facts. He can answer that, under the contract, the action was legally proper. But can he assess the effects on employee morale, future labor-management contracts, or even the possibility of a strike? Can he then in any but the most limited sense determine whether

---

[284] Forrow, "Special Problems of Inside Counsel for Industrial Companies," 33 Bus. Law. 1453, 1466-67 (1978).

the manager's action was "proper"?[285]

The fragmentation of legal work may also affect how clients exercise responsibility over it: "During litigation, I have a great deal of contact with the responsible managers. But, there is another level of decision-making. You talk to those involved, not the VP's who can make the decision about settlement. You don't talk to the VP's with the frequency you talk to middle-level managers." Consequently, this outside counsel admits he "all too often processes the case," instead of having the client responsibly control it.

Fragmentation also limits the lawyer's ability to determine if the manager is acting responsibly. It contributes to the lawyer's inability to distinguish between the goal of the manager with whom he has contact and the goals of the corporation. The lawyer doesn't, for example, know "if the managers are cutting each other's throats" in the marketplace. The lawyer can act only as an advocate for a position. He cannot be a clearinghouse for relevant information. Consequently, when fragmentation exists, it is particularly important that the lawyer try to insure that the choice of which risks to take is being made at appropriate levels within the organization. As an inside counsel prescribed: "You make sure his supervisor knows the risks. You write letters saying, 'You need to get these people to sign off on this.'"

Unfortunately many lawyers, especially outside counsel, argue they need not take the correlates of fragmentation into account: "Have I checked up on whether they have followed my advice? It has never been the role of the lawyer to walk through a client's books and records to see if they have followed the advice;" Or, "All I do is give advice. X told me my client was Charlie. I gave Charlie my advice and he chose to ignore it. I have discharged my responsibility." Fragmentation requires lawyers to consider the fragmentation of responsibility if they are to be loyal to the corporation as an entity.

(4) *Fragmentation and Corporate Adaptivity.* Fragmentation decreases a lawyer's ability to recognize and correct deficiencies in corporate learning processes.[286] When a lawyer "deals with a case as a case," he is unlikely to concern himself with the replicability of cases:

> I don't feel it is part of my job to follow up. That's management's decision. I don't feel it is necessary to tell them that if they have had a thousand lawsuits it's necessary to change the product on my thousand and one. Supposedly someone has thought about that. They know the costs and have decided not to change.

---

[285] See Maddock, "The Challenge to House Counsel," in Corporate Law: 1958, Proceedings of the 4th Annual House Counsel Institute 1, 4 (1959).

[286] For a discussion of corporate learning processes, see R. Cyert & J. March, A Behavioral Theory of the Firm 123-25 (1963).

This assumes a great deal of the client. It doesn't recognize that information might get lost. It doesn't recognize that decisions might not be made. Furthermore, fragmentation decreases lawyers' abilities both to detect when this assumption is misplaced and to respond by correcting deficiencies in corporate learning processes: "The tendency of litigation is to focus on each problem and not raise a problem which occurred five years previously."

When his work is less fragmented, the lawyer can use the information he receives, as an inside counsel noted, to "see applications in other areas; I can see trends and fix them." In fact, one of the inside counsel's supposed advantages is their ability to gather information and improve corporate learning processes: "[T]he accumulation of cases (by lawyers) concerning the activity of an operating unit can show that the management of this unit is not acting with the legal precaution that must be demanded of all operating units in a large company."[287]

Even when lawyers do offer advice about trends and repetitions of problems, because of fragmentation, they tend to inform only the involved manager. Such advice is likely to be ineffective unless there is a meshing of the company's long-term interests and the short-term interests of the manager. When a manager is asked to do something he wouldn't do naturally, the lawyer must go outside the bailiwick he and the manager occupy.[288]

In short, to counter the disadvantageous effects of fragmentation, the lawyer must be able to contribute to corporate learning processes. Consider the issue of whether a corporate client should be involved in a trade association. Given the potential antitrust liability and the difficulty of policing trade meetings, there is a tendency to advise the client to leave the trade association. Several of the outside counsel interviewed took this tack, even though trade association meetings are a useful and legal way for competitors to gather together. An alternate view, advocated by some outside counsel and all inside counsel interviewed, was to educate clients so they would be able to avoid getting into problems at the meetings. Instead of giving advice on a fragmentary basis, a bloc solution was found. This is the "preventive law" solution.

---

[287] Kolvenback, The Company Legal Department: Its Role, Function and Organization 34 (1979).

[288] Simply advising the involved manager may be insufficient. Even when a department re-orients itself after getting its fingers burnt by legal processes, it may not incorporate this lesson into its corporate learning processes. Habits can be formed without learning the reason for the habits. Like the child who will keep on spilling his food until he learns the concept of volume, the corporation puts out fires without understanding why the fires ignited. Cf. P. Selznick, Leadership in Administration 29ff (1957).

TIMING

Donnell found role ambiguity and role conflict about "how early counsel should be consulted by the clients."[289] Lawyers can be consulted before a problem has emerged, while it is emerging, or after it has emerged.

The timing of lawyer involvement makes a great difference. It makes a difference for the work the lawyer does ("Corporate attorneys like to solve problems before they become problems and litigators like to solve problems after they become problems."), the extent of his work ("When you get called in early, the practice of law is like shadow boxing. You have to think of all the potential results.... It's the difference between constructing artificial limbs and stopping flowing blood."), and the success of his work ("Lawyers can be called in too late for them to do any good.").

In a general discussion of experts in organizations, Merton concluded that the expert's value to the organization depends on when in "the continuum of decision" he is called: "The earlier in the continuum of decision that the bureaucratic intellectual operates, the greater his potential influence in guiding the decision...When problems reach the intellectual at...[a] later stage in the continuum, he comes to think largely in instrumental terms and to accept the prevailing definitions of objectives."[290] How does this general tendency play itself out in legal representation?

(1) *Timing and the Circumscription of Influence.* As Merton predicted, the later the lawyer is called, the more circumscribed is his influence. Although both inside and outside counsel can be consulted late in a problem's development, outside counsel more often find their influence is restricted. As an outside counsel related: "Business people don't call us in early, claiming disorganization, not enough time, this is what must be done with this customer, and so on. This gets us into a scrivener routine."[291]

Conversely, a key boast of inside counsel is that they get involved early in the decision continuum: "A lawyer in a corporate legal department finds himself involved in situations where the legal problems remain to be defined; it is his job to find if any legal problems do exist."[292] When a lawyer's involvement begins near the start of the continuum, problems are less routine and the work is broader ranging. When a lawyer is called in late, loyalty to the client requires the attorney to consider how his influence has been circumscribed.

---

[289] J. Donnell, Corporate Counsel: A Role Study 76 (1971).

[290] Merton, "Role of the Intellectual in Public Bureaucracy," in Social Theory and Social Structure, 1968 Enlarged Ed., 261, 270 (1968).

[291] Litigators have a defense mechanism in such situations. They claim that the fun of litigation is taking a set of facts cast in stone when you arrive and making the best of it.

[292] Hand & Gang, "The Practice of Law in a Corporation," in Practicing Law in New York City 111, 112 (J. Fishman & A. Kaufman eds. 1975).

(2) *Timing and the Reduction of Influence into Power.* The later in the decision continuum the lawyer gets involved, the more his influence will depend on exerting power. Power is a costly method of control. Yet, it may be all that is available to the lawyer late in the game. For example, if the lawyer is brought in after a commercial is already in the can he might advise, "You can't say that," but the manager can respond, "Well, we already have. Find us a way so we can use this thing which we have spent a $100,000 to produce." The manager is not asking for alternatives. He is telling the lawyer that the costs are sunk and the lawyer will have to test his power against that fact.[293]

When problems have not jelled, the lawyer also need not fight strong personal positions:

> Managers don't want their "big enchilada" to be wrong. If the lawyer gets in early, it's not a test of wills or ego. By the time things normally get to outside counsel, resources have been invested, many departments have been involved, and consultants have been called. If the outside counsel then says that doing it is a violation of something obscure, the client says, "Change the law or get us another partner who will say it's fine." At that time, there is a lot of pressure on the outside counsel to go back and research it and find a few cases in our favor or at least come up with a grey area opinion letter.

This does not mean that a lawyer who is called in late can't meet this pressure. It does mean that he must exert power to do it.

The relationship between late timing and the lawyer's need to exercise power has not escaped managerial notice. A typical way clients seek to evade legal constraint is by casting the decision as an "emergency." Emergencies are a regular feature of organizational life. Managers, like lawyers, are always responding to fires that need to be put out immediately.[294] But, emergencies also can be created. The manager may purposefully sit on a problem, passing it to the lawyer only when the lawyer would have to stop many spinning wheels to halt the process.[295] In emergency situations only immediately realizable costs and benefits are considered relevant. "If you are brought in late, it goes from being a give and take to an all or nothing situation." This sharply reduces the lawyer's autonomy. Rather than an equal partner in the

---

[293] Put another way, early in the continuum, you influence decisions. Late in the continuum, you have to control actions.

[294] See S. Young, Management: A Systems Analysis 146 (1966).

[295] In one sense, emergencies defuse conflicts. In emergencies, the lawyer and client may assume they share the same expectations about how the lawyer should perform his service and what the service entails. It appears that the problem is transient. The corporation in this instance lacks sufficient resources to fulfill these assumptions. This aspect of emergencies reduces the likelihood the lawyer will try to exert power. He will let the manager "get away, this time."

relationship, the lawyer is subservient unless he chooses to exercise power. "When there is a full court press on to do something and legal is the hold-up, everyone knows it." To resist conformity, the lawyer must be willing and able to exert power.[296] A lawyer alert to the effects of the timing of his work on organizational dynamics consequently will seek to create a relationship with the client in which he is not contacted only when the problem is an emergency.

(3) *Timing as an External Signal.* Clients know that when they involve their attorneys they are signaling something to the other side. For the most part, what they are signaling is either indistinct or too peculiar to the situation to be generalizable. When transactions are regular and routine, however, the signal of lawyer involvement may affect the nature of the relationship.

Consider, for example, the relationship between the corporation and its regulators. When lawyers are involved early, government regulators don't perceive the corporation as stiff-necked[297] and don't adopt a guards-up and "going it by the book" approach: "If you assume basic integrity, you can work things out. If not, you get bars raised you can't cross." Having lawyers involved early in this process is an external signal of corporate integrity. As a manager noted:

> With a new product, the people at the regulatory agencies have a hard time figuring out what standards to impose. Some are very conscientious and others say, "Let me see everything so that nothing will come back to haunt me," thereby artificially screening out good things. The solution is to work openly with the agency. The lawyers are independent and objective voices in this process. They are better able to communicate with the agency people because they are closer to them in terms of background attitudes and interests. The lawyers don't take a sow's ear and turn it into a silk purse. But they can make it understandable to the regulatory people. They can tell the regulators, "Sure the people who are making it have self-interest in it, but I can tell you that you can trust them. I'm on the job."

A lawyer who does not ignore what is being signaled by his involvement will be alert to the responsibilities being imposed on him.

(4) *Timing and Intra-Corporate Political Processes.* When a lawyer tackles a case in its early stages, he becomes involved in planning. At a minimum, a

---

[296] Compare this with the strategy of totalitarian regimes to cast all situations as emergencies. See I. Berlin, "Does Political Theory Still Exist?," in Philosophy, Politics and Society, 2d Series, at 79 (P. Laslett & G. Runciman eds. 1962).

[297] Notice how this differs from one-shot transactions. If I bring my lawyer along when I file a complaint at the department store, they are likely to think I am stiff-necked.

lawyer's involvement in planning provides the company with more information. It thus creates the possibility of decisions more in keeping with the law's intent. Yet, this is not necessarily the result. Information is only one aspect of planning. Information also must be filtered and alternatives selected.

Where lawyers only contribute information to the planning process, their early involvement may work against corporate legal compliance. For example, Good Labs' inside counsel argued that lack of information is essential for the lawyer to render an independent judgment:

> As an inside counsel, I will understand better than outside counsel why the client wants to violate the regulations. I will find the extra amount of wobble. More information gives you more considerations, more alternatives.

> Inside counsel can get talked into interpretations because they know the client's competitors. I can open my drawer and see the competitors' products. So I can seek the wobble they use to make their products and feel justified in so doing. It's information about our competitors that make me want to play with the law.

In this argument the lawyer's ethical behavior depends on transaction costs. It is a perverse argument for ethical behavior, but a recurrent one. The argument, however, only applies if information is the only contribution the lawyer makes to planning. Then, the commercial community's ethics, not the law's purposes, rules.

In other words, the lawyer's behavior depends on his role in the corporate planning process. At Good Labs, lawyers only report information. Although it is a highly politicized corporation, lawyers are not involved in conflicts between units or in controlling the pathologies that may result. Once they make their report, they opt out of the goal-setting process. Even though they are "present at the creation," they still "think largely in instrumental terms and...accept the prevailing definitions of objectives."[298]

Early involvement, however, should signal to lawyers that their work is neither the end-product of corporate decision-making nor a datum that will be unproblematically ingested by corporate decision-makers. Lawyers should be alert to their role in corporate goal-creation.[299]

---

[298] Merton, *supra*, at 270.

[299] The relation of timing to intra-corporate political processes simply generalizes a commonplace of litigation practice. Everyone knows that having a lawyer involved early can help prevent and settle lawsuits, both by steering the company away from problems and by defining the client's objectives. In litigation the parties often only see what is really at stake very far down the road. Although legal rights are frequently tossed back and forth in the litigation process, they may be tangential to the settlement posture. Compromise and settlement will not occur until the parties decide what the case is really worth to them.

PROBLEM-SETTING AND PROFESSIONAL IDEOLOGY AND ETHICS

Like other professionals, lawyers need not accept problems that are pre-set.[300] They can respond to signals their work sets off. They can openly negotiate and bargain about what their work requires. With non-professional workers, such negotiation is often covert. At stake for them is merely "convenience and ease on the job." For the professional, however, "self-respect, reputation, and career are at stake.... *[T]he negotiation takes place from a position of professional worth and values and involves a whole rhetoric of professional claims.*"[301]

The first level for analyzing the insensitivities attested to by the cases introducing this chapter, therefore, must be at the level of professional values. Why doesn't building a practice mean creating a relation in which the lawyer can give the client more than the client immediately wants? How do lawyers with good judgment recast the problems given to them? What are a lawyer's duties in investigating a problem? Why are the elite lawyers involved in the cases introducing this chapter satisfied with saying "It's not my job"?

In the ideology of the profession, the lawyer's independent judgment does set the problem on which he works:[302] A client in need contacts a lawyer. The lawyer learns the facts of the case as the client understands them. The lawyer then searches for other facts to diagnose the true problem. He deposes and interrogates. He filters out distortions, probing to the heart of the matter. Then, based on his training, the lawyer informs the client of the true nature of the problem and the appropriate remedy, saving the client.

Yet in practice, lawyers do not always set the problems on which they work.[303] They may accept client control over the definition of the problem, the lawyer's access to the facts, and the choice of remedies. Or, the lawyer may not redefine the problem, finding it undesirable to invest too much effort on it.

---

[300] The centrality to professionals of control over problem-setting is demonstrated by Miller's study of scientists and engineers. One might have thought that client control over problem-setting would have been less of a problem for engineers than for scientists: engineers are trained to receive problems and solve what is given to them. But Miller found that client control over problem-setting was directly associated with alienation, and in comparable degrees, for both scientists and engineers. Miller, "Professionals in Bureaucracy: Alienation Among Scientists and Engineers," 32 Am. Soc. Rev.755 (1968).

[301] Bucher & Stelling, "Characteristics of Professional Organizations," 10 J. Health & Soc. Behav. 3, 1969 (emphasis added), reprinted in Colleagues in Organization: The Social Construction of Professional Work 121, 125 (R. Blankenship ed. 1977).

[302] See, e.g., ABA, Code of Professional Responsibility DR 5-1, EC 5-24 (1969).

[303] Interestingly, in one study, no difference was found between inside and outside counsel with respect to bureaucratic controls on legal work. Hall, "Professionalization and Bureaucratization," 32 Am. Soc. Rev. 92 (1968); Hall, "Some Organizational Considerations in the Professional–Organizational Relationship," 12 Ad. Sci. Q. 461 (1967).

This gap between ideology and practice is reflected in lawyer self-consciousness. When corporate lawyers talk about their work, they oscillate between asserting the transcendental independence of a lawyer's role, deciding power balances and helping individuals out of deep trouble, and the mundane servility of their work, greasing corporate wheels and following the dictates of the market. Lawyers try to repress this fundamental contradiction by telling war stories and by stressing the dollar value of the problems they handle. But practicing attorneys know their situation often is an ironic one. All too often each of them is like the clown at the circus who, by waving his arms, seeks to convey that he is the master of the ceremony.

There is a defensiveness in the lawyer's "kiss-off," "It's not my job." The "kiss-off" attempts to repress the fact that a lawyer's role is not the same as the work he does. Roles are not totally defined by how they are played.[304] While it is true that the actor makes the role, it is also true that the role tests the actor.[305] Roles include generalized expectations that serve as reference points for actors' performances. Professionals, whose attitudes, in part, are formed and maintained by professional schools and organizations, are keenly aware that they have a role they may not play well.[306]

The gap between the profession's role-concept and the ways lawyers act evidences the fact that a profession is composed of both attitudinal and structural components and these "do not necessarily vary together."[307] A profession has attitudinal components which affect how a professional views his own work. A profession instills beliefs and generates a sense of calling in its practitioners. A profession idolizes exemplars to whom individuals compare their work. A profession also has structural components which affect how a professional works. A profession institutes or sanctions a division of labor and rules governing work. A profession authorizes controls and definitions on its practitioners' work. A profession's attitudinal and structural components may have different sources and supports. These components are relatively independent of each other.

This relative independence explains why the legal profession's view of itself vacillates between the cynical and the optimistic.[308] The structural components of the legal profession appear to contradict the profession's attitudinal components, its role-concept. Others have seized this apparent contradiction, concluding that the role-concept's only function is to merchandize the lawyer's importance and morality to attain and maintain the legal profession's monopoly status.[309] This conclusion incorrectly assumes

---

[304] R. Dahl & C. Lindblom, *supra*, at 111.

[305] See T. Parsons & E. Shils, Toward a General Theory of Action 23 (1951).

[306] See T. Parsons, The Social System 38-40 (1951).

[307] Hall, "Professionalization and Bureaucratization," 32 Am. Soc. Rev. 92, 103 (1968).

[308] Simon, *supra* at 29.

[309] See, e.g., Rhode, "Why the ABA Bothers: A Functional Perspective on Professional

that the legal profession is internally static. The apparent contradiction arises because of the relative independence of the profession's attitudinal and structural components. But, these components are not totally independent. They challenge each other.

Admittedly, too often the challenge is blunted. I found that today the primary function of the role-concept is to prevent lawyers from becoming disenchanted with their work by making their structural subservience appear transient.[310] But, thus the mandarin is defeated. When systematic discrepancies with the professional role-concept are taken as transient exceptions not worth confronting, lawyers tend to conform to their clients' demands and claims of professional independence merit cynical responses. The attitudinal components of the profession today do not challenge its structural components. The lawyer's only refuge is irony.

The relative independence of the profession's attitudinal and structural components, however, provides some reason for optimism. The attitudinal components of the legal profession can be the basis for change. Expansive role-concepts can challenge current work agenda and their structural determinants.[311] Expansive role-concepts can facilitate role-taking.[312] The profession's concept of its role can inspire lawyers to fight externally set agenda and structure their role to allow for autonomy.[313]

The profession's role-concept, while relatively independent from the profession's structural components, however, has responded to them. While the dominant professional image stresses the lawyer's independence, there is a counter-image which encapsulates the servility of practice. In this image lawyers are hired guns or resource-persons obeying client directions.

There is a truth in this counter-image. Lawyers are client-serving professionals who must not dominate their clients. Consequently, the Model Rules of Professional Conduct stipulates that "[a] lawyer shall abide by a client's decisions concerning the objectives of representation,"[314] and comments that "[t]he client has ultimate authority to determine the purposes to be served by legal representation."[315] The norms of independence and of client service are in tension.

Codes," 59 Texas L. Rev. 689 (1981).

[310] Cf. E. Friedson, Professional Dominance: The Social Structure of Medical Care 93-102 (1970).

[311] See A. Carr-Saunders & P. Wilson, The Professions 40304 (1938); R. Pavalko, Sociology of Occupations and Professions 101 (1971).

[312] P. Selznick, Leadership in Administration 3 (1957).

[313] *Id.* at 121-22.

[314] ABA Comm. on Evaluation of Professional Standards, Model Rules of Professional Conduct, Rule 1.2(a) (Report to the House of Delegates, dated June 30, 1982) [Hereafter "Model Rules"]. Cf. ABA Code of Professional Responsibility EC 7-8 (1969).

[315] Model Rules, Comment to Rule 1.2, "Scope of Representation," at 11.

The counter-image, however, too quickly resolves this tension by retreating to client dominance.[316] Instead of an expansive role-concept, it imposes a restrictive one. This counter-image has led even those concerned with legal ethics to flirt with an unprofessional stance. For example, an analyst of conflicts of interest in legal work adopts the following definition of the lawyer's principal duty: "The lawyer should take that action that is best calculated to advance the client's interests, *as the client defines them.*"[317] In other words, the client, like the customer, is always right.

The dominant-image resolves the tension between independence and client service by stressing the lawyer's duty of loyalty to the client. By characterizing the client as a customer, the counter-image eschews the good lawyer's well merited reputation for fidelity to the client. Loyalty is not obedience. Loyalty to the client may require the lawyer to transcend the problem as set by the client.

The Code of Professional Responsibility does emphasize client control over choices within a problem. But, this is not identical to control over the scope of the problem.[318] In the language of organizational analysis, the client controls vertical but not necessarily horizontal specialization. In other words, an ethical lawyer in the dominant-image is required to exercise some control over problem-setting. The lawyer tends to the "whole" client, probing problems.[319]

Whatever is the general salience of the counter-image, its pervasiveness in corporate work is surprising. Corporate lawyers typically pride themselves on their autonomy. They demand and receive high fees because of their independent judgment. Furthermore, to render professional service in the corporate context, the lawyer cannot quickly retreat to servility. As the Code of Professional Responsibility explains: "A lawyer employed or retained by a

---

[316] Cf. "Professional Responsibility: Report of the Joint Conference," 44 A.B.A.J. 1159, 1159 (1958): "One who undertakes the practice of a profession cannot rest content with the faithful discharge of duties assigned to him by others."

[317] Note, "Developments in the Law: Conflicts of Interest in the Legal Profession," 94 Harv. L. Rev. 1244, 1255 (1981) (emphasis added). The Note then restricts this duty by the lawyer's duties to the legal system and the public. *Id.* at 1260ff.

[318] Compare ABA, Code of Professional Responsibility EC 3-5 and EC 7-8 (1969).

[319] This analysis extends beyond standard interpretations of the duty of loyalty. It explains, however, why a lawyer may not represent adverse clients in unrelated actions. See Fund of Funds, Ltd. v. Arthur Andersen & Co., 567 F.2d 225 (2d Cir. 1977); Grievance Comm. v. Rottner, 152 Conn. 59, 203 A.2d 82 (1964). See generally "Annotation: What Constitutes Representation of Conflicting Interests Subjecting Attorney to Disciplinary Action," 17 A.L.R. 3d 835. The problems may be different, but the lawyer's loyalty extends to serving the whole client. Loyalty requires an expansive horizontal conception of the lawyer's work. That the horizontal demands of loyalty can be waived by client consent does not contradict this interpretation. Such a waiver should occur only after full discussion of the client's entire legal picture. This discussion is precisely what is missing when the client sets the problems for the lawyer.

corporation or similar entity owes his allegiance to the entity and not to a stockholder, director, officer, employee, representative, or other person connected with the entity. In advising the entity, a lawyer should keep paramount its interests and his professional judgment should not be influenced by the personal desires of any person or organization."[320] Because the lawyer's true client is the corporate entity, the interests and problems as defined by agents of the corporation need not always be served. The lawyer's loyalty is to the entity. In corporate work, in a practical sense, the customer—the corporate agent—is not always right.[321]

Part of the reason why today the profession's role-concept fails to challenge the work lawyers perform is that the profession has failed to detail the requirements of the duty of loyalty, especially when serving the "client as an entity."[322] This chapter has attempted to develop this duty through organizational analysis. There are organizational reasons why the interests of corporate agents may differ from the interests of the corporation "as an entity": Bureaucratic and political pathologies require the lawyer in being loyal to the entity to exert control over the setting of the problems on which he works.

Instead of an organizational analysis, a consequentialist analysis is used by the Model Rules of Professional Responsibility to elaborate the duty of loyalty: "[W]hen the lawyer *knows* that the organization may be substantially injured by action of an officer or employee,"[323] loyalty requires the lawyer to transcend the customer's definition of corporate interests and problems. This analysis is incomplete. As the cases introducing this chapter reveal, lawyers can be blinded to the consequences of their actions. When lawyers do not actively control how problems are set, they need not confront the adverse consequences of their representation. Thereby, they may misserve their clients.

Although Parsons and Blau and Scott have shown that professionalism

---

[320] ABA, Code of Professional Responsibility, EC 5-18(1969). Cf. Model Rules, Rule 1.13(a): "A lawyer employed or retained to represent an organization represents the organization as distinct from its directors, officers, employees, members, shareholders or other constituents."

[321] See Model Rules, Rule 1.13, Comment "The Entity as the Client": "In transactions between an organization and its lawyer...the organization can speak and decide only through agents, such as its officers or employees. In effect, the client-lawyer relationship is maintained through an intermediary between the client and the lawyer. This fact requires the lawyer under certain conditions to be concerned whether the intermediary legitimately represents the client."

[322] See G. Hazard, Ethics in the Practice of Law 43-68 (1978); Rotunda, "Law, Lawyers and Managers," in The Ethics of Corporate Conduct 127 (1977); Pierce, "The Code of Professional Responsibility in the Corporate World: An Abdication of Professional Self-Regulation," 6 U. Mich. J.L. Ref. 350 (1973); ABA Formal Opinion 202 (23 May 1940).

[323] Model Rules, Rule 1.13 Comment "The Entity as the Client" (emphasis added).

and bureaucratization share similar normative orientations,[324] one similarity these scholars failed to pinpoint is that both professionals and bureaucrats can be blind to the substantive goals and consequences of their work. "Bureaucrat" is a pejorative because a bureaucrat simply follows orders without analyzing them in relation to underlying purposes. As Merton puts it, a characteristic pathology of bureaucracies is that means displace ends.[325] Similarly, a characteristic pathology of one set of professional choices is that professionals emphasize their tools over the actual dimensions of the problems on which they work. Lawyers can adopt the worst aspects of bureaucrats and choose to blind themselves to the consequences of their actions.

When lawyers say, "This is what the client gave me to do," they are denying responsibility for the consequences of problem-setting. As the cases introducing this chapter demonstrate, lawyers thereby may misserve their clients whose welfare they supposedly serve by rejecting control over problem-setting. A restrictive view of lawyer duties with respect to the horizontal dimension of legal work not only misserves clients. When the SEC tried to make lawyers responsible for the consequences of their work, one outside counsel interviewed said the typical response of his colleagues was, "Let's find out what makes us guardians of the public interest and write it out of our retainer agreement." Although lawyers also should be faithful to public interests, this book has questioned the central rationale for the "kiss-off," servicing client goals.

Another frequently invoked explanation for the limited scope of a lawyer's problems is that the law itself determines how the problems a lawyer works on are set. This argument, however, depends on a naive formalism. One seeks a good lawyer precisely because the law doesn't totally determine the scope of a lawyer's work. Yet, elite lawyers at times profess such a naive formalism. Lawyers work on cases, they say, but do not generate cases. Lawyers are merely reactive and are not responsible for the situations leading to legal problems. Lawyers are not responsible for the context. They merely operate independently within the context.

As the cases introducing this chapter reveal, this is true to some extent but it is not always true. A lawyer can be proactive. Legal work can generate other legal work. And lawyers and clients may differently define the context of legal service.

Legal work need not only be parasitic and lawyers have opportunities and responsibilities for serving their clients which are not realized when lawyers

---

[324] They share orientations to rationality, universality, affective neutrality and achievement. Parsons, "The Professions and the Social Structure," in Essays in Sociological Theory, Rvsd. Ed. (1954); P. Blau & W. Scott, Formal Organizations 60 (1962).

[325] Merton, "Bureaucratic Structure and Personality," in Social Theory and Social Structure, 1968 Enlarged Ed., at 249 (1968).

respond, "This is what my client gave me to do." By recognizing that problem-setting is a dependent variable affected by choices both the lawyer and client make, we can move away from a self-serving professional ethic to an ethic of responsibility. Where problems can be framed in alternate ways, lawyers to some extent should be responsible not only within contexts but for the contexts. To be loyal to the client "as an entity," lawyers must be both sensitive and responsive to recurrent problems in serving organizational clients. They must be alert to signals which indicate the need to confront the setting of their problems.[326]

CONCLUSION

This chapter has focused on the lawyer, the supply side in the equation of the delivery of legal services. It has touched only indirectly on the demand side, the creation of legal work by lawyers and clients. Like other workers, lawyers' tasks are conditioned by occupational, organizational, client and social control systems.[327] What factors in the market and delivery system for legal service affect how problems are set?

Answering this question is beyond the scope of this chapter. At this point, it is sufficient to indicate that research on the demand for legal services can facilitate role-taking. Such research can help strengthen the profession's role-concept. It will enable us to create demand structures facilitating autonomy, lessening dependence on professional and personal norms to produce autonomy. Instead of depending on moral individuals motivated to do the right thing, such research would enable us to reconstruct legal work to generate autonomy. Combining such research with the argument of this study would allow us to supplant the profession's experience of irony and its sense of underlying contradiction. It would allow us to utilize the fact that the profession's attitudinal and structural components are both independent of each other and dependent on each other.

Arguing that clients shouldn't set problems for their lawyers might appear ill-timed and naive given current dissatisfaction with the legal profession. One prong of the current critique of the professions is directed at the professions' claims that they are capable of formulating client interests.[328] Yet, the need for professional autonomy remains. The market is an

---

[326] Cf. "Professional Responsibility: Report of the Joint Conference," 44 A.B.A.J. 1159, 1218, 1217 (1958): "Whether he considers himself a conservative or a liberal, the lawyer should do what he can to rescue that discussion [of public issues] from a world of unreality in which it is assumed that ends can be selected without any consideration of means." "The practice of his profession brings the lawyer in daily touch with...the problem of implementation as it arises in human affairs."

[327] See Varieties of Work Experience: The Social Control of Occupational Groups and Roles (P. Stewart & M. Cantor eds. 1974).

[328] For the legal profession, see Leubsdorf, "Three Models of Professional Reform," 67 Cornell L. Rev. 1021, 1023 (1982); Morgan, "The Evolving Concept of Professional

untrustworthy mechanism for policing professional services. Professionals can create demand.[329] The lack of information about the quality and effectiveness of professional services makes it extremely difficult for the client to contract for what he requires. In addition, the client cannot readily exit from professional relationships. Reconstructing lawyers' work may, therefore, strengthen, not undermine, the ability of lawyers to serve clients.

I have tried to show in this chapter some of what lawyers must confront to be loyal to the corporate client "as an entity." Bureaucratic and political pathologies are ever-present possibilities in organizational life. The way legal problems are set often fuel, rather than dampen, such pathologies. Corporate pathologies challenge the current ways in which legal problems are set. Corporate supervision of the work lawyers do for them is inadequate and corporations often inadequately process lawyer reports. As a result, lawyers are likely to misserve their corporate clients.

These conclusions may seem to expand a lawyer's duties. If they do, it is important to understand that these additional duties do not derive from the lawyer's duty to serve the public. To assist the lawyer in *role-taking*, I have emphasized client service. Mending information nets and engaging intra-corporate political processes are required to serve organizational clients. Quality service demands that lawyers be both boundary-spanning organizational actors[330] and autonomous professionals.

Professional service does require independence. But, independence misserves organizational clients when it functions to insulate lawyers from responsibility for their clients' actions and hinders lawyer involvement in client goal-selection. Many would be troubled by recognizing that lawyers in serving corporations are organizational actors. They would be troubled especially by recognizing that lawyers are political actors within the corporate organization. But, as we have seen, organizational analysis reveals that lawyers perforce must perform such roles.

The problem is not whether lawyers are responsible or paternalistic. As any student of organizational behavior knows, the question is not whether lawyers give corporations goals. The proper question is what goals do lawyers advance? Serving organizational clients requires lawyers to confront that question.

Responsibility," 90 Harv. L. Rev. 702 (1977); for the professions generally, see Barber, "Control and Responsibility in the Powerful Professions," 93 Pol. Sci. Q. 599 (1978-79); I. Illich, Disabling Professions (1977).

[329] Evans, "Professionals and the Production Function: Can Competition Policy Improve Efficiency in the Licensed Professions?," in Occupational Leisure and Regulation 225, 250-59 (S. Rottenberg ed. 1980), cited in Leubsdorf, *supra*, at 1027 n.43.

[330] See Adams, "Interorganizational Processes and Organization Boundary Activities," 2 Res. Org'ale Behave 321 (1980).

Chapter Three

SALIENT CONFLICT: THE BUSINESS-LAW CONTINUUM

Lawyers face the continual threat of conflict with clients. A lawyer "constantly tries to resist pressures to go along. It is a constant struggle to tell clients that they can't do what they want to do." Because the lawyer serves at the client's pleasure, he must manage conflict to prevent it from sundering the relationship. On the other hand, the lawyer, faced with professional obligations, cannot simply cave in, allowing the client to determine his actions. Consequently, the private bar agonizes over the problem of client conflict.

Conflict in the lawyer-client relationship is neither accidental nor unfortunate. It fulfills important social functions.[331] It allows for a decentralized system of legal control. In resisting client pressures, lawyers serve a social control function. In being receptive to client needs, lawyers enable general policies and rules to be tied to and tested by local information.

Certainly, lawyers' response to conflict is not merely a function of their own senses of value. To some extent, they adapt their behavior to the organization they serve. The organization of legal services partially explains the variations found in this study. Yet, to a degree, lawyers determine their responses to conflict. As professionals, they have some autonomy and organizations are not so restrictive that initiatives cannot be taken. Especially in intra-organizational conflicts, the uses of organizational resources are not pre-determined. This chapter, then, will focus on how differences in organizational structure and participant use of resources affect conflict-resolution processes.[332]

Conflict situations reveal the choices involved in determining the character of one's legal practice.[333] Conflicts between lawyers and clients, like conflict between any staff personnel and managers, "is a function of disagreement over the reality of interdependence."[334] Studying conflict, therefore, requires an assessment of the relationships between lawyers and managers. As interdependent actors, lawyers and managers must share power and values. Because this sharing cannot be complete, conflicts often

---

[331] For a discussion of the general social functions of conflict, see G. Simmel, Conflict and the Web of Group-Affiliations (1955); L. Coser, The Social Functions of Conflict (1964).

[332] Cf. P. Lawrence & J. Lorsch, Organization and Environment 205 (1961) (noting the paucity of research in his area).

[333] These choices are discussed in Chapter One.

[334] V. Thompson, Modern Organization, 2d Ed., at 108 (1977).

arise in any relationship, the parties must decide questions of their respective powers. In the corporate context, this raises issues such as: Who has the right to make decisions? Has the staff member the right to be consulted? Has the staff member the right to make inquiries? In any relationship, the parties must decide how values will determine their actions. In the corporate context, this raises questions such as: Who has the right to set decision goals? Has the staff member the right to reorient the manager's decision process? Has the manager the right to reorient the professional's values or techniques?

The processes discussed in the last chapter minimize conflicts. When their clients consult them in the latter stages of a problem or provide them with fragmented problem lawyers can avoid conflicts and accept diminished responsibility. Problem-setting, however, doesn't eliminate conflict. Lawyers or the law may demand that the problem as set by the client not be accepted.

Consider a common lawyer activity, writing opinion letters. Smigel, in his study of Wall Street lawyers, was greatly impressed by opinion letters, considering them to be instances of private law-making:

> The opinion letter (a document in which the law firm says that in its judgment "such and such" is the law or within the law) in itself tends to induce the client to take conservative business positions and perhaps to increase his economic conscience in terms of a broader distribution of profits. It often gives advice on laws not yet written, what Adolf Berle calls "inchoate law."

> This means that the lawyer tells his client there is no law preventing a certain behavior; nevertheless, if he does "such and such," his action will ensure that such a law will be enacted. The lawyer then, as the conscience of the businessman, is saying: "So far as the law goes, you can do this—but you must not."[335]

Yet, opinion letters, in the corporations studied, most often were highly stylized documents that were neither intended to act as a conscience for business nor served to uncover the inchoate law of business transactions by pulling law and business together. As a lawyer admitted: "There is always a tendency to give the opinion that the client wants and to qualify it so that it is legally defensible and the lawyer can straddle the fence." If the lawyer succumbs to this tendency, he resolves a potential conflict. As with other retreats into an excessive emphasis upon technique, this tactic leads to the appearance of professional responsibility and the reality of structured client irresponsibility. Although many lawyers would condemn this approach, few would notice a similar result produced by a different process—problem-setting. Late entry and fragmentation are often elements in opinion letters.

---

[335] Smigel, The Wall Street Lawyer 6 (1964), citing A. Berle, Power Without Property 113-16 (1959).

An opinion letter is often seen as only a "piece" of the transaction. As lawyers will tell you, they often get called in late to give an opinion letter because "the client wants" him "only to sprinkle holy water" on the transaction. If the lawyer has difficulty sprinkling the holy water, fragmentation can be used to salvage at least a saving portion of the transaction: the question answered is not the question asked.

But there are situations where the law cannot be sidestepped. To go through with the deal, an opinion letter is needed and the lawyer can't frame the problem in any way that will save the deal. Short of lying, one other way is available to avoid conflict. The lawyer often can write the letter so that the decision, over which there is a conflict, is a "business" one, not one the lawyer must decide or even attest to. This is a classic method for avoiding conflict: put the ball in the other person's court. In corporate life, "the idea that there is a division of labor...opens the way to the evasion of responsibility even within the more narrow fields. When...decisions are especially difficult, dealing with vague and unpredictable elements, it is convenient to allow the decision to be made on other grounds."[336] Putting the ball in the other person's court "solves" the problem of interdependence by denying its reality. The next sections examine the conditions that give rise to this "solution" and its consequences. Less evasive means for dealing with the reality of interdependence are then considered.

LEGAL SERVICE AS RISK ANALYSIS

THE NORM OF RISK ANALYSIS

In corporate practice:

> Clients want to know what it is to comply and how far they can go in a certain area. It would be a conflict of our responsibility to the client if we would factor in their responsibility to the public and it would be a conflict of our responsibility to the profession if we would factor in their business realities.

In litigation:

> Our job is simply to advise the client about the legal risks. The effect of the case on employee development and morale is the client's concern. It is not ours. Yes, it is important to the client, but we don't think about it.

These statements express the predominate view of the legal task: lawyers

---

[336] P. Selznick, Leadership in Administration 76 (1957).

report on the law and analyze legal risks. The talented lawyer is both a talking law book and a sociologist of the legal system. In practice, however, the sociologist threatens to undermine the law book. As Hazard explains, a lawyer's "professional function consists largely of providing counsel about how to escape or mitigate the incidence of the law's obligations."[337] The talented lawyer is the Holmesian positivist: he looks at the law like a bad man. He advises clients about the risk of exposure to the legal environment. The talented lawyer is an expert not in jurisprudence but in risk analysis.[338]

Many claim that it is only realistic to define the corporate lawyer's task as one of providing risk analyses. Corporate clients actually want the lawyer to convert the law into business' metric: dollars. Businessmen are amoral profit maximizers and their only concern is the legal environment's effect on profitability.[339] As one lawyer put it, "It doesn't work if I talk to clients from my professional bent. I have to go back and demonstrate to them why the pieces don't fit together from their perspective. I have to show them the potential costs." Consequently, lawyers can induce client compliance only when legal sanctions make it economically efficient for the client to comply.[340]

---

[337] G. Hazard, Ethics in the Practice of Law 2 (1978).

[338] Considerable evidence supports the view that the legal profession considers risk analysis to be the norm of professional behavior. See, e.g., Vagts, "Legal Opinions in Quantitative Terms: The Lawyer as Haruspex or Bookie," 34 Bus. Lawyer 421 (1979). "What we are doing when we give opinions is predicting the probable reaction of tribunals to the issue of law that concerns the client. This is true even though the 'odds opinion' is apparently rare—at least when lawyers are called upon to commit themselves to writing." Id. at 421. "The lawyer's subjective view as to what the applicable law should be is not, after all, worth much to the client unless there is a reason to believe that it will be shared by the authorities with power over the situation." Id. at 422. "After you advise your clients of these risks (in murky areas of the law), do you have any affirmative duty to counsel your client not to go into a transaction merely because you believe that a court might or should hold that the debt is not a good debt for tax purposes? I suggest you do not." M. B. Adinoff (a practitioner), quoted in Professional Responsibility of the Lawyer: The Murky Divide Between Right and Wrong 7 (N. Galston ed. 1977); even the Code of Professional Responsibility speaks of lawyers giving advice in terms of "what the ultimate decisions of the courts would likely be as to the applicable law." ABA, Code of Professional Responsibility EC 7-3 (1969). See also EC 7-4.

[339] On businessmen as amoral profit maximizers, see, e.g., M. Green, The Closed Enterprise System 162 (1972); M. Glenn, "The Crime of 'Pollution' The Role of Federal Water Pollution Criminal Sanctions," 11 Am. Crim. L. Rev. 835 (1973); Manaster, "Early Thoughts on Prosecuting Polluters," 2 Env. L.Q. 471 (1972). This view is also prevalent in general culture: B. Stein, The View From Sunset Boulevard (1979) (novel); The Media Institute, Crooks, Con Men and Clowns: Businessmen in TV Entertainment (1981) (more than 50% of CEO's depicted on TV are shown engaging in criminal behavior).

[340] Of course, lawyers may overestimate or underestimate sanctions. Overestimating sanctions may produce compliance by making actions in accord with the law appear economically desirable. This not only hides the lawyer's exercise of discretion, it also fails to establish a general basis for corporate legal compliance. Overestimations apply only to the instant case and, since such predictions will be belied by experience, lawyers can't

Although recognizing legal risks requires talent, it does not require the lawyer to assume responsibility. The lawyer does not influence the client, the sanctions of the legal system do. As a lawyer put it, to win conflicts, "the lawyer always has to say there is some outside power. You are effective not because of your strengths as a lawyer but because of the strengths of the outside power."

Yet, even lawyers who adopt a risk analysis approach admit that at times a lawyer can forcefully and convincingly present the law independent of its sanctions. This occurs mainly in routine work. Lawyers filter, store and consolidate information about the law that is passed on to the client. This information processing, which often affects client choice, is not always tied to the inevitability of sanction. Also, clients are not always the amoral profit maximizers that risk analysis assumes. Finally, lawyers often possess the personal skills to motivate their clients to care about the law. It is claimed, however, that these opportunities are incidental. In non-routine situations, the lawyer is forced to fall back on risk analysis when the client wants to pursue a course against the lawyer's initial advice.

Analysis of the delivery of legal services to the corporations studied reveals, however, that luck is not the only factor that enables a lawyer to present the law independent of its sanctions. The organization of legal services and the corporate resources used in the conflict affect the lawyer's ability to tackle conflicts with more than risk analysis.

Legal sanctions have often been inadequate to induce corporate legal compliance.[341] Given the difficulties of detection, corporations' ability to hide sanctions in balance sheets as "non-recurring losses," and the absence of any stigma within the business community resulting from violations, the law's

---

overestimate risks too often. It is more likely that lawyers will underestimate legal risks. This may result from a competitive market for legal services or from the rule-skepticism that legal practice generates. Recognizing the unreasonableness of governing complex behavior by fixed rules and the vagaries of rule-application, many lawyers lean toward a relativism where they do not blink at improprieties. On lawyers engaging in rule skepticism though which the "sense of legal obligation suffers," see Probert & Brown, "Theories and Practices in the Legal Profession," 19 U. Fla. L. Rev. 447, 461 (1966-67). Parsons long ago argued that because the law is ambiguous, lawyers will often yield to expediency, exaggerate the acceptability of merely formal compliance, or sentimentalize client interests to reduce the strain of coming into conflict with their clients. Parsons, "A Sociologist Looks at the Legal Profession," in Essays in Sociological Theory, Rvsd. Ed., at 370, 377 (1954). Given the difficulties of second-guessing risk estimates, the discussion in the text assumes that, for the most part, lawyers accurately report legal risks. It should be noted, however, that inside counsel, who often do not have effective resources for monitoring enforcement, sometimes overestimate legal risks. Managers and inside counsel seeking results and conflict reduction know that they can get a different evaluation from outside counsel. As a consequence, in the two corporations studied where inside counsel provided risk analyses, they were dominated by outside counsel. In these two corporations, outside counsel had the trust of management the corporate legal department lacked.

[341] See sources cited at Kriesberg, "Decisionmaking Models and the Control of Corporate Crime," 85 Yale L.J. 1091, 1106-08 (1976).

sanctions often do not deter corporate action. Corporations, who can insulate themselves from the competitive market,[342] have little difficulty immunizing themselves from interference by the legal environment.

Not only is the corporation unresponsive to sanctions, so too are many managers. Given bureaucratic and political pathologies, in some instances, managers will have incentives to violate the law and will not be disciplined for so doing.[343] Furthermore, managerial animosity to the ways in which the legal system assigns risks weakens the ability to gain client trust and respect of lawyers who are technicians of legal risks.[344] As a result, as Stone concludes, "[c]ontrolling corporations," by legal sanctions constitutes "a misplaced faith on 'negative reinforcement' (trying to teach people through punishing undesired acts rather than by rewarding good ones) but it is also the worst sort of negative reinforcement, one administered almost randomly (or so it seems) by a nonrespected source."[345]

Calling for tougher enforcement policies is a common response to this problem. Not only would such policies avert some illegalities by dipping into a corporation's pocketbook, but also they would have a global influence on corporate compliance. Tough enforcement induces the corporation to hire regulatory specialists, including lawyers, and to devise compliance programs.[346] A strong regulatory policy, however, may lead risk-averse managers to "over-comply" with the law and thus weaken productivity.[347]

Risk-prone managers also may frustrate tough regulation through con-

---

[342] See J. K. Galbraith, The New Industrial State (1967).

[343] This is the brunt of Professor Stone's work. For a discussion of the failure of the risk analysis approach to control corporate behavior, see C. Stone, Where the Law Ends: The Social Control of Corporate Behavior, Ch. 6 (1975).

[344] As one manager expressed his views about regulations:"[S]ome unilateral action in Washington could make right wrong, or, for that matter, wrong right." Clee, "The Appointment Book of J. Edward Ellis," reprinted in Readings in Organization Theory: Open Systems Approaches 406 (J. Maurer ed. 1971).

[345] Stone, *supra*, at 42.

[346] E. Bardach & R. Kagan, Going By the Book: The Problem of Regulatory Unreasonableness 95-96 (1982). It is important to distinguish between the amount of legal activity and the threat of legal activity. The multiplication of regulations may increase the need for lawyer input but it does not necessarily place more discretionary judgments within the lawyer's ambit. In my study, the company that faced the most highly regulated environment had the weakest lawyers and the highest proportion of violations.

[347] Beckenstein & Gabel, "Organizational Compliance Processes and the Efficiency of Antitrust Enforcement," at June 1980 Law & Society Assn. Meetings: "Risk-averse corporations and managers are faced with an uncertain enforcement environment, changing definitions about what constitutes a violation, and imprecision about the final impact of compliance efforts after they are processed through a complex corporate hierarchy with interdependent actors. Furthermore, there is an incentive to avoid the costs of litigation even when you expect to win it because of a lack of faith in the outcome of complex litigation. Economically, it is even wise to avoid investigations by enforcement agencies."

tinued resistance. Furthermore, only the most egregious problems will compel tighter enforcement. Otherwise, the law will continue to set only minimum standards of conduct. Increasing risks only in selected areas will be insufficient to produce generally responsible corporate behavior. Consequently, we must seek additional bases for influencing corporate behavior. For all of economic incentives' importance in corporate decision-making, they are not the sole determinants of corporate action. To use these other determinants, the lawyer must be a talented student, not only of the legal risks, but also of his corporate client.

RISK ANALYSIS AND ORGANIZATION THEORY

Comparing two schools of organizational analysis—resource dependency theory and strategic contingency theory-reveals an inescapable problem in limiting the lawyer's task to risk analysis. Resource dependency theory highlights organizations' dependence on their environments. In all organizations, the ability to meet the problems facing the organization is a basis for power. When the problems have uncertain outcomes and are important, power is up for grabs. Resource dependency theory argues that when individuals or departments are able to successfully navigate the corporation through environmental uncertainty, they gain power. Consequently, "when an organization faces a number of lawsuits and legal difficulties, the legal department will gain power and influence over organizational decisions."[348] I did not find this result in the corporations studied. To understand why, strategic contingency theory must be called into play.[349] When the organization will be harmed if it doesn't cope with the environment, resource dependency theory is a sufficient tool for analysis. When, however, the feedback between the environment and organizational success is blocked or distorted, strategic contingency theory is required. Strategic contingency theory emphasizes that intra-organizational negotiations decide the problems critical to an organization. Organizations can devalue certain ways in which they are dependent on the environment. They choose their "strategic" contingencies. Whether lawyers or law departments can influence corporate choices depends on their ability to make legal contingencies critical.

Strategic contingency theory has developed principles of organizational analysis that determine an organization's critical contingencies. The greater a

---

[348] J. Pfeffer and G. Salancik, The External Control of Organizations: A Resource Dependence Perspective 230 (1978). Resource dependency theory is often stated in terms of "departments." It applies as well to individual corporate actors and outside consultants. To simplify the discussion in this section, outside law firms are considered to constitute a boundary-spanning department of their clients.

[349] Hinings, et al., "Structural Conditions of Intraorganizational Power," 19 Ad. Sci. Q. 22 (1974); Hickson, et al., "A Strategic Contingencies Theory of Intraorganizational Power," 16 Ad. Sci. Q. 216 (1971).

department's "centrality," the greater its power. Centrality can be measured on two dimensions: (1) pervasiveness, and (2) immediacy. "Pervasiveness" refers to the extent a department's work connects to the work of others in the organization. When a corporation faces many legal problems, lawyers may be involved with several different departments which could be the source of the problem, the source of a solution, or the source of relevant documentation. "Immediacy" refers to the extent the department's work affects the final output of other departments. Given important legal problems, lawyer decisions may be required for other departments to proceed with their work. Consequently, one would expect the same conclusion as in resource dependence theory: lawyers gaining corporate power. But power is not given; it must be organizationally created. An organization can constitute itself so that legal problems are not central.

Lawyers also may negotiate relationships so that their work is neither pervasive nor immediate. Strategic contingency theory explains that a department will not gain power if its work can be performed by other departments. The greater the "substitutability" of a department, the less its power. Given the professional nature of legal service, one would expect that lawyers would not suffer from the "substitutability" problem. Professional service, however, can be restricted so that critical contingencies do not fall within the professional's control. These contingencies may be defined as matters for non-professional decision-making. Lawyers may leave the critical decisions to "business judgment." Whether lawyers gain power will depend on their ability to effectively monopolize the critical contingencies in responding to legal difficulties.

Expressed another way, corporations choose what risks to address. Whether a legal contingency is critical to the organization depends on the risks of exposure and the ways the company is organized to sense the contingency. That the company uses lawyers shows it is receptive to the legal environment. Receptivity does not mean, however, that legal information will be correctly processed or decisions will be appropriately reached. To understand corporate action, we must comprehend the processes through which the legal environment influences corporate actors.[350]

As strategic contingency theory emphasizes, the fact that choice of risks is negotiated raises an important normative question. Because resource dependency theory assumes feedback between the organization and the environment, it implicitly contains a normative theory of organizational power: An individual or a department should have just the amount of power that enables the organization to meet environmental problems. Hence, for an organization, "[t]he theoretically interesting aspects of the development and conferral of power include the extent to which influence extends beyond the

---

[350] For the distinction between receptivity and influence, see Sonnefeld, "Structure, Culture and Performance in Public Affairs: A Study of the Forest Products Industry," 4 Res. in Corp. Soc. Perf. & Policy 105, 177 (1982).

immediate functions of the subunit...."[351] In resource dependency theory, the power lawyers gain poses a problem. It is disturbing that "the power of a legal department derived from its handling of the organization's legal difficulties may extend beyond the legal function and involve the department in decisions about product design, advertising, and production."[352]

This problem can't be readily solved, however, because there is no simple mechanism for environmental feedback. Given an inadequate feedback mechanism between a corporation and its legal environment, an organization and its lawyers have no basis for easily identifying the limits on lawyer power. The corporation must then rely on organizational processes to determine, through negotiations, the critical contingencies. We know from the history of power struggles and the character of power wielders or seekers that rational decision-making is often distorted. But we have not sufficiently considered the other side of the coin. Given that organizations can easily be deflected from rational decision making, organizational and personal resources must be utilized to enhance corporate rationality. What effect do various methods of delivering corporate legal services have on corporate rationality?

RISKS MUST BE CHOSEN

I will develop this answer by focusing on the managerial task. As was pointed out in the last chapter, organizational pathologies may limit the lawyer's ability to make the law salient. Yet, even in the absence of pathologies, a lawyer may not be able to bring the law to bear. To a certain extent, this is because managers may discount the risks down the line.[353] To a greater extent, it is because managers need to balance many risks. Managers must pick and choose the risks to consider. Managers treat risks as contingencies to be minimized but not eliminated. Their job requires them to accept that risks are ever-present. When lawyers attempt to forestall managerial action because of the possibility of sanction, they are not addressing the manager's problem.[354] To view the lawyer's job as simply that

---

[351] J. Pfeffer & G. Salancik, *supra, id.* They continue: "...and the extent to which influence is used in the interest of the subunit independent of the goals and interests of the organization as a whole or of others in the organization."

[352] *Ibid.*

[353] In all the corporations studied, there was an emphasis on "being positive." While I certainly cannot generalize about how this attitude has affected productivity, lawyers felt it precluded adequate consideration of legal risks.

[354] Cf. Bardach & Kagan, *supra*, at 79-80: "[T]he tendency of businessmen [is] to think of regulation as an ongoing process of encountering problems and searching for cost-effective solutions.... Accustomed to trying to achieve their goals in the face of the competing concerns of other departments and workers, managers expect the problem solving to proceed through negotiation and compromise, according to a 'morality of cooperation' rather than by legal fiat. Thus managers criticize inspectors who walk through the plant

of communicating risks to which the manager responds is to misunderstand the manager's job: balancing risks, developing a risk-portfolio, securing support from others to minimize risks. Managers do not see legal risks as different from other risks, such as those engendered by customer and supply markets, that they must balance.[355] The law may insist upon compliance, but that is not the way managers approach risks. A quality control manager, who often fought lawyers who asserted the risks of sanction and frequently won, explained it this way:

> It is ludicrous to say that I don't care about quality or the consumer. An ex-regulator wrote an article about the personality of guys who feel the need to ask the government questions. Regulators are trained to answer 'no' to questions. That is the official policy. All sorts of questions are asked that shouldn't be asked. Companies take business risks. If you are in a grey area, the question is weighing risk. Some people call it unethical. I have no problem with that. Other people ask, 'What do we do if the regulators come in?' They play the game by saying that the government could ask us to recall the product. That is probably technically legally true. But the question is what in reality would they have us do. They would say, 'Cease and desist the advertising.' Now, you wouldn't want to do a lot of this. You have to balance the whole thing. That is the key. In most of these conflicts, there is no right and wrong. We all agree on the black and white. It is the grey stuff.
>
> A lawyer shouldn't be a white knight. It is like pure science versus what I do. I work with analytical people who are smarter technically than I am. I don't have a problem with that. Yes, to some extent, I have bastardized my technical training because I am not doing 'science.' I have chosen to broaden myself and go into management. If the lawyer wants to do pure, zero-risk kind of law, then they should be in the government. I get into fights with my technical people like I get into with lawyers: 'Can we read the data in this way?' You have to take risks in management. You try to make it black and white but generally you can't do that. There is often a lot of uncertainty and a lot of misunderstanding of why there is a problem.

When lawyers attempt to secure compliance by risk analysis, they do not acknowledge that managers have a different perspective on risk. Especially in

---

looking only for 'violations' of the rules...with no...concern with the problems involving in 'coming into compliance.'"

[355] R. Miles, et al., Organizational Strategy, Structure, and Process 202-03 (1978) (survey of managers in food processing and electronics industries that found that manager viewed legal risks as no more uncertain than other risks).

technical companies, where many managers wear two hats (they are managers and also have a technical profession), the risks of sanction will not make the law salient. As these managers cut short scientists who only talk about technical problems, so they cut short lawyers who raise "technical" problems. As one respondent put it, "Look, it is dangerous to get up in the morning. The bomb may go off tomorrow. The lawyer is just trying out his fear scenario." Given that the manager must choose the risks to be concerned with, how can legal risks be made more salient? How can legal risks, when necessary, become the critical contingency? One option, which will be explored first, is for the lawyer simply to engage in risk analysis. Other possibilities also will be considered. One lawyer in rejecting risk analysis correctly assessed the managerial task: "I'll write a memo telling then there is this risk and that risk. But getting out of bed in the morning is risky. A risk has to be picked. Uncertainty is not complexity. If on one side there are 62 considerations and on the other there are 64 considerations, that is not a complex situation. That is a dead heat. Business people are used to living with uncertainty. They don't need lists of considerations. All they need to know is that they could go either way." This may sound as if the client has a great deal of license. Or, it may sound as if the lawyer has great potential for domination. After assessing the inadequacies of risk analysis, we will evaluate the strengths and weaknesses of rejecting it.

RISK ANALYSIS: CONFLICTS AS POWER CONTESTS

There are certainly many instances when all the corporation wants or needs is for the lawyer to supply a risk analysis.[356] Yet, lawyers often supply nothing but risk analysis in situations posing trade-offs between legal and business interests. In determining at what level a company complies with the law, these trade-offs are common. Corporations then must choose risk levels.

When the lawyer only provides risk analysis, conflicts between lawyer and client that require risks be chosen often descend into power plays. Power struggles between the lawyer and involved managers decide the corporate response. As a senior Vice-President said:

> It is easy for the lawyer to argue his point of view. He throws out a legal fear scenario. He can scare the client. He can always say, "you never know what the judge will hold." He then gnaws at the manager until the manager's judgment is warped. This happens all the time. The lawyer scares the hell out of the businessman. He raises a lot of legal red flags along the route he wants to strike, while the route he wants to go on has probably as many red flags, if

---

[356] The corporation may need only to predict the likely behavior of legal officials. For example, in pricing their securities, corporations may only need lawyers to tell them the risk of legal action against the issue.

not more. It is all a con game.

A lower-level client, a marketer, expressed it this way: It is marketing's job "to be creative as possible with claims and let others help them restrain the claims. It is legal's job to keep in everybody's mind the zero-risk position. In every instance it is a judgment call and everyone's judgment is going to be different. Judgments are made according to who has power. In a power struggle, even the lawyer's predictions of the court's response will be up for grabs. According to the marketer, the law "is all opinion and not based on much fact. It is all judgment and people differ about these judgments. So legal conflicts are noisy."

Lawyers recognize power plays result from risk analysis. As one put the difficulties of the legal task: "If the lawyer keeps the legal issues in the forefront, he is trying to dominate the play. If he breaks down all the legal issues in a problem that is a way for him to enlarge his role and it makes it more difficult for the business guy to do a risk evaluation."

In this situation, lawyers and managers tend to negotiate a bifurcated order. Lawyers have audit functions on certain issues, usually limited and routine ones. Certain types of decisions are formally required to pass over the lawyers' desks and often lawyers must sign-off on them. Otherwise, lawyers adopt a wait-in-the-office attitude, letting the client define when and on what problems to seek legal risk analysis. Both these approaches tend to maximize the pathologies described in the last chapter. Nevertheless, there remain issues over which—because of the legal risks—conflict will ensue. As in all corporate power struggles, the question facing the lawyer is a political one. Does he seek support from powerful others? Does he try to build coalitions? Does he seek organizational support for establishing auditing functions?

When lawyers restrict themselves to struggles over whether the manager's decision adequately incorporates legal risks, their ability to win conflicts is limited. They can win conflicts only by raising the issue before higher levels of the hierarchy for reconsideration. The issue then becomes whether the particular manager has adequately performed his job: has he adequately assessed the risks inherent in the task assigned to him?[357]

As one inside counsel complained: "There are often conflicts in deals. A manager wants to do something and the lawyer says he can't because it will cause problems. Even if the lawyer says, 'This will get you into hot water and X will write a memo to your boss if you persist,' the manager will respond, 'Go ahead. Write your memo. I am taking full responsibility.'" This result

---

[357] Organizational theorists find that as decisions are reviewed, they become translated into the language of money. This enables the reviewer to make decisions between homologous alternatives. R. Marris, ed., The Corporate Society 240 (1974). Consequently, the question becomes whether the manager made the proper cost-benefit decision, i.e., whether he did his job.

occurs because the issue, from the manager's perspective, is control over one's job. Those higher in the hierarchy recognize this issue. As one senior manager said, "You handle conflict between lawyers and managers by seeing how far people are willing to go. They are betting their jobs on the line and seeing who is going to back down. You get the truth out by seeing how willing each is to put their job on the line. If no one backs down, you call in someone else."[358]

There are strong pressures to defuse conflicts of this sort. Managers may respond to the conflict by claiming the conflict is simply one of personalities. The lawyer will be called, for example, a "nit-picker." This indicates a rather intense power struggle. Fair play flies out the door.[359] Perhaps more important, so does the substance of the law's requirements.

Even when the lawyer wins the power struggle, managers do not consider legal compliance to be a corporate commitment. They perceive that the balance of power was against them in this instance. Managers therefore often attempt to reduce legal strength by making lawyers battle over everything. As an inside counsel explained:

> At my previous employer, if an ad came to me and I had to make a lot of comments on it, it was a bad reflection on the guy. If he could write an ad which was legally O.K. the first time through, his supervisor applauded him. Here, people purposely put stuff in which they know I will take out. They say, 'I just wanted to see if I could get that by you.' Here, the attitude is let us see what we can get by legal. It is not, 'Let us develop something in concert with legal.' They always want to get stuff through. I ask them, 'Why

---

[358] At one company studied, the absence of organizationally defined risk-levels means that "a lot of this gets knocked up to the President." Even then, whether a rational decision is reached depends on the manner in which the power struggles continues: "Conflicts in this organization go to the President. Each makes his case and the stronger one prevails. Unfortunately, it has occurred that one party was travelling and one side put his case before the President without the other side being present and the decision was made. This is sniping and breaks down trust. If both sides air their GRIEVANCE and the President decides, no problem. It creates difficulty when the decision is made without that. We have to train managers throughout this company not to make decisions when they know there are conflicting viewpoints without ferreting out the viewpoints. Differences of opinion can be legitimate and both sides should be heard." That these conflicts are seen as "grievances" highlights that participants perceive power, not reason, to be at the root of the battle. The President in this company often sided with legal. Managers explain this by noting that the President often calls on an outside lawyer, who is his personal friend and who has his trust. The managers do not acknowledge that the President has chosen to commit the company to a policy of compliance with the law. They just see that they do not have the power of the President's friend.

[359] See previous note. And, as a client said, lawyers will "gear their opinions to who is going to win or lose. If there is a maldistribution of legal knowledge in the company, the inside counsel will defer to those with the greater knowledge. In a conflict between finance and personnel, where the financial person knows ERISA, the lawyer will side with finance."

throw it in when you know I won't let it through?'

Clients "throw things in" because they know the costs to the lawyer of power struggles.[360] They know they can hamper lawyers' abilities to win conflicts by increasing the number of conflicts. The lawyer must choose his fights. He knows that even though, "management looks to us to keep the company out of legal trouble," the lawyer is also "expected to try to find a way for management to do what it wants to do."[361] Consequently, "I have to decide when legal issues should prevail. On the outside, I used to say, 'Here is my opinion and the risks. It is up to you to decide whether you want to assume the risk.' On the inside, it is the same principle, but if we put up enough of an argument against something, chances are it won't go through. You have to pick and choose when to do that. It requires some judgment about how strongly to say no."

How is that judgment made? The seriousness of the violation is the first level of analysis: "Line managers learn that we don't cry wolf unless THERE IS SOMETHING OUT THERE. So when we say, 'no,' it is more likely to be taken seriously." Once he makes such a decision, a power struggle ensues: "You have to have a strong weather vane because the winds will try to push you and you have to know where you won't budge."

To reduce conflict, lawyers resort to the actual risk of sanction. Another lawyer volunteered: "There are two types of risk: There is the risk of this being a violation of the law and there is the risk of getting caught and the size of the fine. I don't employ that. A defensible position is not enough." But, when pressed to explain how he responds to a client who claims to need a certain result, he said: "I say to the manager, 'This is the risk under the law. We have a good argument but there are three cases against us. If we are wrong it will cost us x dollars.' Then I let the client do the risk analysis." Or as an inside counsel at another corporation put it, "If there is a colorable or reasonable legal defense, you advise on that basis. Only if the client commits an illegality, do you take it upstream."[362] These lawyers, at least, will not engage in conflict no matter how high the risk so long as the problem lies in a gray area of the law. Lawyer independence is a flimsy concept when all it means is a lawyer will not abet a clear illegality. It is further attenuated by the notion that illegalities are acceptable if approved by an appropriate level

---

[360] They also waste corporate resources because much has to be re-worked. It is not easily solved by organizational controls. Rewarding managers who get things by legal on the first try might spawn over compliance or increase the incentives for improper collaboration. Furthermore, such a device would support the notion that anything that gets by legal is acceptable to the corporation. It inhibits pride in responsible behavior.

[361] This dual task is a difficult one. Another lawyer forcefully asserted his independence' "In conflicts, you are accommodating, understanding and helpful without forsaking legal or ethical absolutes." But, he later said, "Our task is to let clients do whatever they want to do in a legal way. If you have sharp edges, the clients will refine you."

[362] Within the corporation.

of the corporate hierarchy.

In the risk analysis mode, legal compliance depends on the pressures the manager feels.[363] Lawyers can stop actions only when there is little pressure behind them. Although lawyers do filter out some actions, risk analysis generates a very permeable filter. Lawyers all too often can eliminate conflict by using the manipulability of the law. Consider a case in which a manager learns from the attorney of regulations concerning the marketing of a product: "Legal won't let us say it fits into that specific category. But we can say, 'This product is present wherever good things are found.' The natural connotation is that if it is not there, you won't have a good thing. But we've never said that. In effect, legal said, 'You can't make this claim, but, if you word it like this, that is fine. That is a defensible position.' That way, we can lead the horse to water." Actually, the lawyer was upset by this evasion of regulatory intent. He thought the campaign was sleazy. But he had done his job as he conceived it—limiting the legal damage to the company. In the face of management pressure and maneuverability in the law, he had to cave in.

Because corporations are used to assuming risks, the lawyer's position is weakened further: "This corporation accepts certain risk levels. Often there is something done which is wrong. I always call it to the manager's attention. I tell him it is wrong, you can't do it that way and outside counsel would say it was wrong. But, then I have to make the decision whether I will go to the mat on it. Whether I will go to his supervisor depends on the risk levels and it depends on how often I can go to the well and say, 'I don't go further than this.'"[364]

Instead of altering their service to fit the realities of the managerial task, risk analysis lawyers often justify caving in by claiming legal risk is just another business risk. This leads to a self-justifying cycle that increases the number of times lawyers cave in to avoid conflict. Consider the following example:

> We misprinted some labels. To the letter of the law, it was a misbranded product. But we had a million dollars worth of labels and it would have been an economic loss to the company and ultimately the consumer would have paid more for the products. It would have been real economic foolishness to scrap the labels. We took the practical position: you can use the labels until you run

---

[363] These pressures may not be identical to the pressures on the corporation.

[364] How often a lawyer must "go to the mat" depends on the organization of the corporate law department. At this company, the corporate law department was organized by legal specialties. Thus, some lawyers did corporate work and others did regulatory work. The regulatory lawyers could not contest all the decisions they wanted to because they would have been in a position of always telling their clients "no." Assigning lawyers to divisions with back-up specialists, minimizes this problem. Lawyers are then able to draw on the constructive work they do for the managers when they go to the mat to stop managerial action.

out. We agreed to take the risk because the government has approved such schemes and it is an accepted practice in some circumstances.

In fact, the product was seriously misbranded and substantially less than a million dollars worth of labels were involved. The lawyer could avoid conflict, claiming to be pragmatic, because the corporation was used to taking risks akin to that of getting nailed in this regulatory environment. Outside counsel suggested the arguments that it was accepted practice and that destroying the labels would result in pass-through costs to serve defensive purposes in the event of an investigation.

The choice may have been correct, but it reflects the lawyer's inability to make the corporation follow through on its enunciated policy of complying with the relevant laws and regulations. Instead of a commitment to legal compliance, a risk-taking attitude pervades the whole corporation and its legal choices.

In risk analysis, lawyers are not able to pursue conflicts. Whether the lawyer fights depends on the violation, which is filtered through an assessment of the risk of sanction, which is filtered through the corporation's general level of risk-taking, which in turn is filtered through the lawyer's willingness to make an issue of it. The result is of concern not only to the public but also to the corporation. Even when corporations have lawyers engaged in risk analysis, they seek attorneys who can control managers' discretionary judgments. The two risk analysis companies studied formally established a two-tiered test. At the first tier, the lawyer informs the appropriate manager of the risks and the manager makes the decision. At the second tier, the lawyer is relied on to appeal decisions that are "too violative." As a divisional manager put it:

> Part of developing subordinates is to give them experience with taking risks. The lawyer should point out the risks. The lawyer never has final authority. The manager can say, 'I hear you, but I'm not going to do that.' It's the lawyer's responsibility then, if he is uncomfortable with the position taken, to go up the line and say, 'I think there is a problem here.' We've worked out by trial and error what is pushed up. If it is a substantial business risk or a risk of my going to jail or the corporation paying a high penalty, then I want to be informed. This is also how we handle non-legal matters. If the question involves less than $100,000, I don't want to be involved.

Because organizations reach decisions based on how far each side will go and because such conflicts are costly, lawyers let a great deal slip through. Both the manager and the lawyer is putting his job on the line and the question often is who will break first. Lawyers feel that at the first management level, the immediate supervisor, "the manager often comes out good because his ability to take risks is valued to keep things off his manager's desk. It is only if it is kicked up much higher that legal has a chance. Top management is not so frightened of losing a deal and are more frightened by legal risk." But lawyers often break first. They justify their unwillingness to go to the mat by lauding the importance of practicality. As one lawyer rationalized: "People have very narrow interests until you get to the top. So very little looks grossly out of line and so we accept the manager's risk taking." At higher levels, they claim the decision is no longer legal. It is a business-policy one for which they have no responsibility:

> I am not getting paid to impose my values on the company. If the Corporate VP for Personnel says, 'I understand what you are saying and I understand that case and how it might affect us, but it is going to cost too much to change. I am going to take the risk, hoping it won't come up,' as far as I am concerned, that is his decision. I don't know what the long term best interest of the company is. I could only appeal it by going to the CEO. That doesn't make sense. I have a personal rule of never going over someone's head unless he is grossly out of line.

This process defeats organizational controls. Instead of a two-tiered test implementing corporate risk-levels and developing the corporate risk portfolio, these lawyers exacerbate organizational weaknesses by letting managers take the risks that they have chosen. All too often, lawyers cave in when the manager says, "It's my exposure." In risk analysis, lawyers cop-out, saying, "We gave good legal advice, but the management made a bad business judgment."[365] Without power or influence, lawyers retreat into safety of their prestigious technical role. In so doing, they claim that they are merely respecting the corporate hierarchy: It would be paternalistic to do more, since "this is the manager's problem." The lawyers' perspective presents a limited view of the corporate organization, which, after all, sought to organize, if ineffectively, a two-tiered test to control managers' discretion. By stressing their purely technical function and viewing the corporate organization as a simple hierarchy, lawyers misserve the corporation and become the worst sort of company men.

This problem is well illustrated by the contract administration work at Drafter, an industrial company where sales are "the bread and butter of the business." A principal activity of the corporate legal department is drafting

---

[365] Or, "If the contract is detrimental to the company, that is not my business. The underlying economic assumptions are the corporation's business, not mine. The ABC deal went sour, but they were good contracts which perhaps limited our exposure." Or as another inside counsel in the same company put it, "If the issue is impact, it is a business decision. If the ultimate business decision is not to my liking, but it is within the strictures of the legal advice I rendered, that is fine. That is my function."

sales contracts. At Drafter, the legal department is responsible for supervising contract terms and conditions. The legal department writes standard warranties, indemnification clauses, and the like, and managers who wish to waive them need formal legal approval. Drafter has a production department, a sales department, and a form-creating department. The operating manager makes widgets, the lawyer makes documents. But, as a Drafter lawyer explained, there is a significant difference "between the widgets and the contract documents. The customer uses the widget. The customer does not use the document." Contracts often are not adhered to.

Drafter's inside counsel prided themselves on their expertise with the company's contracts. They denigrated outside counsel who "prepare excellent legal documents but not ones which are workable in our marketplace." They explain that managers do not want "legal positions." Managers want something they can "work with." Drafter's lawyers cast themselves as "craftsmen" of widget sales contracts. Drafter's managers, however, denigrate inside counsel's understanding of business realities: "There would be no sale if the lawyers were always involved. Lawyers write things in ways we can't understand.... Contracts are useless in most relations.... Only in court is what is on paper important."

At Drafter, managers use lawyers because the hierarchy demands it. They use lawyers, as one said, because "that's the way the company is organized. It's part of my job. But, lawyers work for us and the laws don't fit the situations we find ourselves in. There is a great difference of opinion about what antitrust laws require." Managers feel free to renegotiate contracts according to their perceptions of the marketplace. As a lawyer said: "They work things out with the customer. Unless they ask us to get involved, we let them work it out by themselves. We only find out after the end of the contract, or when it must be revised, what the marketplace requires. We rewrite the contract to conform to the market conditions."

Claiming that their expertise does not meet practical needs, lawyers do not perform their control function. Managers waive terms without their approval and even when legal advice is sought, it often is not followed. As a lawyer admitted, "People in the company don't always listen to us." Managers look to lawyers only in the event of litigation. Because contracts only rarely go to litigation, one lawyer wondered, "Why do I do this? But, it's my job."

Drafter lawyers experience one of the ironies of risk analysis. They attempt to secure managerial compliance by raising the specter of litigation, but when litigation is a possibility, they speak in terms of commercial realities. As a lawyer said, "In such situations, you have to be a realist and tell the manager that the contract language is not necessarily going to be adhered to, that it takes three years to get to trial and even if you win in court, you lose a customer." It is little wonder, then, that managers approve contract variances on their own and don't request legal advice when customer disputes arise.

At Drafter, lawyers pride themselves on being able to write contracts for a settled market. When the market is not settled, they play a game of catch-up, adjusting clauses for new contracts as necessary. Although the corporation formally wants its lawyers to set policies to limit managerial discretion, the lawyers avoid this function, and its potentialities for conflict. They defer to managerial problem-setting: "Managers don't want to listen to us. We get called in at the last moment. I know they automatically want to keep the lawyers out." Lawyers defer to managers in the choice of risks. Managers work out contract variances with the customers. Drafter lawyers may be expert craftsmen of widget contracts, but they do not help make corporate choices.

Drafter marketers therefore must rely on their judgment alone to reconcile two conflicting corporate goals—obtaining the strongest marketing position for the corporation and keeping customers. Lawyers, rather than salesmen, formally administer contracts because the corporation knows "salesmen want to satisfy their customers. They are gauged by the amount of sales, not the profitability of each sale." Having reduced themselves to technicians of litigation risk, however, Drafter lawyers are not in a position to insure that sales are fair to the company. Furthermore, even contracts that may be excellent for a particular sale can create legal problems. Robinson-Patman questions are raised by differential treatment of customers. Because contracts are re-made at informal levels by individual managers, lawyers are not involved. Drafter lawyers rationalize this result, which contradicts the company's formal delegation of responsibility, by claiming conflict situations demand "business judgment." Lawyers are not responsible for that: "This company doesn't want lawyers involved in business decisions. They want legal advice presented, packaged and evaluated if possible."[366]

When lawyers only provide risk analysis, the law does not help organize corporate processes. In the mislabeling example, for instance, the company made no attempt to prevent a re-occurrence. The corporation has repeatedly misbranded products, each time assuming it will not get caught or severely sanctioned. Another corporation's product safety group, which is dominated by risk analysis lawyers, also demonstrates this problem. The safety group's mission is not to make safe products. Its mission is one of "reviewing that risks are justified, that the returns will offset the risks." Instead of providing input on the manufacture of safe products, the law is just another cost. As a client said, "We have systems to provide feedback if the product is faulty. That is for us to do. There is not much lawyers can do. They can't protect us. Either we get sued or we don't. They don't know what should be done. I just shake my head at what the courts have done. If anything goes wrong, you get

---

[366] The solecism in this quote is important. Managers ("They") do not want lawyers to struggle with them over business judgments. This does not mean, however, as the lawyer implies, that the company (an "it") doesn't want lawyers to exercise a control function over business judgments. Drafter lawyers equate the company with the managers to avoid conflicts.

a suit." Thus, the law does not pressure companies to make safe products and the risk analysis lawyer's function is only damage control. The lawyer may control damage to the company, but he does nothing to prevent damage to the consumer.

The law doesn't affect corporate processes because risk analysis lawyers rely on raising the specter of litigation to influence corporate action. Even when effective in individual instances, the threat of litigation cuts against the company's anticipating legal problems. As a manager explained: "The lawyer has power because even if I think we did a good job, if the lawyer says we will go to litigation and lose with an inexperienced jury and lose big, his recommendation will prevail. Even though our operating people think they did it right, we recognize that as a large company, many people are going to take pokes at us and in this crazy legal system, we will often lose." The unpredictability of exposure in litigation lessens managers' willingness to implement systems to prevent legal liability. Managers come to see the law as a "crazy system." When the lawyer tries to get involved in planning, it "ruffles feathers." The company does not respect the law and adopts a defensive posture. The company rarely learns from the threat of litigation. As a manager reported, his fellow managers always "are yelling they acted perfectly well and the fault lies elsewhere." In the end, "if it comes to a small enough settlement we will settle. It all comes down to economics." The lawyers gain a certain kind of power by stressing the exposure in litigation. They gain the power to settle suits. They do not gain the power to bring the law to bear to organize corporate processes.

When lawyers see their job as one of damage control, they don't consider rights, especially those of third parties. When asked about the Pinto case, a risk analysis lawyer described it as a case where Ford's lawyers failed to effectively disclaim their warranties. When asked about the complicity of Ford's lawyers in the decision to balance lives against increased production costs, the lawyer claimed I misunderstood the function of lawyers: "The problem is that product liability is expanding all the time. Our job is to find ways to protect us. Disclaimers are necessary, even if they don't always protect us." The lawyer offers no indication the company or its lawyers had any duty to protect others, such as Pinto drivers.

Or consider a company's introduction of a product that did not meet a published regulation. The regulation had been rejected by federal courts on procedural, but not substantive, grounds. Without a controlling regulation, the product could be marketed legally: "I asked them how long it would take to develop the product. They said about three years. I told them, 'You are taking a hell of a risk that the regulators won't be able to get out a standard to satisfy the courts in three years.' They took the risk. Now, since the regulators under Reagan are doing nothing, we are the only company marketing the product." This lawyer drew a thick line between the law and business; his role was cast only in terms of risk analysis. His advice on legal sanctions side-stepped the question of responsibility. Even though the product is defective, the lawyer considered his professional role as one of helping the company take advantage of the public because of a procedural irregularity.

It is easy to ascribe these lawyers' actions to control by the client and the client organization. This view, however, assigns too strong a role to clients in determining professional behavior. The importance of professional orientation is made clear by noting that one of the two corporations where inside counsel took a predominantly risk analysis approach was poorly organized and was the scene of many intra-corporate power struggles over the choice of corporate goals. This corporation's lawyers ignored the possibilities for influence and simply avoided the conflicts. Even though a leadership vacuum existed, the lawyers made no attempt, when conflicts with managers arose, to make the dispute an organizational issue. As a lawyer admitted:

> At my previous employer, I would know what management would do. Here, it is a new battle each time. No one knows which way the company will go at its junctures. It simply depends on the politics at the time. At my previous employer, we had a calculated risk mentality based on business experience and our legal experience. But, here we haven't have had the continuity of people to create a corporate sense of what is an acceptable risk. In various areas, there is no company position on what are accepted risks. It is always a balancing act.

Because the lawyer did not have a sense of what would be acceptable up the hierarchy, he often did not engage in conflict. Interestingly, during his sharpest conflict situation, he moved away from risk analysis. He made a weak feint to the organizational problems at the company:

> Someone wanted to do something I knew was wrong. The manager had no reason not to comply with the law except it didn't look right to him. He didn't know he would get more sales. His response to my asking him about verifying the sales was, 'Are we going to get caught?' I told him not everyone who drives at 70 gets caught, but do you want to make it an established, spelled out company policy that everyone who drives for the company drives at 70? It didn't work.

But the lawyer left it there. He made no attempt to try to develop organizational policies or risk-levels. His only additional move was to bring in outside counsel to second his opinion and do battle with him. That also didn't work.

That this conflict remained at the level of individual power struggles with the lawyer not making any significant effort to address the organizational problem can be explained only by the lawyer's professional orientation. Unlike the lawyer, the involved manager knew the battle could have gone against him had the lawyer drawn on potential allies. But the lawyer saw himself as distinct from the rest of the company and battled first alone and then with a brother at the bar. He made no attempt to address the corporation's weak organization, which allowed individual managers to choose the company's direction. The manager was all too happy to keep the conflict at the individual level. He publicly derogated the lawyer's personality, labeling him "extreme." The manager kept the personality issue in the forefront because he knew the lawyer had organizational support that could have been brought into the conflict. The manager admitted:

> There are other non-legal people in the corporation who also prefer the zero-risk position. They feel they are right and are protecting the company from people like myself. I think that doing what is right doesn't mean not taking risks. The question is right for whom. It is not 'What is good for GM is good for America.' That is a little gross. Everybody has to decide what they believe in. I think we must state the technical facts and not worry about the implications. We state the facts and let the customers imply what they want into these facts. Others say what we are doing is having the cookie crumbs leading you to the cookie and are not hot about that. But, I don't normally worry about that. In other companies they have decided to do what is right for the consumer. They take things off the market because they don't want to send out a signal that they don't care about the consumers. People argue that here, but they are just making a play to get power.

In risk analysis, lawyers do not seek to understand or change the organization they serve. They direct their attention to the risks of the legal environment. They adopt a position of professional independence and do not get involved with the corporation. Consequently, individual managers, not corporate policies, often decide risks. The risks chosen are usually based on the lowest common denominator of what any competitor is doing. The lawyer cannot respond, "Yes, they do it, but we won't." To make that argument, he would have to draw on corporate resources: policies, coalitions and culture.

In risk analysis managers do not call on lawyers to re-think corporate processes, commitments, and risk-level choices. When the lawyer's job is one of reporting on the legal environment's risks, the law is external and remote. Where the law is external, the manager's perceives it as demanding compliance, requiring the manager to give in which is "a loss of discretion, a constraint, and an admission of limited autonomy."[367] Furthermore, each time the manager gives in he fears his admission will result in ever more losses, ever more attempts to control his behavior.[368] The law, interest groups

---

[367] J. Pfeffer & G. Salancik, The External Control of Organizations: A Resource-Dependency Perspective 94 (1978).

[368] E. Bardach & R. Kagan, Going by the Book: The Problem of Regulatory Unreason-

"out there," and lawyers are seeking to limit his power and take over his job. Where the law is external, the manager tries to go as far as possible and the lawyer tries to limit him. The manager, to the extent he can, therefore will try to limit the lawyer's involvement. He will demand the privilege of choosing when to initiate contact with the lawyer and will avoid the lawyer's scrutiny by not encroaching on the lawyer's territory and by covering his tracks. Power struggles are common and "managers are not rewarded for anticipating outside power."

Certainly, many lawyers try to make the legal risks appear to be not merely external. Sometimes lawyers make this move in the spirit of risk analysis. Lawyers, who try to persuade managers that their and the lawyers' moral lives are at stake, will frequently talk about the risks in the court of public opinion.[369] As with narrower conceptions of risk analysis, this information's import depends on how the corporate organization processes it. Some corporations are risk averse and will not pursue actions that arouse public feelings. Others have responsible management, ready and willing to meet the ethical issues raised by the invocation of public opinion. And still others, perhaps the majority, consider negative public disapproval as yet another risk, requiring specialized staffs to measure and report on it. The effectiveness of these staffs, paralleling legal risk analysis, will depend both on the sanctions of public opinion and public relations officers efforts to make their risks critical ones.

In this context, consider a drug company's decision to release a new drug. How will the corporation determine the best way to make its product safe? The company's toxicologists know an unlimited amount of work can be done. Testing the product for 20 years doesn't guarantee there won't be adverse affects after 30 years. The toxicologists may want, therefore, to keep the product from release. The medical staff may want the product available immediately for experimental evaluation. The manager in charge may want both to use the lab facilities and staff talents for other research and to boost this quarter's earnings. How is this decision to be made? There is no clear answer. The answer will always depend on questions such as, "Safe compared to what?" and "What alternative use can be made of the resources?"[370] The decision will be made based on contributions of different departments, with different understandings of the decision's risks. In light of these varying assessments, the company must choose certain risks. If the departments provide only technical risk estimates, a power struggle will almost certainly

---

ableness 11 (1982) (quoting a corporate safety official about OSHA: "Give them an inch and they'll push you a mile.").

[369] In so doing, they draw on the publicity requirement of ethical decision-making. See S. Bok, Lying: Moral Choice in Public and Private Life (1978).

[370] Milton Wessel argues that the law has shifted its focus to managing precisely these sorts of decisions and that recent key corporate litigation has concerned them. M. Wessel, The Rule of Reason: A New Approach to Corporate Litigation, Ch. 1 (1976).

ensue. Yet, the corporation's character is at issue in this decision. When lawyers and managers in other departments move away from technical risk analysis, they can contribute to a decision that defines the corporate character.

EMERGENCE OF TERRITORIALITY

To defuse risk analysis generated power struggles, managers typically not only reduced conflict to the level of personality clashes, they also created territorial regimes. As a manager expressed it, "We know where the lawyers are coming from." Managers consider the legal perspective unique, quite separate from the life of the company. Lawyers, in turn, establish themselves in enclaves and accept they are not part of business planning or policy setting: "We try to discourage making business judgments. We give off the record feeling about business questions, but it is not our bailiwick, or province."

Where enclaves are created, the lawyer has a hard time doing work outside his province. The lawyer favors a reactive stance, waiting for work to come to him.[371] Lawyers are able to secure compliance only where the law has specific, certain and harsh sanctions.[372] They limit their advice to instances in which the law is so clear they can present their opinion in a take-it-or-leave-it form. Lawyers are either heeded or ignored. They are excluded even from areas where they have developed expertise of use to the corporation, unless the expertise is tied to a clear legal issue. Consider an example of a decision about how strongly to push in a negotiating position. As a lawyer said, "That's a decision for the business SIDE. I point out the expense and problems in enforcing legal rights under a contract and tell them whether it is worth pushing FROM A LEGAL POINT OF VIEW." Or as the client put it, "Lawyers primary job is to give LEGAL PERSPECTIVES and let the business-man decide."

Conflicts are waged on terms that work against legal compliance. As a lawyer put it, "They [my clients] think they are the company and legal is the policeman." Lawyers are not part of the "real" company. Conflict may be reduced because it no longer centers on the manager's job definition, but conflict remains. As another lawyer said, "People are always unhappy with us. There is always a conflict between aggressive marketers and legal. You are unpopular. You are seen as a major impediment to the reason for the company existing—to sell the products." One of the givens of the lawyer's role is that he is "working to someone else's schedule, who has an inflated view of the importance of his own problem and no understanding of other issues." In

---

[371] See Kreisberg, *supra*, at 1124 n.125, and Coffee, *supra*, at 1127 n.89. (At Gulf, because of territoriality, inside counsel did nothing about overseas payments.)

[372] Cf. Bardach & Kagan, *supra*, at 99 (when the laws didn't specifically and forcefully apply, compliance experts were not able to generate compliance).

such a setting, lawyers' influence depends on their effectiveness as police-men. Lawyers always play a game of catch-up, trying to apply the brakes. They are the "brake department." As one manager said, "The corporate legal department is the department in this company responsible for catching us."

Territorial conflicts are disputes over turf. They are not conflicts over the correct decision or whether the manager properly performed his job. Relegated to a separate enclave, lawyers have little ability to get the manager to reconsider his decision. As one manager put it:

> Some lawyers can take their responsibility. They write memos saying, 'I've told you the risk and you are willing to take it.' They present it as, 'for the record, I told you this.' Others can't handle the responsibility. They are paranoid and take a zero-risk position. It is important to state the zero-risk position, but just once. I can sit here and tell you what the zero-risk position is. I don't need to go to inside counsel or worse an outside counsel and pay billions of dollars for what I know.

Legal risks are viewed as tangential and unrealistic. As another client put it: "A good lawyer says, 'I understand marketing's position, technical's position, and this is legal's point of view. This is where we draw our line.' The good lawyer knows he can't be dogmatic. The lines are not black and white. They are all wavy. In a good company, you need lots of flexibility and few hard positions taken. In Japan, going to a lawyer is a mark of failure because it means that two intelligent people have failed to reach agreement." To this manager, in a good company, territories are respected, lawyers inhabit their own province, realize they are external to the corporation's purpose, and are subservient.

Territoriality, then, often involves the ritualization of conflict. Most conflict is decided by "agreeing to disagree." The lawyer is allowed to express his position, but is denied any real chance to affect the decision. The doubting position is made explicit and distinct; the organization thereby engages in the "domestication of dissenters."[373] The lawyer's ability to influence outcomes decreases when the manager "knows where legal is coming from," but at least the attorney's conscience is "assuaged."[374]

Because lawyers only have power over their own turf, they fear client education. As a manager said, "If I know it's a gray area for him, a turf problem results." The more the client knows, or thinks he knows about the

---

[373] Thompson, "How Could Vietnam Happen? An Autopsy," Atl. Monthly 47 (1968), cited and evaluated in A. Hirschmann, Exit, Voice, and Loyalty 115-116 (1970).

[374] Hirschmann, *supra*, at 115. Of course, there is some truth to the rationalization that "if it had not been for me, an even more sinister decision would have been taken." Id at 116. But the lawyer may be overestimating his influence and cannot know whether he could have taken more meaningful measures to combat the decision.

law, the more he will argue and push. As a lawyer said, "I lose clients because they feel I'm in their area. The manager tells me what is the law. I have to respond, 'No. This is what the law says.' To which the manager responds: 'I read the law differently.'" The lawyer's turf is compromised and he has little power to retain it. As the lawyer continued: "When they think they know the law better than me, it is upsetting. But, maybe his boss really should have the right to decide who his lawyer is." Lawyers respond to this territorial incursion by trying to keep their terrain esoteric. But educating clients, in law as in other staff functions, is necessary to promote client use of expert knowledge.[375]

This doesn't deny the many instances when the lawyer's input has important consequences. Certainly when the law's sanctions are immediate and render the option inefficient, corporations tend to comply with the law. And sometimes a manager consults a lawyer because he wants to do the proper thing, but doesn't want to appear "weak." If the lawyer finds the law is on the manager's side, the manager can argue, "The lawyers won't let us do it." Other managers will approach lawyers with cynical intentions. They want the lawyer to take their side in a struggle with other managers. When manager and department boundaries become an issue, the law is often used as a scapegoat: "The lawyers say the risk is unacceptable." The consequence of this use of lawyers, however, is to reinforce territoriality. Managers come to see the law as a body of rules and lawyers as stumbling blocks: "They think legal problems are insoluble. They don't know you can bargain with legal." The law is presented in a take-it-or-leave-it form. Sometimes, the lawyer will be heard. Other times, he will be ignored, his recommendations cast as unrealistic and outside the company's real concerns.

Given territorial divisions, lawyers do have strength in limited areas of conflict. If a salesman wants to waive a warranty because a customer insists upon it, the lawyer can win: "Lawyers say 'no' a lot. THAT'S THEIR JOB. People tend to stray. They say, 'this time the light doesn't look red to me' when they get to the intersection." The lawyer's power is based on the awareness that each manager wants to better his numbers and will do things in his short-term interest that are not in the company's long-term interest. As the manager explained: "Most of the time it's the buyer wanting a price consideration and the salesman wanting the sale, so the lawyer's decision carries." A similar situation was presented in another area: "Pricing is a seat of the pants, intuitive decision. There is then a great desire to get information on customer prices and determine what the market will bear. It is natural where there is no scientific means for pricing for people to get together to skirt the law. This is an area where we need lawyers."

Lawyers have power in those areas where managers know and accept the company wants to restrict their decision-making abilities. Because lawyers address only issues delegated to their province, they do not examine other

---

[375] W. Kornhauser, Scientists in Industry: Conflict and Accommodation 192 (1962).

areas where they might be needed. In a territorial system, lawyers' ability to extend legal input is limited because they only have the authority of their position. Although these lawyers think their power derives from the possibility of legal sanction, their power actually arises vicariously from the organization. As a result, when lawyers try to extend their influence, managers consider them to be domineering.[376] This attitude reinforces turf boundaries and limits lawyers to areas, usually routine ones, where clients will accept "take-it-or-leave-it" instructions.

Corporate lawyers always work as surrogates for management. With territorial divisions, they are policemen or auditors. But they are rendered ineffective by operating from an enclave: "Lawyers can be confined if people want them to be. The lawyers were not located where the activities were taking place. Since the central management wasn't orchestrating it, you needed to get lawyers out in the field so that they could have lunch with the managers and find out what they were doing. The lawyers didn't have time to go out and look for problems. Lawyers didn't know and people didn't let them know."

In the auditing mode, both lawyers and clients exhibit defensiveness. Contacts are structured. The lawyer is passive, completing his auditing work by rote. Managers see his suggestions as sniping. Managerial hostility and noncompliance are generated. Furthermore, a division of responsibility is institutionalized so that much slips through and short-cuts and other co-optive compromises develop. Reciprocal relationships emerge; managers give lawyers the bare minimum both sides can accept so that no one will be "embarrassed." Instead of trade-offs between legal and business concerns, decisions become trade-offs between territorial boundaries so that both sides can "wink while they work."[377] The result is what Simon calls "Gresham's law of planning," where "programmed activity tends to drive out non-programmed activity."[378] The lawyer's work is rationalized and compartmentalized. He occupies a territory and is not used as a consultant. His functions are limited and to reduce conflict it is likely he will accept that limitation.[379]

Consider a company's adoption of a marketing scheme. The choice was

---

[376] Cf. Kanter & Stein, "Life in the Middle: Getting In, Getting Up, and Getting Along," in Life in Organizations: Workplaces as People Experience Them 80, 95 (R. Kanter & B. Stein eds. 1979).

[377] Cf. R. Golembiewski, Organizing Men and Power: Patterns of Behavior and Line-Staff Models 114 (1967). These accommodations reduce conflict and constitute a mutual greasing by individuals who must only perforce cooperate. Beside an accepted degree of illegality, this cooperation prevents upper-level managers from being informed of distortions in the implementation of corporate policies.

[378] H. Simon, The New Science of Management Decision, Rvsd. Ed., at 53 (1977).

[379] Lansbury, "Generalist versus Specialist in an Era of Change," 3 J. Gen. Mgmt. 55 (1976) (finding this to be a general phenomenon for staff groups).

between two approaches, one at the margins of legality and the other clearly legal. Management informs the lawyers that the marginal program has been selected and their job is to limit its potential damages. Depending on the strength of the law department, they may be able to place certain restrictions on the marginal marketing idea, such as insuring that the work on it is subject to their inspection at various points. But the lawyers will always be in a game of catch-up with managers, who seek to evade the lawyers' control. Only by admitting their limitations can lawyers push for the other program. To make such an admission, however, the lawyers must confess that they can't effectively operate from an enclave. In a corporation where lawyers were unwilling to cede their territory, the attorneys responded by developing a series of limited warranties. The adoption of the marketing scheme generated a set of programmed activities for the law department. The lawyers knew managers evaded certain of their controls and operated beyond the law in others. A mutual relationship developed where the lawyers did not press the managers and the managers accepted limited legal control. Although the chosen marketing plan may have worked well with appropriate legal guidance, in this corporation it led to numerous violations and penalties. If the corporation, chastened by this experience, could choose again, it might have recognized it was in its economic interest to change the organization of its legal services or to adopt the other marketing scheme. In the context of territorial boundaries, the chosen marketing strategy proved to be unworkable. Lawyers couldn't even perform the task of damage control.

RISK ANALYSIS: CONCLUSION

When confronted with litigation, damage control and risk analysis may be all a company needs from its lawyers. Litigation, however, is past oriented. Obtaining compliance, like developing marketing programs, negotiating deals, performing securities work and structuring mergers, looks forward not backward. It cannot be tied to existing rules or facts, but must anticipate future events. The lawyer's task is to construct workable and defendable programs.[380]

Corporations know that developing workable programs requires more than restricting managers' discretionary power by threatening sanctions. Organizations often seek to encourage workers to pursue goals in the absence of sanctions. Corporations do not rely only on surrogates who question managers' risk assessments and perform audit functions because these activities can only create adversary relationships. Then a situation develops where managers don't pass information because they see the surrogate as always ready to play-off a confidence to increase his bargaining strength at a

---

[380] On the difference between the litigation stance and a future orientation, see Swaine, "Impact of Big Business on the Profession: An Answer to Critics of the Modern Bar," 35 A.B.A.J. 89, 91 (1949).

later point.[381] Furthermore, such surrogates are weak motivators. Consequently, corporations develop cultures, policies, and imprecise goals, as well as targets to be reached.

In performing risk analysis, lawyers are ineffective surrogates for management. When lawyers are pressed about illegal activities, they often say, "What could we have done?" Normally, they claim, they lacked information. Good managers realize that you often have to convince subordinates you can help them with their job to get necessary information. When a violation occurs, lawyers should wonder why no one came to them to find out "Are we protected?" "Am I protected?" Good managers understand that to get information you sometimes need to consider the situation's politics. Good managers comprehend that management is not homogeneous and they are willing to use this fact. When a violation occurs, lawyers should wonder why someone didn't come to them and ask, "Do you know what Joe, my enemy, is doing?" Good managers discern that they must be sensitive to more than just direct orders. They must pay careful attention to the corporation's attitude about itself. They often advise subordinates about and vie with other managers for control of the corporation's culture. When a violation occurs, lawyers should wonder why they weren't asked, "Is this (and perhaps, Should this) be our corporation's way of doing things?" When lawyers merely provide risk analyses, they will not be asked any of these questions. The law is then seen as external, a stumbling block irrelevant to the emergent consensus within the corporation.

The lesson to be learned from the risk analysis approach is that the lawyer must approach managers in a constructive fashion to effectively serve the corporation. The lawyer must approach the manager from the position of helping the manager realize his objectives. If the lawyer doesn't adopt this stance, the client will not consult him and will find ways to circumvent him.

This lesson is not unfamiliar. In fact, it simply restates the traditional basis of the lawyer-client relation. Lawyers serve clients and clients use lawyers to achieve their objectives. Risk analysis sunders this relationship. In it, the goals of the lawyer differ from the goals of the managers. Managers will say the sales department's function is to be as aggressive as possible and the legal department's function is to hold them back. The failures of risk analysis reminds us that an effective lawyer helps develop his client's goals. Where there is a gap between the lawyer's and the client's goals, lawyers will not be effective. In risk analysis, the lawyer does not have the resources to develop client goals. He simply has information the client can take or leave. To be effective, as in the traditional lawyer-client relation, the lawyer's first step must be to understand what the client is doing. The lawyer must learn "why" the client wants to pursue a certain path. He cannot simply say "yes" or "no," but must be constructive, helping and guiding.

---

[381] Cf., R. Golembiewski, Organizing Men and Power: Patterns of Behavior and Line-Staff Models 21 (1967).

Yet, this lesson is somewhat surprising. One might think the lawyer-client relationship would not hold when the lawyer functions as a surrogate for management. The traditional relationship is premised on the lawyer not being an enforcement official. In risk analysis, lawyers dispense with the traditional relationship, replacing it with organizational authority. Yes, risk analysis fails for the same reasons that effective corporations rely on management tools other than pure authority. Risk analysis fails because the lawyer must secure client assistance. When the lawyer only provides risk analyses, a client won't be motivated to work with the lawyer or comply with the law. Like any other individual who supplies intelligence to an organization and then retreats into expertise, a risk analysis lawyer "remains too distant from the intelligence user, too ignorant of policy needs, and is forced to compete with other producers for the support and guidance of the user."[382]

LEGAL SERVICE AS MIXED LAW-BUSINESS ADVICE

LAWYERS AS DECISION CONSULTANTS

Inside counsel at four of the companies studied provide another model of the lawyer's task. They rejected risk-analysis as the predominant mode of legal advice. Instead, they held themselves out as consultants to their companies. They had little formal authority. Instead, they relied on knowledge of their client's business combined with their legal expertise to influence corporate action.[383]

The lawyer who has formal authority and views his task as conducting risk analyses either presents his information to the manager and engages in a power struggle, or retreats into his enclave. The lawyer often says, "We gave good advice. They made a bad business judgment." Where law and business advice are joined, the decision may be the manager's but the lawyer influences the manager's choice of risks by presenting alternatives: "Lawyers must be problem solvers. If you go to meetings and say, 'you can't do this,' you will be fired. People chew up lawyers who are just naysayers. You have to say, 'Why do you want to do this? You can't do it this way, but maybe you can do it this way.' " By becoming consultants on managerial choices, lawyers meet the challenges presented by having both little formal authority and

---

[382] H. Wilensky, Organizational Intelligence 50 (1967).

[383] This result is consistent with Donnell's that inside counsel find it difficult to separate law from business. J. Donnell, The Corporate Counsel: A Role Study 37 n.10 (1971). At two companies, legal, ethical and business advice were conjoined, a result that goes beyond Donnell's findings. Donnell found that inside counsel thought they were not wanted to advise on issues of corporate social responsibility. But, consistent with the finding of this study, Donnell also found that clients wanted advice from inside counsel on corporate social responsibility. *Id.* at 83.

considerable responsibility to serve the corporation.[384]

Although there are differences in the knowledge and experience of all lawyers, inside counsel have unique opportunities to learn the business side of certain decisions. They can assess the facts, the corporation's risk portfolio, the corporation's business style, and managers' fears. As a result, inside counsel are often asked to suggest alternatives.

Mixing legal and business advice is a way to reestablish the traditional lawyer-client relationship. The manager trusts such advice because it appears to advance his interests. It appears to be aimed at improving his performance. As a lawyer said: "The way to get clients to obey you is to learn other people's jobs. I have to know what this guy has to do in order to do his job." Like the manager, the lawyer's emphasis is on the decision not on whether the risks have been presented. As one lawyer explained his combining of legal and business advice: "If you are ignored, you will be ineffective. If you become a pain, they will leave you. You always have to be diplomatic. Ask if there is another way of doing it, rather than saying, 'No.'" From the manager's perspective, the lawyer helps the manager perform his job by presenting a choice that can mobilize corporate support. As a product developer said, "Good legal people, like good technical people, will effect a compromise situation. 'If you just re-word that in this way I can live with it from a legal point of view and marketing will say, 'that's enough.' The decision is in the range between the two." To both the manager and the lawyer, the lawyer's efforts are aimed at identifying the risks within the choice and establishing the direction of corporate efforts. The lawyer's decisions are not craft-based but mission-based. Inside counsel recalls that when they were outside lawyers they were "almost never able to give an immediate answer to any legal question." As inside counsel, they are sometimes surprised that their answers are derived from simply knowing "our system of common law." When emphasis is not on legal risk, but on the goals of decisions, inside counsel find that they are "constantly reminded of the truth in Justice Holmes' statement that: '[e]mphasis on the obvious is often more important than elucidation of the obscure.'"[385] They find their

---

[384] A different explanation can be advanced for inside counsel's involvement in business consulting. This explanation is based on inside counsel's apparently frustrated aspirations to be lawyers. They bring to their positions values and expectation engendered by their professional training and experience, only to find themselves frustrated. Instead of retreating into alienation, they "begin searching for opportunities to embellish their roles." H. Aldrich, Organizations and Environments 95 (1981). Although this explanation has an unfortunate reductive quality, inside counsel's reasons for mixing law and business are not as important as whether the combination improves the organization. Whether mixing legal and business advice is a crown for a nest of thorns, it can still be a source for constructive change.

[385] Klots, "The Need and Utilization of Retained Counsel," in Proceedings of the First Annual Inst. on Corporate Counsel 61, 63 (1959).

work contributes to corporate goal choice.[386]

In joining legal and business advice, lawyers recognize two basic facts of organizational behavior. First, managers need to choose risks. Second, in an organization, alternatives are not simply given, they must be sought and then presented.

The lawyer seeks, in mixing legal and business advice, to develop alternatives which instance and reinforce corporate commitments to law compliance. The lawyer tries to transform the law, from a check on corporate action, into a generator of solutions to corporate problems. The lawyer asks, "Why do you want to do this?" to move legal compliance from a side constraint on the manager's choice to the goal of choice. One always can anticipate resistance to side constraints and attempts to minimize their significance. When the lawyer, acting as a consultant, generates a genuine alternative, rather than simply throwing up a roadblock, the ensuing battle can be waged over the action's goals not the lawyer's power.[387] As a lawyer explained, noting the limitations of the risk analysis approach:

> When managers ask, 'Can we do something?' that gets us into grey areas. Management is bottom line oriented. For example, if a manager wants to terminate a distributer, he will come to us not wanting to know all the legal ramifications of termination, but: Can we do it? Are we likely to be sued? What would that cost us? And, does the corporate legal department think it is worth it? If this went to an outside counsel, the manager would get a big memo, in which, by the time you get to the recommendation, you can't tell whether they agree with it or are just hedging their bets. Here, we begin with there being conflicting opinions of law and give an opinion based on what we would feel comfortable with. When they come to us asking what are the requirements of a regulation, we try to use a broader perspective. We view the corporation as a whole, instead of as rival profit centers. This gives us a broader perspective which we use whenever people come to us for interpretation of the law. This way, when people come to us asking whether they can do something, we can turn it into a

---

[386] The move to a mission-based decision framework can be explained by the highly variable subject matter of mixed law-business advice and by the fact that techniques for manipulating such subject matter are less certain than are legal techniques. Cf. Perrow, "A Framework for the Comparative Analysis of Organizations," 32 Am. Soc. Rev. 194 (1967). An emphasis on affecting corporate goal emergence has been found with other staffs, see, e.g., Goldner & Ritti, "Professionalization as Career Immobility," 72 Am. J. Soc. 489 (1967) (discussing engineers). This result also helps explain why, in a study of top management of 300 companies, 16.4% were found to have moved into management from the practice of law. Lynch, "The Growth of In-House Counsel," 65 A.B.A.J. 1403 (1979).

[387] For the distinction between constraints as checks and as solution-generators, see H. Simon, Administrative Behavior, 1st Ed., at 258-62 (1947).

question of what they should do.

Serving as a consulting group can be a high-risk method for insuring compliance to the law. What the manager perceives as a compromise, the lawyer may consider a sellout. The manager may find no alternative, which bears fidelity to the law acceptable. In such a case, the lawyer, who lacks formal authority fears he will be pushed around by management. As a consultant, the lawyer can't "pull rank." He can't use the law "as a club to get the decision the lawyer wants." But it also isn't the case that management alone decides, after the lawyer has assessed and communicated the legal risks, how far to push its chances within a permissible zone. The lawyer is part of the team. When the lawyer succeeds in establishing himself as part of the business decision process, he can influence the choice. As one lawyer advised: "[Instead of holding yourself out as] the only witch doctor who can interpret the results, be empathetic, sympathetic and identify with the success of the enterprise. Give your client support and confidence and you will get the results *you* want." An atmosphere of "cooperative problem solving"[388] allows the lawyer to be part of the risk choosing process, gives him some responsibility for the decision, and makes it more likely that legal risks will be salient:

> My clients want to hear my recommendations. They want to know how they can reach their objectives. When I was an outside counsel, I would say, '60% chance this way, 10% that way, you decide.' As an inside counsel, my clients want me to answer the question, 'If you were in my shoes what would you do?' Many outside counsel wouldn't go that extra step. They would say it was a business decision.[389]

When companies use lawyers as consultants it is an implicit recognition of the fact that lawyers who act as legal auditors do not produce legal compliance. Because the lawyer can't be everywhere, because much of legal compliance depends on good-faith action by managers, and because when the law is perceived as external to the company's basic function it tends to

---

[388] Bardach and Kagan, *supra*, at 146.

[389] As one inside counsel described this experience: "[I]nside counsel is part of the decision making process...whether he likes it or not. Often he is forced to make recommendations that outside counsel has the luxury of walking away from and he is put to the test more often on more close questions than outside counsel ever gets involved in." Forrow, Discussion, 33 Bus. Lawyer 1473 (1978). In one corporation studied, the lawyers had so successfully become part of the management team that they were used as "super-staff." They were used to review internal debates of little legal significance because they were thought to know how the company worked, to understand what options were realistic and to have no stake in the outcome.

"oil the fire" of noncompliance,[390] the lawyer must try to secure managerial support for legal compliance. The lawyer must be a salesman, who is at his best, not when painting the sky dark, but when suggesting alternatives. He can show managers that legal compliance works and teach them that legal compliance is not only a legal concern but also good business practice.

Certainly, in some areas such as benefits, compliance does mean drawing up the right documents. In those situations, giving lawyers formal authority can insure compliance. "But lawyers are not going to shore up leaking tanks or put up place cards." Then, the lawyer must develop cooperative relationships. At four of the companies studied, the lawyer reaches this result by being "a participant in the compliance process. His task is not determined by a written charter and does not begin at a particular point. He is part of the whole process. There is no mandate that an attorney be involved." Instead of possessing a mandate, the legal department is organized to facilitate consultation. Its task is to get there before a problem develops. Its mission is to educate managers to follow "the company's express and implied philosophy on citizenship." Its task is to help organize work and reporting systems so managers are not inclined to "shove the problems on someone else." The lawyer is of counsel. Even though "a lawyer doesn't have to sign off on anything at this company," he has influence. There is little territoriality. The law is not a separate area needing a policeman. It is part of the process of developing and choosing among alternatives.[391]

---

[390] See discussion of risk analysis, *supra*. See also Marx, "Ironies of Social Control: Authorities as Contributors to Deviance through Escalation, Non-enforcement and Covert Facilitation," 28 Soc. Problems 221, 223-26 (1981); Bardach & Kagan, *supra*, at 106 (cognitive dissonance creates a vicious circle where managers denigrate the law and retaliate with noncompliance).

[391] In the companies Donnell studied, he found similar movement away from the auditing to the counseling mode. Donnell, *supra*, at 108. Those who have examined the internal audit function also witnessed a similar development. Modern internal auditors, we are told, must achieve a relationship "no different from that which exists between a lawyer and his client.... The modern internal auditor...must carry out his responsibilities so that the manager will look upon him as a counselor, a problem-solving partner, not as an adversary or an object of fear and distrust. And he must maintain that relationship despite the fact that, as an internal auditor, he may ultimately report what he finds to levels above the manager. The lawyer who is not thoroughly acquainted with his client's business and its goals, functions and operations cannot provide an able, professional service. And modern internal auditors who do not understand the functions, responsibilities, theories, and practices of management cannot ably assist and counsel managers." L. Sawyer, The Manager and the Modern Internal Auditor: A Problem-Solving Partnership vii (1979). "The time has come for the internal auditor to equip himself to be more than an after-the-fact critic and to become at last a counselor and adviser to the tread milling problem-beset manager." *Id.* at 4. See also G. McAleer & G. Jager, Salaries and Attitudes: A Profile of the Internal Auditing Profession 37, 43 (1979). For a study claiming that accountants misserve their companies and the public by retreating into technique, see Montagna, "The Public Accounting Profession: Organization, Ideology and Social Power," 14 Am. Behav. Sci. 475 (1971). Acting as consultants may be the most effective technique for all staff functions to secure managerial compliance. Consider, a lawyer's comments about the payroll staff: "I

To see how this works in practice, consider a lawyer faced with one of any lawyer's hardest problems—knowledge of continuing illegal activities:

> My clients had commercial practices which amounted to price-fixing. I had to convince them that it was in their best interests to change their commercial practices. I knew change took a period of time. My job was to get them to change. The general counsel's attitude was that the corporate legal department had to be policemen. He had every manager sign off that, they didn't violate the [Sherman] act. It blew up on them because no one was going to confess they were acting unethically. When the corporate legal department is the policeman, the higher ups may or may not be protected by representations that the operators are complying. But, compliance won't result from these representations. What you get is an adversarial relation. I realized that you couldn't change business practices overnight. The company called in big law firms who set out rules. This shut off conversation. I took the approach that the point was to reduce violations gradually. I had to learn as much as possible about their work and get them to change. Such a change does not yield a paper program which is violated as soon as pressures rise. There are always incredible pressures and rewards to make the bottom line. You have got to change their notion of business professionalism. You have got to get them to develop a sense of pride in doing it lawfully. I've been here three years and I now have certain managers and writers who will come to me beforehand and ask me to help them write it. We have been able to convince them that the system works.

By being a team-member and suggesting alternatives, the lawyer is able to secure managerial cooperation for legal compliance. Managers come to view lawyers as necessary to their decision and planning processes. When inside counsel were able to become trusted consultants, it was not uncommon for managers to say: "The lawyer increases the efficiency of our department." Managers perceived increased efficiency for several reasons. When lawyers are involved in the planning process they can suggest better methods and defeat organizational pathologies. They also are able to reduce managerial resistance to lawyer suggestions, which hardens after the manager has chosen a pet project. They also are able to minimize conflicts and reduce the amount of work that must be redone.

Securing managerial cooperation and developing organizational alter-

---

used to get pissed off at payroll. It seemed like they had a million rules and they were just a stumbling block bureaucracy. I wasn't trying to see their problems. They started a payroll department bulletin and I now see they have problems too and weren't just trying to be arbitrary." This lawyer prevents payroll from doing its job. He understands, as manager's come to understand with respect to legal compliance, that it is not unduly burdensome.

natives also prompts lawyers to seek the creative interplay of law and business that characterizes the best legal advice. In the risk analysis mode, settlement decisions are made by finding a price; in the mixed law-business mode, lawyers also pay attention to the settlement's effect on corporate morale and development and on the company's continuing relations. Because lawyers and managers are not isolated in exclusive enclaves, creative collaboration becomes possible. For example:

> We were sued by someone we had previous dealings with. We owed them $100K. I decided to hold onto that money in order to be able to send it out of synchrony to the President of the suing company. Out of synchrony insured that it would be noticed and, anyway, the head of a major company doesn't know what to do when he gets a big check on his desk. Their President called up our President. Our President, briefed by us, acted like a statesman and got a statesmanlike response. They settled the thing themselves. Two great geniuses of American business couldn't allow themselves to mess up the deal.

Not only was a favorable settlement reached, but it paved the way for future good relationships between the companies.

In offering mixed law-business advice, lawyers not only gain knowledge of the business but clients gain knowledge of the law. The lawyer must demystify the law so lawyers and managers can be involved in joint decision-making. As a client said: "It's easy to understand the federal regulations. They aren't complicated. What is difficult is applying them." As a lawyer said, "Law is a combination of common sense, contracts and reading the fine print. It is not an objective profession. Unlike accountants, we are interpreters."[392]

Cooperative relationships, of course, are difficult to maintain. In the risk analysis mode, educating clients in the law diminishes the lawyer's power. Turf battles frequently result. In risk analysis, bureaucratic rules are an alternative to education. When lawyers are part of the management team, a client's limited legal education often results in conflicts over the law's application to particular cases: "Because the salesman wants to make the deal, he has a vested emotional stake in having his interpretation of the UCC be right. This allows him to conflict with the lawyer on the basis of his self-education in the UCC, over the lawyer's expertise." Because of the importance of a cooperative relation, the lawyer cannot simply shut off the manager's attempts to read the law. The lawyer must find a way to establish the need for interdependence in this continuing relation. As one put it, "Consider the Foreign Corrupt Practices Act. It is four pages. If a business-

---

[392] Unlike accountants, or attorneys using risk analysis, lawyers in mixed law-business situations can retain client trust by sharing the manager's task. This respondent continued: "Accountants are viewed as putting the bad news together and therefore the accountant-business relation is not friendly."

man were to read it, he would find a way to get around it. He would read the fine print and if he didn't see anything negative, he wouldn't pay attention to the act. If the lawyer reads it, he knows it is to be interpreted broadly."

Put another way, when lawyers become consultants, they risk deprofessionalization. Their monopoly on legal expertise is threatened. Managers may decide to make legal decision on their own. When lawyers claim to be able to analyze business problems, managers will not be amenable to claims they can't analyze legal problems. When lawyers retreat into an excessive emphasis on technique, such as only performing risk analyses, managers don't consider their advice legitimate and often don't respond to it. When lawyers educate their clients, however clients may improperly use their limited legal knowledge.[393]

Lawyers can respond to the threat of deprofessionalization in two ways. First, they can follow through on client education. When lawyers are effective consultants, consulted before decisions are made, they need not be afraid of client education. A little bit of knowledge, of course, can be dangerous. But, if lawyers are effective consultants, they can generate continuing educational processes:

> Making managers know as much about the law as I did made them able to argue. I like that. When marketers don't know the law, they don't accept my decisions either. The more educated the client is, the more I trust him. The more they know about the law, the more they will keep me sharp and the more attention they will pay to it in their everyday existence. I give my clients the old reg's. When they call me up, we go through it. We look at what the preamble says and then the reg's. If they get bored, I back up a little. It is a way of getting them excited and getting them to know what I am looking for. I try to get them to look at it from the regulator's point of view; what 'fairness' means to the regulators and why.

Lawyers' second response to client education is to structure the range of client discretion. In mixed law-business advice, lawyers use the organization to limit the problems of mis-education. They create situations in which all the alternatives available to manager are legally acceptable.

Take Educator, a corporation, like Drafter, where sales contracts are the business' bread and butter. Unlike Drafter, at Educator lawyers function as consultants and are not subservient to client demands. At both companies,

---

[393] This problem parallels a major problem in democracies. Professional expertise threatens to create a technocracy, not responsive to democratic concerns and unlegitimated by democratic values. The rule of the demos, however, is neither efficient nor trustworthy. This tension is resolved in democratic thought by universal education and by creating separate spheres for technical and for democratic choice. Much of administrative law concerns the instability of these resolutions.

corporate commitments to maintaining "friendly" relations with customers, regardless of contractual rights, threatened the legal function. At Educator, the lawyers sought to educate managers about the potential problems. The lawyers emphasized teaching managers the trade-offs between the law and the business. Their approach was to have the client attempt to draft the sales contract by himself. The client then had a stake in the contract language and the lawyer could discuss that language with him more easily. Clients came to appreciate the way various terms were used and to understand better the conflicts between them and their lawyers. Clients also perceived that contracts had uses other than support in litigation. Contracts were important both for planning individual transactions and for developing overall corporate strategies.

By taking a role in corporate planning, the Educator lawyers were able to make the law generate alternatives. They could organize the ways clients sought alternatives. Instead of fighting power battles over particular decisions, lawyers helped develop corporate choices. At Educator, "once every six months, we sit down and talk about their problems, what they are doing and plan to do. We negotiate among ourselves. Once *we* understand what we are trying to do, the business really gets going. The managers know what the trade-offs are, what to offer the other side if they object, what their series of fallbacks are, and so on. After these meetings, I write a memo discussing the markets and what to do in various situations."

A situation diametrically opposed to the one at Drafter resulted. While Drafter managers stressed that lawyers were external to the corporation's real needs and were ignorant of commercial realities, Educator managers stressed that "our attorneys know the industry. I respect their advice on what will fly in the marketplace." Instead of evading lawyers' advice, as was the situation at Drafter, managers called on lawyers for assistance. As a result, Educator was able to minimize antitrust problems and "giveaways."[394]

By holding planning meetings, inside counsel can avoid dissipating power struggles, where they often bow to immediate managerial need. At another company, the law department arranged for a meeting with the corporate governing board to strengthen its role in managerial planning:

> We put together a program for the executive committee to ask them where on the liberal to conservative spectrum they wanted us to give antitrust advice. We wanted to hear from the governing board of the company where they wanted our advice to be, as opposed to being pulled by our noses by the clients. Clients want to know if their position can be defended. They don't want to hear the

---

[394] This is preventive law. At Drafter, established policies require lawyer to approve certain choices. As described above, these policies are paper programs, bowing to managerial perceptions of economic necessity. Educating clients combined with continuing consultation and planning allowed preventive law to flourish at Educator.

conservative position. They are being pressured into a more aggressive position and we have to advise consistently. Otherwise, no one will come to us. We went to the governing board and told them that they had to make the decision.

The legal department presented various options to the board, and then assessed both the possibility of securing managerial compliance to each option and each option's effect on corporate development. The board chose the option preferred by the legal department. The department now feels it can give responsible advice that the company follows. Unlike lawyers who only perform risk-analysis, these lawyers do not function merely on a case-by-case, item-by-item basis. They function at the corporate planning process level, giving them power even in the face of recalcitrant clients. As a manager who did not use lawyers as consultants said: "To set the legal department up to second guess all decisions or to be a conscience means that you need a new President. Legal here often second guesses. But they shouldn't play that role forcefully. The lawyer should tell the personnel manager that in his opinion these things are required. The Personnel manager should institute them and a year later both should sit down and see how things are working out." This manager admits that lawyers can plan organizational changes, even if individual decisions remain within the manager's prerogative. The lawyer tries to limit the manager's discretion by reducing, through planning, the number of available alternatives and by showing the manager he can be a helpful consultant on individual decisions.

As the lawyer suggests alternatives, becomes part of the team, and helps to make business decisions, managers both allow them more power and develop a greater respect for the law. They learn to play less games with the law. Inside counsel at these companies repeatedly said, "You have to be helpful." By being helpful, the lawyer earns the client's trust, changes the legal department's relationship to the company, and develops the basis for corporate commitment to legal compliance. Mixing legal and business advice also minimizes power struggles between lawyer and client in three ways. First, the lawyer can suggest a business alternative that wins managerial support. Second, the lawyer can help plan business activities so managers seek options consistent with the law. And third, through experience and education, the lawyer can train managers to make legal compliance a goal of their decisions. In short, knowledge is both a component and the honorific of gaining power. When lawyers have amassed power, their clients will say about them, "They know how our company works." Then, clients will say, "What would you do if you were me?"

When the lawyer becomes a trusted consultant offering business advice, he can present the law independent of its sanctions, even becoming involved in issues of corporate social responsibility:

> If the lawyer is accepted in all other areas, then his decisions in social responsibility are also accepted. He is really part of the

management team. I get involved in decisions about what the contract is, how we should do it and whether we should do it. I don't get involved in whether we should give money to the symphony. But, I do get involved on corporate morality. If my outside counsel says that a question is close to the line but we can get away with it, I tell management what he said and then I tell them, 'I can't play it so close to the line.' I make them recognize the possibility of bad publicity. I explain the ethos of the law as well as the details of the law.... It surprises me how much I talk equity. I ask management three questions: (1) What do you want to happen? (2) What do you think is fair? and (3) What do you want to see on the front page of the newspaper? When the managers ask me, "Suppose we get sued, what will happen?," my answer is based on notions of equity.

A rather intense conflict at another company highlights the ability of lawyers who are part of the decision making team to raise issues of fairness:

It was not a violation of policy but I thought we oughtn't to be doing business in that way. The other side was a foreign party with little knowledge and without a lawyer. I felt we were not in good faith representing our position to the other side. The client wanted to shave the language on the deal to keep it ambiguous. I felt it wasn't appropriate for us. A kind of trickery was being attempted for short-run opportunity. The same thing has been tried to be played on us and I felt it was wrong for us to do it. I wouldn't bend to the client's wishes. I took the issue above the client. I took it up not as a legal issue but as an issue of business ethics: How ought we to do business? The client felt I was out of line and was unhappy about it. I was sustained in the courts above. The clients are the final decision makers and I am not free to make such decisions. But, I am free to have my day in court and raise the issue. The relationship with the client was strained for a while but it blew over.

I did this because I am an employee. It is a subtle issue of business ethics. Outside counsel wouldn't have felt it or gotten involved with it. But, for me, it is a question of what is my corporation going to be like. Part of being inside is that you feel part of a community. The object is to do well and do it correctly. The focus is different from that of outside counsel. An outside counsel wants to give good quality service and to cultivate return business. An inside counsel is interested in the quality of his work not for its quality but to help the company accomplish what it wants and to accomplish it in a way he feels good about.

An outside counsel gave this example of inside counsel's ability, based on his involvement in the corporation's business, to inject notions of fairness:

> The client wanted to know if he had to pay the debt. I found that the statute of limitations had run and that there was no legal requirement. I had known the client for a while and we talked about what was fair. He left wondering whether it was a waste of corporate resources to pay. The inside counsel then talked to him about just what the debtee had done for the company. He was needed to convince the client that in light of all the circumstances, it was proper to pay. I just couldn't do that.

Notions of fairness, however, are often very vague and lack content. Even when lawyers raise the issue of fairness, it is quite possible that managers and corporations will decide to act immorally or to take a self-interested view of the demands. Furthermore, by being involved in the process, by suggesting alternatives, lawyers may adopt the perspective of those they are advising. Acting as a consultant is a high-risk option not only because the lawyer can only pull rank occasionally, but also because he may become a captive of the client's self-interested viewpoint. As a manager expressed it:

> There is a great difference between a professional sitting around an office and a member of the management team. The inside counsel want the trapping of management. They want the offices, cars, and so on. But, in their own minds, they want to be lawyers. Others in the company assume that if you want the trappings, you must become part of the team. Law school training and private practice hasn't taught the lawyers how to become proactive and make qualitative judgments. All technical people like to avoid qualitative judgments. But, if they want to be managers, they have to learn to be pragmatic and to make balances and have a decent perspective about things as well as a legal perspective. We want to look at inside counsel as managers with a technical training. Their technical training happens to be legal as opposed to engineering, or what have you.

"Pragmatic" and "decent" are the client's code words for captured. When lawyers suggest alternatives, there is an ever-present possibility that they will adopt the corporate perspective as their own. There is a great difference between an engineer saying, "You can't do this because of what I know about engineering, but I will find a way to get around it," and a lawyer saying, "You can't do this because of what I know about the law, but I will find you a way to get around the law."

In situations where lawyers use risk analysis, they win conflicts by gaining the power to control the manager's job. In mixed law-business situations, lawyers win conflicts by gaining the authority to speak as a corporate actor. To do that, they must not represent simply the external law; they must represent the corporation. If they aren't able to do this, conflicts can regress to power struggles, which is a particularly dangerous possibility because lawyers-as-consultants can suggest alternatives that frustrate the law. To prevent this regression, the lawyer must be able to draw on corporate resources. To prevent being captured by these resources, the lawyer must be able to challenge them.

Unlike lawyers who provide only risk analyses, lawyers who mix legal and business advice recognize that they have responsibility for the corporate decision. Unlike the lawyers quoted above who assume this responsibility requires them to raise issues of fairness, however, some lawyers limit their responsibility to advancing the corporation's economic interests. As one explained: "Those who live by the sword, die by the sword. If you stick your nose into business, you can't keep on playing the role of impartial umpire and if your grand plan collapses, you should be held liable."[395] In these instances, the lawyer is simply another manager. Moving beyond risk analysis provides lawyers with opportunities to acquire resources to buttress their position in conflicts. To improve corporate legal compliance, however, these opportunities need to be crystallized. The next sections discuss methods for crystallizing these opportunities.

The move to mixing legal and business advice is a recognition that cost-benefit analyses are not amoral. They are always made against a background of moral valuation, which decides what counts as costs and benefits. Although the cost-benefit method assumes decisions are made simply on the basis of a neutral uncovery of facts, it also presumes that all agree to the background valuations.[396] In moving away from risk analysis, the lawyer makes the background salient and controversial. By broadening the range of possible alternatives, the complexity of the background and the relevance of the actors' moral beliefs in drawing on it are revealed.[397] Acting as a consultant and insisting that managers choose risks reveals that decisions depend on values and aren't reached through amassing amoral arithmetic computations. As a result, the corporation's and the manager's conceptions of their character become relevant. It then becomes possible for the lawyer to make salient the long-term benefits of legal compliance: "[D]ecision-making in the light of long-run benefits presumes a concept of the institution. The enterprise as a going concern, as a relational entity, becomes the focus of

---

[395] Another lawyer at the same company put it this way: "If you are at a management meeting which is going for red widgets and you want blue, and you say, 'Red is not a hot idea because I hear the regulators are about to come down on red widgets and the market is in blue anyway' and the blue market falls out, you have to share responsibility for that."

[396] This analysis is based on A. MacIntyre, "Utilitarianism and Cost/Benefit Analysis: An Essay on the Relevance of Moral Philosophy to Bureaucratic Theory," in Ethical Theory and Business 266 (T. Beauchamp & N. Bowie eds. 1979).

[397] The introduction of some new products demonstrates the importance of actors' values. For example, safer automobiles and quality paperbacks were introduced in the absence of consumer demand because managers valued them. *Id.* at 271.

policy and strategy."[398] In risk analysis, the lawyer can't make long-run concerns salient because the decision doesn't focus on the organization's sense of identity. When the lawyer mixes legal and business advice, he can redirect the focus toward that identity.

CULTURE

Corporations develop norms and routines to motivate workers and guide the exercise of discretionary judgments. "As one sales manager put it, 'Only lazy sales managers rely on commissions to get their salesmen to sell.' "[399] Norms and routines that create a corporation's culture may further legal compliance. Corporations may develop a normative framework in which managers take "professional pride" in complying with the law: "[W]hen top managers emphasize professional pride and the distinction between clean and dirty profits, the commitment to achieve profits through legal means is clearly driven down the line."[400] In organizations that inculcate the idea that "if we're not smart enough to make reasonable profits without resorting to any form of price fixing, we'll simply get out of the business," individual managers believe, "I'd rather quit than stoop to getting my results that way."[401] On the other hand, a corporate culture may further illegalities, by informing managers that policies may be evaded as long as the manager doesn't get caught.

For norms to be effective, they must be tied to specific routines.[402] The corporation's array of procedures makes corporate cultures complex ones. Procedures both question existing norms and generate new norms. Consequently, corporate norms and policies may be undermined. Furthermore, managers' values are not solely determined by the organization for which they work. As members of society, managers bring to the corporation their values as well as the values of the professional groups to which they belong.[403] As a result, even in a single corporate division, the normative worlds of managers are heterogeneous. Since each normative world is complex, with norms capable of being crystallized at various levels of generality, even in corporations with "strong" cultures, managers have great leeway. Each manager interprets the culture. Unless norms are tied to

---

[398] P. Selznick, Law, Society, and Industrial Justice 47 (1969) (emphasis omitted).

[399] Sonnefeld & Lawrence, "Why Do Companies Succumb to Price Fixing?," 56 Harv. Bus. Rev. 145, 153 (1978).

[400] *Id.* at 156.

[401] *Ibid.*

[402] E.g., norms against antitrust violations are supported by evaluating salesmen in terms of volume of sales, rather than price or profitability. *Ibid.*

[403] Current writing on corporate culture seems to assume that one must be at IBM to be inspired by Tom Watson. Folk heroes are part of culture and need not be ritualized at individual companies.

organizational procedures, corporations will find that their norms will be only loosely followed.

Lawyers also experience the flexibility of corporate culture. At the corporation studied with the most pronounced culture, "every inside counsel becomes their own lawyer in deciding whether or not to report in grey areas. When we get differences of opinions between lawyers, we get forum shopping. Managers go for the best answer."

Nonetheless, lawyers can use corporate culture. In conflicts with managers, a lawyer can argue that his alternative may not be superior in terms of immediate economic benefit, but is superior in the corporate culture. As one put it: "I challenge their plans from a corporate perspective. I know a lot more of the corporation than those who work for one division. I am using my broader knowledge of the corporate culture to be a highly trained rabbi to tell these guys, 'you are not through rabbinical school yet, you better rethink whether this is kosher.' This challenging is fine. It is not really conflict." It is not really conflict because the lawyer's and client's respective powers are not drawn into the battle. The lawyer acts as a consultant, telling clients: "I am testing the decision to see if it fits in the culture."

Lawyers often are experts on the corporate culture because they deal with many aspects of the corporation and with managers at all levels. The corporate legal department's turnover rate is much lower than other departments. As a result, inside counsel may know the risk levels acceptable to the corporation better than many managers. Because corporate law departments possess much of the documentation of corporate actions, inside counsel often are used as corporate historians. Especially in a divisionalized company, expertise in corporate culture allows for influence.

The chief weakness of drawing on culture in conflicts is that it is not always determinative. Cultures are not univocal. Generally, we believe both "look before you leap" and "he who hesitates is lost." And individuals have considerable leeway in applying cultural norms. As one senior manager put it: "Individuals must be consistent with the corporate philosophy, but they must also diverge. This is the only way to have movement and change and avoid mediocre, average decisions." In any corporation, there are corporate cultures that can be played off against one another.[404]

Furthermore, cultures can induce noncompliance. Noncompliance happens not only in deviant cultures, it also occurs because 'normal' business behavior often supports extension of accustomed actions beyond the legal

---

[404] The organization's structure, to some extent, determines how the conflict between cultures is played out. It gives voice to this or that faction on this or that point. Thus, for this reason too, lawyers must address and, if necessary, seek to change corporate organization.

pale.[405] Lawyers acknowledge that cultures can capture, even when they claim to have evaded it: "It is inevitable, working for a company that you become part of the culture of the company. But that doesn't mean you forget justice. I am definitely more closely tied to the company than is an outside counsel. But, we get sweaty palms. Being a patsy is not the way to win respect." Or, as another said: "My company is very conservative and that makes it easier than working for a company that seeks to go into the grey areas. One reason I came to this company was its strong standing and good sense of business ethics."

In issues involving corporate responsibility where judgments are not determined by the logic of efficiency, the corporation's assessment of itself is particularly important. Without this assessment, opportunism will decide. One lawyer, at a company where the predominant mode of legal service was risk analysis, explained the impact of not being able to draw on corporate culture: "I get it all the time that the competitors are doing this or that. I tell them that I don't work for our competitors. I work here. We are very visible to the regulators. We get a lot of publicity for what we do. There is a price to pay for being one of the largest in our field. You [the manager] have to pay it now. We shouldn't do it, even if our competitors do it." But, as the lawyer said, "this hardly ever wins." His attempt to refer to the particular needs of his company is taken as "just my opinion." Although the company has had regulatory troubles, the marketplace's lowest common denominator still determines corporate choices. The lawyer concluded that if the company's lawyers are "going to restrain their clients," the development of institutional support for a particular corporate identity is what they are "trying to do and have to do."

The lawyers must learn to manipulate cultures.[406] They must use their knowledge of the culture to engage in conflict. When managers claim that they alone must choose risks or that the lawyer is encroaching on their

---

[405] Thus, the electrical industry antitrust violations of the 1960's have been explained as "apparently sensible extensions of accustomed patterns of behavior." Lekachman, "Businessmen and their Rivals," 34 Annals of Am. Acad. of Pol. Soc. Sci. 110 (1962). Furthermore, general business ethics may not deter violations in foreign markets. In a Conference Board survey of executives, 48% responded that corporations can use the "commercial modes and moral standards" of the countries in which they do business. Coffee, "Beyond the Shut-Eyed Sentry: Toward a Theoretical View of Corporate Misconduct and the Effective Legal Response," 63 Va. L. Rev. 1099, 1126 n.86 (1977). Overseas payments were considered a standard business practice.

[406] This knowledge won't be obtained from the current sociologically thin work on corporate cultures, which attempts to make the corporation into a summer camp where peer group approval and besting one's rivals is all important. For all the talk about making the corporation into a religion, see, e.g., T. Deal & A. Kennedy, Corporate Cultures: The Rites and Rituals of Corporate Life 194-95 (1982) (advising corporations to model themselves on the Roman Catholic Church), current analysis speaks more of color wars than of low or high masses. (Compare Deal and Kennedy's descriptions with the summer camp described in H. Wouk, The City Boy (1952).)

territory, the lawyer must be able to respond, as one did in a conflict situation, "Yes, but our company doesn't want to be in a situation which is technically legally right, but doesn't seem right."

At one company, the lawyers in conflict situations drew on the corporate culture in the form of Smith, the oldest member of the legal department. Managers trusted Smith to sense the decisions the corporation wanted. As a manager said: "Smith has been here so long that he has a valuable perspective. He thinks so National that it is difficult to object. There were a number of times he proposed things I wasn't completely on board with. Eventually, I discovered Smith was thinking National. He was responding appropriately within our company's processes." At another company, Jones played the role of articulator of corporate culture. In addition to his experience, Jones' strong personal relation with the Board of Directors made him trusted. As a client put it, "Jones' advantage is that not only does he have tremendous knowledge about our company but he is so heavily relied on by the Board and top management that he can create policy."

Lawyers can draw on the corporate culture. When the corporation has various cultures, some cutting against the lawyers' views, they can be trusted articulators of the dominant culture or be individuals known as able to create corporate norms. Smith and Jones serve these functions. They represent, however, individual solutions. When lawyers crystallize culture into policies and organizational structures, they need not rely so heavily on influential individuals. Lawyers also can forge coalitions to support their positions. Drawing on influential individuals or coalitions, however, threatens to turn the conflict into the power struggles more commonly found in the risk analysis mode. In drawing on these resources, the lawyer must make clear that he is not usurping the manager's role, but testing it against the corporate culture.

In conflict situations, the test of corporate culture can engender what March and Simon call, "politics." They distinguish "bargaining" from "politics" as solutions to intra-organizational conflict.[407] In "bargaining," it is assumed by the various coalitions that differing goals are irreconcilable. In bargaining, for example, when a party invokes norms of fairness, he does not refer to a general corporate goal. Rather, his claim is considered part of a struggle to determine who has the power to make the decision. In "politics," the assumption is that the corporation's goals are complex. When parties engage in politics, they test individual actions by the complex and often opaque goals of the corporation. In conflict situations, lawyers must draw on corporate culture so managers will "acknowledge" the lawyer's goals are part of general corporate goals. When lawyers engage in politics, the law is not external and lawyers are not isolated to their own territory. Conflict "legitimizes [the] heterogeneity of [corporate] goals" and allows lawyers to

---

[407] J. March & H. Simon, Organizations 131 (1959).

have influence.[408] The extent of their influence, however, depends on their ability to acquire the power to shape the corporate culture. At one company, the Chief Executive Officer was not receptive to legal positions and lawyers could not win conflicts by drawing on corporate culture. Nonetheless, the lawyers at this company understood their task: "The General Counsel is trying to figure out a way to convert the CEO to our perspective" and individual lawyers are "trying to teach managers that their goals are legal's."

POLICIES

In delivering mixed law-business advice, the lawyer's knowledge of the business is partially knowledge of corporate policies. Lawyers who act as consultants on the application of corporate policies can help frustrate a manager's evasion of corporate controls, a problem that occurred frequently at the risk analysis companies.

At all the companies studied, the General Counsel was a member of the corporation's policy-setting committee,[409] and therefore the lawyers could claim knowledge of corporate policies. At the risk analysis companies, however, turf battles undermined corporate policies. Managers saw legally relevant corporate policies as the lawyers' business. When lawyers became consultants, however, the company addresses corporate policy issues to managers and lawyers help interpret and apply those policies. At two of the companies, this procedure was formally sanctioned; the companies issued policies through the corporate legal department. Senior management, as well as middle-level management, used lawyers as experts on corporate policy. They asked lawyers how the policies were determined, what they meant and how they could be changed, in the same way they asked marketing about customer recruitment and demand.

When corporate policies are addressed to managers, the policies define managerial tasks and indicate corporate commitments. They are investments in particular behaviors. Lawyers, then, benefit when corporate cultures are crystallized into formal policies addressed to managers. First, compliance with the law is valued in managerial decisions. Second, the managerial task is enlarged to include legal compliance. Third, compliance with corporate

---

[408] *Ibid.* As was stated above: "If the accepted in all other areas, then his decisions in social responsibility are also accepted." Such a lawyer can invoke norms of fairness and reference corporate goals.

[409] AT&T's General Counsel has described his role in such a committee as one of giving "advice on general business matters whether they have legal implications or not." That he was a lawyer and had commitments to "standards that transcend the requirements of his particular employment" was valued. de Butts, "The Client's View of the Lawyer's Proper Role," Bus. Lawyer 1175, 1180 (1978). Today, most companies have codes of conduct. White & Montgomery, "Corporate Codes of Conduct," 23 Cal. Mgmt. Rev. 81 (1980) (survey of 611 companies finding that 77% had codes of conduct and that 97% of those with over $4,000 million in sales had codes).

policies can be a factor in evaluating the manager.[410] Fourth, in the face of conflict, lawyers' attempts to influence the decision by clarifying the policies' application are supported.[411] These benefits, however, depend on whether the corporation can control the enlargement of the managerial task. Will managers have the ability and resources to balance the corporate policies with their desires to improve their individual department's numbers? Will managers be able to evade the corporate edicts?

Policies, which all too often in corporate life are vague, can frequently be undermined. Managers can interpret policies in light of their own interests. Policies are often fragmentary. Like laws, they tend to be literally interpreted, discouraging the consideration of conditions not explicitly included within them. As a result, creating policies often "commits the organization to the familiar syndrome of resisting change and responding to mandated performance with minimal compliance."[412] This problem is exacerbated when policies are promulgated by top management. Collins and Ganotis found that low and middle level managers' feelings that social responsibility policies were set on high and did not take into account their knowledge undermined their desires to act responsibly.[413] In such situations, lawyers must be able to invoke the corporate culture. The culture can check distortions of vague and fragmented policies. Drawing culture and policy into decisions also can make those policies more open to managerial inputs.

If managers can't use them, policies will be ineffective. Operations can both create and undermine formal policies. As has been pointed out, the managerial task involves a complicated set of trade-offs: "Yes, we have a policy against pollution, but we also have a policy to utilize this plant. Furthermore, we are planning future modifications which will solve the problem and these plans will be deterred if we now put controls into this plant." Policies will be paper-thin unless they can be invoked and negotiated when they are applied. Consequently, corporations must use lawyers not only to promulgate policies but also to consult on them. To promote responsible action, it is necessary to develop cooperative relations with low and middle-level managers.

Not only may policies be evaded, but they also may facilitate rather than inhibit corporate noncompliance. When this occurs, the lawyer must again raise the level of conflict. By invoking or altering the corporate culture, the lawyer can deliberately change policies. As Professor Coffee has suggested, in such instances the lawyer must convince management that its self-definition

---

[410] This discussion follows R. Ackerman, The Social Challenge to Business 304, 310 (1975).

[411] Ackerman, "How Companies Respond to Social Demands," in Managing Corporate Social Responsibility 283, 288-89 (A. Carroll ed. 1977).

[412] M. Anshen, Corporate Strategies for Social Performance 148 (1980).

[413] Collins & Ganotis, "Is Corporate Responsibility Sabotages by the Rank and File?," in Managing Corporate Social Responsibility 344 (A. Carroll ed. 1977).

is problematic, suggesting, for example, there is "a difference between the levels of risk aversion that characterize management and its shareholders or between the time frames in which they wish to maximize profits."[414] Only by developing the corporation's sense of professional behavior can lawyers counter cases where laws make immoral actions efficient For example, corporations can wink at certain forms of featherbedding and unreported income, such as petty thefts and padded expense accounts, because they may financially benefit the company; tax laws provide deductions for these expenses at rates different from wage expenses.[415] By developing a corporate sense that these actions are inconsistent with other values it holds, or needs to hold to be productive, lawyers can prod a company to take these violations seriously.

Lawyers' ability to induce legal compliance will then depend, in part, on how lawyers are organized into the policy implementation process. The risk analysis mode tends to encourage policies that eliminate managerial discretion. Because of risk analysis lawyers' inability to effectively guide managerial discretion, policies at their companies usually take the form of definite terms and conditions, waivable only with a lawyer's consent of the lawyer. This type of policy is most effective in corporate relations with outsiders: "We can't do this because it would violate our policies and we can't get a waiver through the lawyers." Nominally, it also allows the lawyer to raise the issue with those higher in the hierarchy: "If you have a serious breach of corporate policy, after discussion with the General Counsel and the client, you go up to the next level or to the Board in extraordinary circumstances. Your real client is the corporation, not the V.P. and the V.P. is also a servant of the corporation." But, for all the reasons suggested above, this only occurs in the most exceptional of circumstances. Managers evade policies, usually with the excuse that the policy concerns the lawyer, not them. They argue that policies must be violated in individual cases and the lawyer should police them. Power struggles result, in which the manager says, "It's my exposure," and lawyers, given the difficulties of policing conflicts, often cave in.

When lawyers act as consultants, they let the internal audit department monitor policy compliance. Lawyers "give specifications and interpretations" of policies. They suggest alternatives so there is "less incentive to violate ethics" and prepare for conflict by structuring choices so that "the manager won't profit from violation." In these companies, lawyers become consultants on the corporation's overall risk portfolio, not policemen of policies. Policies are developed to direct certain behaviors and to create a risk portfolio. When the manager says, "It's my exposure," the lawyer responds, "You can't take

---

[414] Coffee, "Beyond the Shut-Eyed Sentry: Toward a Theoretical View of Corporate Misconduct and an Effective Legal Response," 63 Va. L. Rev. 1099, 1105 (1977).

[415] This example is from Katz, "Cover-Up and Collective Integrity: On the Natural Antagonisms of Authority Internal and External to Organizations," 25 Soc. Problems 3, 12 (1977).

that risk because elsewhere we've got this exposure." The lawyer admits that policies need to be re-worked in practice, but he demonstrates to the manager the need for his input in the reworking process. As a lawyer put it: "Managers come to me with their difficult decisions because the corporate legal department writes the corporate policies and we are keepers of the company's morals. By 'company morals,' I mean that the corporate legal department must know to what risks the company is subject and we know what risks the company feels are appropriate." Corporate processes, rather than individual managers and market forces, determine exposure. Lawyers acquire the power to establish policies because they are capable of balancing and spreading risks. They are in touch with actions throughout the company, as well as informed about the environment. When a manager tries to push his product, lawyers know what else the company is doing. In setting up policies, they can use their professional training to determine how far the company should go with various types of risks. When they do this well, they can inject into the corporate risk portfolio the seriousness of the violation as well as the possibility of sanction.

Lawyers who act as consultants handle policy conflicts differently than do lawyers who merely analyze risk. Because everyone accepts that policies may change, lawyers cannot try to override a manager's decision simply because it violates the letter of a policy. Policies don't enable lawyer-consultants to serve an auditing function; they help inject the lawyers into the decision process:

> Our policies are guidelines, not rules. Their function is to educate clients about the areas of conduct which are of concern. They can't be so rigorous that they are used to fire people. We want the employees to know that in these areas they should call up the corporate legal department or their supervisors and talk about it. If they are worried about jeopardizing their position they might not communicate. Our goal then is to set up the right framework, not write the right rules.

Nonetheless, policies are normally authoritative. At the managerial level, lawyers are consultants. They first "lay everything out on the table and go over the policy. This normally resolves things even when the client wants to make the deal." When it doesn't work, an appeals procedure, different from the one used at risk-analysis companies, is utilized. The lawyer first approaches higher authorities in the corporate legal department to insure his reading of the policy and its application is appropriate. Then, to defeat any power play the manager may be attempting, "the General Counsel meets with the manager," instead of contacting the manager's supervisor. "This can be intimidating because the General Counsel is a powerful figure in the company." If this doesn't work, "the General Counsel will directly contact his opposite number in the appropriate department," rather than contacting the manager's supervisor. Again, this insures the conflict remains at the level of corporate goals.

By keeping the conflict at the level of policy, lawyers can retain power even when they lose individual struggles. After going through the above appeals procedure, the relevant authorities decided to allow a waiver of a certain antitrust policy. The involved manager, however, did not interpret the waiver as a sign the legal department's power had been dissipated or that the company was moving away from its commitment to antitrust compliance: "At that point, legal couldn't hold up the flow. But, ours is a very conservative company and legal was right in their estimate. In application, sometimes you may have to take risks you might want to avoid but that doesn't change our basic orientation."

Lawyers' invoking policy, like their appeal to corporate culture, is basically an attempt to raise the level of conflict. Instead of a conflict between individuals or departments, it becomes a conflict about the character of the organization. This approach to conflict differs from the way most intra-organizational conflicts are managed. Most conflicts are managed by reducing the level of conflict. Conflict is reduced to personality clashes or power plays minimizing its threat to the organization because the issue appears to be one of personal relations.[416] When an actor has little formal power, however, he must often raise the level of conflict to get a fair hearing. Because lawyers will always be criticized for not being sufficiently "pragmatic,"[417] they must raise the level of conflict. Strangely enough, when lawyers who mix legal and business advice raise the level of conflict, they don't destroy the trust between lawyer and client.[418]

THE INTERNAL LAW OF THE ORGANIZATION

When a lawyer mixes legal and business advice and draws upon, the corporation's conception of itself embedded in its cultures and policies, he

---

[416] March and Simon, *supra*, at 131.

[417] This is a normative judgment masquerading as a personality judgment.

[418] This is consistent with Litterer's findings. Litterer, "Conflict in Organization: A Re-Examination," in Resource book in Macro-Organizational Behavior 157 (R. Miles ed. 1980): "[C]onflicts over the means to goal accomplishment are more disruptive of group cohesiveness than conflicts over differing goals." When lawyers are not able to draw on corporate goals, as is normally the case with outside counsel and with inside counsel in the risk analysis mode, conflict remains at the personality level and threatens continuing relationships. This is one reason why such lawyers do not press conflicts. But see Fuller's "Fourth Law of Association" "To the extent than an association is seen by its members as held together by the principle of shared commitment, it will be hostile toward internal groups dominated by the same principle.... [I]n a less uncompromising way, the same tendency holds toward internal groups supported by commitments that are consistent with, or even purposes to (reinforce), the commitment sustaining the larger association. The sometimes uneasy relations between the Vatican and the various Catholic orders provides a familiar case in point." K. Winston, ed., The Principles of Social Order: Selected Essays of Lon L. Fuller 7677 (1981).

becomes an influential member of the corporation, an exponent of not only the external law of the state, but also the internal law of the organization. This lawyer, like the good inspector, policeman, parole officer and teacher "learns how to develop...community resources to gain information and support through the use of a mixture of force and service, threats and appeals to reason, toughness and teaching."[419] This tactic recognizes, as does the traditional lawyer-client relationship, that to be influential the lawyer must approach clients trying to "understand their concerns, problems, and motivations."[420] Sensitivity to client's concerns need not undermine the lawyer's public obligations, because "better compliance most of the time can be secured in most premises if one persuades the occupier of the need for compliance as a matter of good practice, rather than to avoid conflict with the law."[421]

By drawing on the internal law of the organization, the lawyer not only avoids the problem of power conflicts but also makes the law salient. The lawyer can't ignore corporate resources because if he sets himself up as the guardian of the public interest, he is considered disloyal, self-aggrandizing, and is therefore rendered ineffective.[422] Furthermore, by drawing on organizational resources, the lawyer helps make the choice concrete. Compliance with the law is more likely when managers understand that their characters, as well as their corporation's character, are tied up in the decision.[423] By casting his advice in these terms, the lawyer not only evokes the corporation's internal law, but also helps develop it. Corporations, in turn, learn that their organizational choices have normative significance. They learn, as Fuller puts it, that "problems of business...[are] questions of the forms of social order.... For example, a problem of choosing among principles of order is involved in the familiar question of the relative merits of the 'stenographic pool' as compared with a system that assigns steno-graphers to individual executives."[424]

Although it may seem unprofessional to draw on the internal law of the

---

[419] Bardach & Kagan, *supra*, at 126. The account given here is consistent with what might be called the "Berkeley School of Institutional Analysis." It is consistent not only with the work of Bardach and Kagan, but also that of Kadish and Kadish, Muir, Studt, and Selznick.

[420] Bardach & Kagan, *supra*, at 127.

[421] Bardach & Kagan, *supra*, at 133, quoting (British) Inspector of Factories, Annual Report for 1969.

[422] Thompson, "Types of Representative Bureaucracy and Their Linkage: The Case of Ethnicity," in Public Administration: Readings in Institutions, Processes, Behavior and Policy (R. Golembiewski, et al., eds. 1976).

[423] Cf. T. Shaffer, On Being a Christian and a Lawyer: Law for the Innocent 119-20 (1981) (contrasting a lawyer who argues on constitutional grounds for equal pay for equal work and a lawyer who talks about the particular women who will be injured and the con-sequences of this for the corporation).

[424] Winston, *supra*, at 266.

organization as well as the state's law, it actually furthers the ideals of the legal profession. In our society, legal language strives not to be merely esoteric. Lawyers speak to their clients in common language, not just in "legalese." They often tell country anecdotes, drawing on the common culture to make the law relevant and to increase the number of incidents that are seen from a legal perspective. The country lawyer's folksy approach is not unprofessional. Rather, it fulfills the profession's goal of developing a legally sensitive citizenry.[425] It also furthers the profession's aspiration to integrate local interests and information with general policies in rendering client service. For example, lawyers who combine legal and business advice may lose conflicts in settlement situations, when they argue the settlement is cost-effective. Managers counter that to settle would reward the squeaky wheel. When lawyers are able to overcome the initial shock to their pride, however, they can use the managers' arguments to advance corporate commitments to merit and equity, ultimately advancing legal compliance in other situations.

There are serious risks to lawyers who concentrate on the internal law of the organization. An inward focus must not be allowed to compromise the lawyer's commitment to the law. In the company where the lawyers most vigorously used the corporation's internal law, they also aggressively interpreted regulations. They felt "comfortable making pro-operator and pro-management decisions without feeling [that] their objectivity [was] compromised." At this company, the legal department was well organized, had helped to develop strong corporate commitments to legal goals, and had attained a position of power. Consequently, they were able to advance management interests in areas where they deemed the law unreasonable. But it is easy to imagine situations in which lawyers lacking organizational support adopt an almost exclusively internal focus. And, it is possible to imagine that, even after the lawyer has insured full debate, the corporation might take actions the lawyer cannot in full conscience support. What is the lawyer to do in such situations?

For all the risks of lawyers turning a blind-eye toward serious illegalities, lawyers cannot, if they hope to influence the corporation, dispense with commitments to the corporation and its managers. Lawyers must assume these risks to convince managers of the moral concerns at stake in compliance with the law.[426] The lawyer must meet these risks and stand up to serious violations. The lawyer must have "a 'tragic sense' of life—a recognition that law is not the sole measure of morality, that values often are in conflict, that causation and blame are not simple matters. But he combines

---

[425] See Probert & Brown, "Theories and Practices in the Legal Profession," 19 U. Fla. L. Rev. 447 (1966-67).

[426] As Edward Shils has said, civil politics "requires an understanding of the complexity of virtue, that no virtue stands alone, that every virtuous act costs something in terms of other virtuous acts, that virtues are intertwined with evil." Quoted in Marx, "Ironies of Social Control: Authorities as Contributors to Deviance Through Escalation, Non-enforcement and Covert Facilitation," 28 Soc. Problems 221 (1981).

that perspective with passion—a desire to do justice and to protect potential victims...."[427] To maintain both a sense of tragedy and passion, the lawyer must have organizational supports to insure that cases of non-enforcement occur where the law is unreasonable and do not reduce the lawyer's overall power or the corporation's commitment to legal compliance.[428] Because there will always be individual managers who will not be swayed, lawyers must be able to draw on effective appeals procedures, such as the one described above. The lawyer must be able to use a mixture of "threats and appeals to reason." As a consultant, the lawyer should use threats selectively, preferring to earn trust and support but not allowing corrupt decisions to pass.

If the highest levels of management approve corrupt decisions, lawyer options are more limited. Inside counsel can call in outside counsel and accountants. If that doesn't work, inside and outside counsel, if the bar continues to refuse to let them breach confidences, have little choice but to resign. Although mixing legal and business advice tends to minimize the number of cases in which lawyers face this tragic choice, the choice cannot always be avoided. Furthermore even if lawyers resign, responsible corporate action may not result. Public initiatives are needed to develop intra- and extra-organizational structures to control such instances. Just as stronger sanctions are needed to make legal service in the risk analysis mode more effective, regulations geared toward corporate organizational structures are needed to support legal service that mix legal and business advice.

THE SUPPOSED BUSINESS-LAW SPLIT RE-EXAMINED

When lawyers retreat into the technique of risk analysis, they justify their withdrawal by claiming certain choices are questions of business, not of law. This split assumes that lawyers cannot appropriately provide input to or resolve certain issues. Issues are divided into those of concern to lawyers and those reserved for businessmen.

This division is not morally neutral. In corporations, ethical considerations often involve trade-offs between the demands of law and the requirements of business. The lawyer's moral agenda is set, in part, by how he constructs this trade-off. At what point does he say the risks are to be decided by businessmen?

When lawyers are not certain they'll triumph in conflicts, they tend to

---

[427] Bardach and Kagan, *supra*, at 126.

[428] Cf. Katz, "Cover-Up and Collective Integrity: On the Natural Antagonisms of Authority Internal and External to Organizations," 25 Soc. Problems 3, 10 (1977): "Decisions not to enforce become corrupt when, instead of strengthening the authority of persons in officially superordinate positions by recruiting agents for the enforcement process or by inducing cooperation for its goals, they strengthen the independent authority or illegitimate purposes of the persons granted lenience."

accentuate the split between law and business.[429] When the decision is difficult, involves unpredictable responses or requires taking an unpopular position, the lawyer finds it convenient to claim the choice is one for business and simply act as a conduit for choices and positions taken by others.[430] Yet, this retreat affects managers' choices. It invites them into adventurism and opportunism. As the examples in the risk analysis section indicate, when lawyers retreat, managers don't hesitate to become adventuristic, feeling uncontrolled by public norms, and opportunistic, reading the law in the most opportune fashion for their current needs.[431]

This result is particularly troubling because our society relies on corporations to assume responsibility. But in conflicts involving corporate social responsibility, lawyers tend to retreat into their technical expertise. Corporate social responsibility issues are always ineffable; their parameters are hard to set and they are difficult to second-guess. The lawyer, who cannot help but retreat, will set back his corporation's ability to assume responsibility, giving strength to the forces of adventurism and opportunism.

Lawyers also are likely to retreat into technique in precisely those instances when his duty to serve the corporation as an entity requires him to fight legal violations. Given a business-law split, managers must be capable of making clear decisions on their own. They must have identifiable positions and interests that are not unstable, inchoate or conflicting. The trade-offs involved in any legal process—resolving value conflicts, deciding risk-averseness, ranking goals—can be univocally decided by the manager and need not be muddled through with the lawyer. They are capable of a definitive solution. The lawyer can either accept the decision or withdraw. He is not likely to seek reconsideration, mobilize coalitions, and influence the decision-making process.[432]

When lawyers act as consultants, rather than a split, a continuum exists between law and business. The law is not merely the formal derivative of public political processes. Law is part of all social processes. The law not only determines particular behaviors, it informs all behavior. In turn, actors beliefs and desires test the law. The law is not esoteric, but responsive. Private actors are part of the legal process.[433]

---

[429] See J. Donnell, The Corporate Counsel: A Role Study 31 (1971) (separating law and business elements reduces overload and ambiguity for inside counsel. Where they are intertwined, the lawyer sees potential problems everywhere, creating stress (citing R. Kahn, et al., Organizational Stress 59 (1964)).

[430] Cf. P. Selznick, Leadership in Administration 76 (1957). Clients too can use the split to avoid responsibility. This is described in the adage, "If a deal works out, it was a sound business decision. If it doesn't, it was bad legal advice."

[431] Cf. *id.* at 148-49.

[432] Cf. Rhode, "Class Conflicts in Class Actions," 34 Stan. L. Rev. 1183 (1982).

[433] Cf. Anshen, "The Socially Responsible Corporation: From Concept to Implementation," in Managing the Socially Responsible Corporation 1, 8 (M. Anshen ed. 1974): "[T]he notion

To accept the split, to say that 'business' decisions are for the client alone, implies that the choice does not even require the *invocation* of legal norms.[434] When the business-law split forces decisions to be handed over to the client, a premature rejection of the role of standards, policies and principles occurs.[435] Instead of engaging in reasoned argument, the lawyer shuts up. The lawyer asserts that business norms are trumps or that the law lets one do anything within one's sphere of rights.

To assert that business norms are trumps is to make the lawyer's role subservient to a particular theory of business organization. In forsaking reasoned argument, the lawyer lobbies for a particular conception of corporate organization, one that forgets that organizations depend on individual discretion. A concomitant of bureaucratization is the multiplication of rules. To enforce these rules, corporations must generate standards and policies. Certain organizational roles emerge to guide the inevitable ambiguity in the application of rules. One such role is that of the corporate lawyer. When the lawyer steps aside, claiming he can't become involved in 'business' decisions, he fails to recognize the depends of his role and the delicate balance between discretion and command in corporate organizations.

Asserting that the law defines spheres where justice has no place, the lawyer lobbies for a particular conception of the legal process' place in social life. If a split exists between law and business, then the law merely sets up fences and it denies the reality of interdependence. If, instead, law and business are part of a continuum, then the law can be invoked as a standard for action and it becomes part of a social process where agents define themselves and strive against each other.[436] Given a split, public law only affects private action when the law directly addresses private individuals.[437] Without the split, public norms can diffuse into private choice[438] and private

---

that business should look to government...is troubling [because] experienced successful managers have valuable contributions to make to the design of a complex system of incentives and restraints. Managers understand technological feasibilities, administrative systems, and organizational behavior. The absence of this understanding can lead to a misdirection of efforts and gross waste of resources."

[434] For a discussion of the difference between the invocation and the determination of decisions by norms, see Abel, "A Comparative Theory of Dispute Institutions in Society," 8 L. & Soc. Rev. 217, 234-35 (1973).

[435] When legal norms are invoked but are not determinative, they are in Dworkin's language "standards," "principles" or "policies." They are reasons guiding the decision in a certain direction, but not spelling out the conclusion. See R. Dworkin, Taking Rights Seriously (1978).

[436] Cf. Barnes, "Law as Politically Active: An Anthropological View," in Studies in the Sociology of Law (G. Sawyer ed. 1961), cited in Abel, *supra*, at 238.

[437] The above includes those laws designed to facilitate private arrangements.

[438] As, for example, in the diffusion of procedural due process into corporate life. See, e.g., P. Selznick, Law, Society, and Industrial Justice (1969) (also arguing that these norms are emergent from the constitution of corporate institutions).

norms can attain legitimacy.[439] Conceptualizations of the business-law split, then, are conceptualizations of the place of the normative in social life.

CONCLUSION: CHOICES IN CORPORATE LEGAL PRACTICE

Three arguments are advanced to justify the law business split. First, it is claimed that the lawyer is not knowledgeable enough to give business advice. Corporate decisions are complex and the lawyer must retreat into his zone of expertise. Second, it is argued that the lawyer is not sought as an influential counselor. The corporate world is big, with corporations relying on many other actors. Third, it is argued that the lawyer is not responsible for the client's decisions and their consequences. The lawyer is a specialist, who does not expound his own positions in the process of representing.[440]

It is asserted that lawyers do not have the knowledge to advise on complex decisions. Outside counsel, especially, will say that they are too far away from their client's business.[441] As was explored in the previous chapter, this is true to some extent: how involved lawyers become in business considerations is, to some extent, a function of the problems set for them. But, as we explored in this chapter, to some extent, the lawyer's limited knowledge results from the ways lawyers have chosen to position themselves. Lack of knowledge too often masks real choices. It plays the role of an ideological devil. As was demonstrated at four of the companies studied, lawyers can master business expertise. They can assume the role of giving

---

[439] Private norms need not rest on the imposition of power. Their legitimacy may rest on their ability to realize values. The courts recognize this in utilizing private norms to decide cases. See Goldberg, "Institutional Change and the Quasi-Invisible Hand," 14 J. L. & Econ. 461, 484 (1974). See also the work of Ian McNeil. This occurs, e.g., in invoking the codes of ethics of professional associations and in accepting the internal constitutions of trade unions. See Evan, "Public and Private Legal Systems," in Law and Sociology: Exploratory Essays 176 (W. Evan ed. 1962).

[440] These arguments mirror those in Chapter One. As I stated there (p. 49): "There are at least three choices any lawyer must make. First, he must establish how open his expert knowledge will be to other forms of knowledge. Second, he must determine how much influence he wishes to exert in his relations with clients. And third, he must declare allegiance in the face of the conflicting interests associated with his work."

[441] As one said: "My job is to tell the businessman what his options are. I try to be a source of information to them." This doesn't seem problematic, except when it is put in the context of complex decisions. For example, he takes pride in writing memos that provide information on the "way in which the ideal world would work. Because we don't know the situation, we can write a memo on the way the perfect world would work and then the client and his inside counsel can adjust it to the needs of reality." This allows the lawyer to feel independent, avoid conflict, and have little influence. As he explained, "I say, 'This is what the statute says you need to do. Don't tell me about your business realities (the cost in dollars to print new forms, the fact that you have always done things in this way). I am telling you what is required.' "

business advice.[442]

It is asserted that lawyers are not sought as influential counselors. This assertion, however, seems to be made only when ethical responsibilities are at stake. Otherwise, lawyers routinely sell themselves as counselors to their clients. As a prestigious member of the bar said, "The most valuable lawyers in the corporate area are those who are good business advisers. The most sophisticated companies use lawyers as business counselors. It may have nothing to do with the law—they just use lawyers as people who have good judgment."[443]

Yet, when asked if a lawyer serving as counselor has responsibilities for implementing corporate social responsibility, this lawyer responded: "When the client asks, 'What should I do?,' you have the most difficult question because you are not the client.... There is a question of whether it is appropriate for outside professionals to make management decisions."

Lawyers justify their lack of influence by stressing their independence and by pointing to the "bigness" of the corporation: "You expose yourself to greater risks of being proven wrong because presumably they have other advisers. If you give business advice in the tone of expertise, there is also a liability problem." Or, "To give business advice when it is not specifically asked for means that you are on the one hand offending them and on the other hand costing them more than they want to pay." These claims re-capitulate the findings of the previous chapter. Clients control the way legal problems are set and the form lawyers' influence will take. Lawyers, in turn, acquiesce to these restrictions.[444] As a business lawyer in a large firm said, in explaining his low influence: "I have been told many times, I don't want your business advice. I've got Harvard and Stanford MBA's to do that for me. I want your legal advice." Self-interest partially explains lawyers' acquiescence. They can avoid liability problems and the risk of being overruled in conflicts,

---

[442] Note that managers and management consultants, who often move between companies, quickly pick up knowledge of corporate business and culture. Consequently, it's difficult to readily accept lawyer's claims of ignorance.

[443] Sometimes this claim was related to the "bigness" of the client: "What less sophisticated clients want is not just the crossed t's and dotted i's of legal compliance, but judgment based on your experience with other clients to determine whether the transaction makes sense from a purely business point of view." Or, smaller clients "want me to venture recommendations based on my experience with a wide range of companies. It is more satisfying than working for large clients. It is not as cut and dried. You have to encourage them to make the decisions themselves but you also have to determine what they are after." These companies may not have a trusted corporate legal department, so "they are looking to you for general long-term planning." But, these statements were taken back when ethical responsibilities were raised. See also H. Drinker, Legal Ethics xii (1953) (describing lawyers as having business judgment, but denying that lawyer's have business expertise when questions of ethical corporate conduct are at issue).

[444] Lawyers often said, "You can and do give business advice if you have a good personal relationship with the client." Or, "You respond to your clients. There are some clients who want you in and there are some clients who want only purely legal service."

yet continue to ask high fees. Also, this is partly attributable to the ways outside lawyers' problems are set following the rise of inside counsel. As one inside counsel explained, "When I talk to outside lawyers, I ask them about the law. They are the mouthpiece. I rely on myself for equity." But, the justification most lawyers provide is: "Why should corporations be required to pay lawyers to give non-legal advice?" This chapter and the last should provide answers to this question. Purely legal advice on problems set by the clients are not adequately processed by corporate decision structures, with potential costs to the client.

It is also asserted that lawyers are not responsible for the consequences of corporate decisions: "I believe decisions should be made by the client. I can't decide what the consequences are. The biggest problem is that everybody would like someone else to make their decisions. I try not to do that." Or, "We are consultants, not part of the process." While there is something appealing when an ex-Supreme Court clerk claims that "I don't see myself as a fount of wisdom," its charm lessens when it is tied to a denial of responsibility. While the lawyer stresses the limitations of his specialty, actually it is the intervention of the cash nexus that apparently relieves him of responsibilities for the rights of others. His claim relates not to expertise but to the impossibility of discourse. As was seen in the previous chapter, lawyers must be aware of the way the corporate hierarchy processes their information. To insure that their information is used correctly, the lawyer must be the type of consultant of whom clients ask, "If you were in my shoes what would you do?" Therefore, while the lawyer must be aware of the ease with which he could assume a function not properly his, and must be aware of the ways managers might evade responsibility for their work, the lawyer must also be part of the decision process to function properly. To not be part of the team, to function merely as a lawbook, is to misserve the corporate client. The lawyers-as-lawbook can evade responsibility for his actions. The lawyer who functions as part of the corporate team—a function demanded by the weaknesses of corporate organization—must take responsibility for the decisions of which he is part. All too often lawyers evade the choices corporate practice demands. One senior member of an outside firm's situation is typical. He denied facing ethical problems:

> The people I deal with happily listen to what I say. I've never confronted a situation where I say, "This is the law and if you do x, you will wreak havoc on your company," and they don't listen. I've been in situations where I've said, "It's not clear to me. There is an argument here that you may be running afoul of this law." The client says, "O.K. I will consider that and then I will make a decision about what I will do." My job is to tell people what the law is and by the force of my personality convince them that is the way to go. It works.

The lawyer asserts that he has the client's trust, that his explaining the situation resolves conflicts, and that this allows the client to put the law and business together in accordance with the law. He must boast of his clients' respect and his forceful personality. Otherwise, he might have to acknowledge what an inside counsel with whom he works perceives: "He is used for nitpicking questions on regulations and the manager leaves him saying, 'He doesn't know the business,' and the manager doesn't listen to him."

Chapter Four

THE INFLUENTIAL LAWYER: WHO IS THE CLIENT OF THE CORPORATE COUNSEL?

INTRODUCTION: RULE 1.13: THE ORGANIZATION AS CLIENT

Ethically concerned corporate attorneys encounter situations in which they have trouble identifying their client.[445] Identifying "who is the client" raises two different questions.[446] The first question is: what are a lawyer's minimal duties to the client? This question addresses potential conflicts of interest between the lawyer and the client. It seeks to define the minimal requirements of professional service. The second question is: what are a lawyer's maximal obligations to the client? This question addresses third parties' and the legal system's claims on a lawyer. It seeks to define the extent of professional independence. Based on this study of corporate legal practice, the first question can be answered:[447] serving the corporate client requires the lawyer to influence the corporation and conceive of corporate decision-making processes as his client.

Corporate legal service's peculiar obligations derive from the differentiated nature of the corporate organization. As the Model Rules of Professional Conduct states: "An organizational client...cannot act except through its officers, directors, employees, shareholders and other constituents."[448] The Rules, however, demonstrates a very limited understanding of organizational differentiation. It conceptualizes differentiation as merely the bureaucratic division of authority. Bureaucracies contain different offices, posing the threat that officers may not obey hierarchical commands and may make decisions not delegated to them by the chain of command. Consequently, the Rules prescribes that a lawyer's minimal duty to the organizational client is to protect the integrity of the bureaucratic hierarchy. The lawyer accepts commands from subordinate officers, because these commands derive their authority from decisions at the hierarchy's top.[449] To

---

[445] See, e.g., G. Hazard, Ethics in the Practice Law 7 (1978).

[446] See "Developments in the Law: Conflicts of Interest in the Legal Profession," 94 Harv. L. Rev. 1244, 1252-53 (1981).

[447] The two questions are not unrelated. To the extent that minimal duties include actions to promote respect for others and the legal system, the second question will be faced in a different context.

[448] Model Rules of Professional Conduct, Rule 1.13, Comment, "The Entity as a Client," 15 (1983) [Hereafter cited as Model Rules]. Note, lawyers are not included in this list.

[449] Hence, "[w]hen constituents of the organizations make decisions for it, the decisions ordinarily must be accepted by the lawyer even if their utility or prudence is doubtful." *Ibid.*

prevent the violation of hierarchical command, the lawyer who questions a subordinate's commands, will raise the issue up the hierarchy for reconsideration.[450]

This formulation assumes that corporations are bureaucracies, transmitting goals to managers who act on them. It further assumes that corporate decisions result from hierarchical commands, not from processes of organizational decision-making. To a considerable extent, these assumptions do not fit the work patterns and decisions of the lawyers and managers at the six companies studied. Moreover, other students of organizational behavior have also rejected the assumptions in Rule 1.13.[451] Rather than operating as a bureaucracy, large corporations act as "a coalition of interests groups, sharing a common resource base, paying homage to a common mission,"[452] where decisions are "political resultants," not the results of command.[453]

As Pierce recognized, this prescription is not useful in any instance in which corporate decision-making doesn't follow hierarchical command, as where different groups within the corporation have different interests, goals and powers. Then the lawyer cannot be subservient to the hierarchy; he must be "counsel to the situation." Pierce, "The Code of Professional Responsibility in the Corporate World: An Abdication of Professional Self-Regulation," 5 U. Mich. J.L. Ref. 350, 362 (1973). Before acting in the face of such conflict the "corporate attorney [must] predetermine the corporate interest." Id. at 361. If, as is true in the six corporations studied, such conflict is endemic, the professional codes' advice is of little value. As Pierce concludes, they do not spell out any standards "about the attorney's obligation in the face of...internecine disputes." Id. at 363 n. 45.

[450] Model Rules, Rule 1.13(b). Cf. ABA Comm. on Professional Ethics, Formal Opinion #202, 489 (1967 ed.) (ethical conflicts resolved by orderly movement up the hierarchy). In the Rules of Professional Conduct, as enacted, the lawyer's duty clearly is not to prevent or try to prevent an injury. His only duty is to seek a reconsideration. The Rules provides no indication as to how high up the hierarchy the lawyer should go. While he has permission to go all the way to the top, Rule 1.13(b), this is for the "extreme case." Comment at 15. Normally, the lawyer must judge who has "responsibility in the organization" to make the decision. Rule 1.13(b). This judgment cannot rest on hierarchical principles. In most cases, the manager seemingly will have authority. To determine whether or not to seek reconsideration, the lawyer must look not to where authority is found within the hierarchy, but to where the authority should be placed. This requires organizational analysis and the profession provides little guidance on how to make this judgment. Practicing attorneys are left not knowing how high up the hierarchy they should go. See O'Neal & Thompson, "Vulnerability of Professional-Client Privilege in Shareholder Litigation," 31 Bus. Lawyer 1775 (1976).

[451] March, "The Technology of Foolishness," in Ambiguity and Choice in Organizations 69, 72 (J. G. March & J. Olson eds. 1971): "It seems to me perfectly obvious that a description that assumes goals come first and action comes later is frequently radically wrong. Human choice behavior is at least as much a process for discovering goals as for acting on them." See also W. R. Scott, Organizations: Rational, Natural and Open Systems 264 (1981).

[452] Miles, "Introduction," in Resourcebook on Macro-Organizational Behavior 1, 5 (R. Miles ed. 1980).

[453] G. Allison, Essence of Decision 162 (1971): "Resultants in the sense that what happens is not chosen as a solution to a problem but rather results from compromise, conflict and unequal influence. Political in the sense that the activity from which decisions and actions

These inaccurate assumptions lead the Rules to exclude lawyers from corporate decision-making processes: "Decisions concerning policy and operations, including ones entailing serious risk, are not as such in the lawyer's province."[454] This dismisses the lawyer's role in shaping the "political resultants" that are the corporate decisions. Furthermore, lawyers are directed to don a bureaucratic mind-set, oblivious to everything not directly related to hierarchical command. Hence, the lawyer's duties are restricted to matters "related to the representation."[455] Is it in the corporation's best interests to limit lawyers in this way? How would they treat a manager who saw a serious problem and decided not to do anything because it was outside his job definition? Managers, because they serve the corporation rather than their office, would not be praised for sticking to their job descriptions. Their task is to "manage," which can require transcending hierarchically-defined offices.[456] Only if corporations were simple bureaucracies would corporate officers need to consider only clearly defined and directly assigned tasks.[457] Similarly, the Rules does not recognize the responsibility managers have to exercise their discretion. A lawyer's minimal duties begin only when "the lawyer knows that the organization may be substantially injured."[458] How would a corporation treat a manager who failed to warn the corporation of a potential problem because he was not certain it would lead to substantial injury? The discretion granted to managers entails more responsibility than that.

---

emerge is best characterized as bargaining among regularized channels among individual members." (Emphasis omitted.) See also W. E. Moore, The Conduct of the Corporation 186 (1962) (describing corporations and their staffs as "pluralist governments").

[454] Model Rules at 15.

[455] Model Rules, Rule 1.13(b). In determining how to proceed, the lawyers must consider "the scope and nature of the lawyer's representation." *Ibid*. This formulation rejects the 1979 draft formulation (in Rule 1.12) of "lawyer employed or retained by an organization" whose minimal duties are ones of "allegiance" that arise when he "knows" of a problem. This language is broader than that adopted since it potentially includes knowledge not related to the representation.

[456] The Rules appears not to understand this point. In considering the ways the manager may fail in his responsibilities, it considers only violations of hierarchy. These violations may occur without malfeasance; the manager incorrectly assesses his stated responsibilities, corporate policies or the risks. It may also occur through various forms of self-dealing. Rule 1.13(b). In the Rules, there is no discussion of a manager failing to meet his responsibility to "manage."

[457] Compare that in a study of Fortune 500 top executives, 74% responded that "the legal staff should initiate involvement in corporate activities." 106 N.J. L.J. 124 (Aug. 7, 1980).

[458] Model Rules at 15. This language, in the comment to Rule 1.13, appears to be more inclusive than the Rule. In the Rule, the duty is only incurred when the lawyer, in matters related to the representation, knows that the action "is likely to result in substantial injury." Rule 1.13(b), *id*. at 14 ("may be" is less restrictive than "is likely"). But, the comment hedges by requiring the lawyer to have "clear justification." *Id*. at 15.

Why should corporations limit their lawyers more than their managers? According to the Rules, if lawyers were granted broader duties, it would risk the "disruption of the organization,"[459] a fear better associated with bureaucracies than with current corporate forms. Managers, unlike lawyers, know that conflict is endemic in business and that to get along, you don't have to go along.[460] Managers, unlike lawyers, know that policies may be stated or informal,[461] may come from various sources and may not be easily distilled from the corporate culture.[462]

Corporations understand the costs of bureaucratic control. They utilize consultants, develop staffs, cultures, and formal and informal channels to marshal information outside bureaucratic channels. Corporations seek to transcend their formal organization chart by developing a constitutive organization. Lawyers are a part of this more developed organization. They are part of corporate decision-making processes. They play a part, sometimes forming an interest group, in shaping the political decisions that propel the corporation. Just as it would be a failure for managers to serve a corporation by simply obeying its hierarchical commands, so it may be a failure for lawyers to adopt such a passive stance in their service.[463]

The Rules portrays the lawyer as henchman and sometimes auditor for the corporation. The argument here is that Rule 1.13's account of a lawyer's minimal duties disregards the corporation's organizational dependence on the lawyer. It ignores the lawyer's involvement in corporate decision-making.

Corporate differentiation is not merely the bureaucratic division of authority. Consequently, lawyers are forced into roles other than those to which Rule 1.13 applies. Lawyers do not merely follow policy, they also make policy. A suggestion of these other roles is found in the Comment to Rule 1.13: "The stated policy of the organization may define circumstances and prescribe channels for...review, *and a lawyer may encourage the formu-*

---

[459] Rule 1.13(b). The Rule is formulated to minimize disruption except in the most exigent of circumstances.

[460] See P. Lawrence & J. Lorsch, Organization and Environment 222 (1969); Thomas & Schmidt, "A Survey of Managerial Interest with respect to Conflict," Acad. of Mgmt. J. 315 (1976).

[461] Rule 1.13(b) directs the lawyer to consider "the policies of the organization." It is unclear whether this means both stated and unstated policies. The thrust seems to be to consider only stated policies, which is in accord with the bureaucratic image of the corporation, as well as the discussion in the Comment. Model Rules at 15.

[462] Rule 1.13(b) directs the lawyer to look at "the seriousness of the violation," "its consequences," and the "injury" to the corporation. It appears to assume that these are objective and do not require the lawyer to examine corporate norms and culture.

[463] Lawyers and managers do not have the same duties. They have different professional bases, tasks, and roles in the constitutive organization and decision-making processes. But, a lawyer's minimal duties derive, like a manager's, from serving not a hierarchy but a constitutive organization.

lation of such a policy."[464] This recognizes that the lawyer does have a role in corporate decision-making. No account, however, is given of the source of this right.[465] By mentioning the lawyer's potential influence, the Comment raises the question of whether other incursions into corporate decision processes may be justified. The conclusion reached here is that to serve the client, as Harold Williams has put it, "lawyers—along with their more mundane responsibilities—must be architects of the accountability process which provides the corporate structure with the discipline necessary for effective decision-making."[466]

THE CASE

To understand the deficiencies of the Rules in practice, it may be helpful to consider an actual case. This case began for the lawyer, an inside counsel, when he received a call from a divisional personnel officer. The personnel officer reported that a manager, recently transferred to a new unit, wanted to fire a black woman employee who had worked in that unit for the past five years. The personnel officer asked the lawyer to call on the manager and "explain to him the law on firing members of protected classes." This lawyer had two years experience in the corporate legal department, after a career with a prestigious outside firm. He met with the manager, explained the possibility that the employee might contest the firing, admitted his ignorance about how to best protect against such litigation, and put the manager in touch with an outside firm specialist. The outside counsel then met with the manager and advised him on how to leave a paper trail to protect the corporation in the event of litigation. The manager proceeded to construct the paper trail.

The personnel officer then called on a second inside counsel, with whom he had previously worked and whom he respected. The personnel officer explained to the second inside counsel that he did not like the events which were transpiring. He said "he knew" that the manager was firing the employee for racist reasons: "She got along well with previous managers, he finds her 'difficult' because he doesn't like her color." The second inside counsel suggested transferring the employee, but, for various reasons, that was an unacceptable solution. The personnel officer explained that he had wanted the first inside counsel to "lay down the law; get the manager to see that he couldn't get away with racist firings."

---

[464] Model Rules at 15 (emphasis added).

[465] In line with the Rules' conception of the organization, this right may be seen as derivative of the lawyer's joint obligations to minimize disruption and to raise certain limited problems.

[466] H.Williams, speech before the ABA, 8/5/80, reprinted in Legal Times, 23, 25 (Aug. 11, 1980).

At this point, the second inside counsel reminded the personnel officer of something that had transpired during the ERISA negotiations they had worked on together. Under ERISA, to discriminate between workers with broken service and with unbroken service, you must document the gaps in service. Outside counsel had advised the corporation that the documentation was expensive and that it was not worth developing such procedures. The personnel officer had objected, arguing it was essential to signal to the workers that they would get out of the corporation what they would put into it. Given his commitment to meritocratic principles and equity, the personnel officer argued it was worth the expense to differentiate between workers based on their work records. The second inside counsel reminded the personnel officer that they had opposed the outside counsel, standing together to win the day. The second inside counsel suggested that this case involved similar principles. This woman had invested five years in the corporation and was not being rewarded for it. The second inside counsel recommended that he and the personnel officer talk to the manager along these lines.

In their discussion with the manager, they avoided the issue of race, knowing they could not get the manager's cooperation if they suggested he was a racist. They also did not mention established corporate policies on equal opportunity employment. Instead, they emphasized corporate commitments to merit and reward. The talk stopped the firing. At the time of the interviews, the woman was still working at the corporation, although she had not been promoted in four years.

Several features of this case are appropriate for analysis. First, note that neither the personnel officer nor any of the attorneys consulted the manager's supervisor. The reasons the issue was never raised up the hierarchy are critical to understanding the Rules' approach's limitations. Firing this low-level employee was not an appropriate decision to raise up the hierarchy. The manager, for reasons of efficiency, had the authority to fire the employee. Corporations are a complicated combination of command and discretion. A corporation could not function if every time a problem was raised it required decision further up the hierarchy. Instead, the corporation develops an organization, staffs, policies, and culture to deal with individual problems. At the same time, however, the corporation is subject to political pathologies that disrupt this organization. In this case, the first inside counsel and the outside counsel assumed a decision had been made and they were simply conduits for it. They assumed that they came into the decision late, on a fragmentary basis, and ended up exacerbating the political pathology.

Corporate policies against racist firings also were not drawn into the case. The first inside counsel knew of the policies and saw the possibility for racism in this case, but as he explained, "I had to make up my mind whether I was certain the firing was racist. I was not certain and adopted the manager's perspective that she was 'difficult.'" The outside counsel made a similar argument, but added "that's the corporation's problem." He speculated that had the manager explicitly stated he was firing her for racist reasons, he would not have provided him with the paper trail. Although the outside counsel thought he had withdrawn from some representations, he could not remember any particular case. Like the first inside counsel, his relations with clients alternate between subservience and paternalism. To avoid a power struggle between themselves and the manager, both these lawyers relied on the law's potential sanctions to discipline the manager. The legal sanctions were not only ineffective in producing legal compliance, they also deflected the lawyers from considering the resources the organization created to guide behavior. Neither lawyer asked why the personnel officer had initiated the case. Neither considered the possibility that the personnel officer, who was rather expert in employment law, approached the lawyers, not for expertise about the law's sanctions but for authoritative statements that racist firings would not be tolerated. Neither understood that the corporation, in using personnel officers, had made a commitment to restrain managerial discretion in firings.

Neither the personnel officer nor the second inside counsel invoked corporate employment policies. They knew that the policies could not be directly implemented without alienating the manager and thus guaranteeing the firing. They drew on resources other than legal sanctions and stated policies to develop responsibly the manager's exercise of discretion. They realized that corporate decisions occur at various levels and that the corporation had created resources to influence these decisions. By drawing on corporate culture and character, they developed the internal law of the organization. They fulfilled their task in the constitutive organization.

Two Proposals

Two proposals for altering the corporate lawyer-client relationship elucidate the corporation's organizational dependence on lawyers in its decision-making. The first proposal highlights the inadequacies of hierarchical command. The second highlights the connection between lawyer advice and corporate decision-making processes.

The first proposal is an indirect attack on current corporate lawyer-client arrangements. It recommends developing satellite mini-boards[467] as an alternative to counsel for implementing the board's policy decisions. Mini-boards would serve as policy enforcers by launching investigations and protecting "whistle-blowers."[468] They would have the "clout" necessary to compel corporate legal compliance.[469] In a corporation, however, power

---

[467] Coffee, "Beyond the Shut-Eyed Sentry: Toward a Theoretical View of Corporate Misconduct and an Effective Legal Response," 63 Va. L. Rev. 1099, 1148ff (1977).

[468] *Id.* at 1153.

[469] *Ibid.* Although Professor Coffee believes that the legal staff could not gain this power, his

alone is insufficient. To implement policies, managerial cooperation is also required. For mini-boards to be effective, they must earn the trust of the managers. Furthermore, they must have bases for bargaining. They must understand the manager's work well enough so they "could bargain for compliance...and, where necessary, credibly threaten sanctions."[470]

Analysis of organizational behavior, however, suggests that these two further requirements—trust and bargaining capacity—favor developing staffs, not mini-boards. Mini-boards cannot readily earn trust because they are not part of the work group and are likely to be seen as supervisors trying to second-guess the managers. Lawyers, like other staff members, can earn trust because, operating as consultants, they are part of the manager's work group.[471] Lawyers also have bases for bargaining because they can make positive contributions to the manager's work. A lawyer's suggestion commonly improves a manager's career prospects.

A board sufficiently involved with the manager's work to suggest alternatives is likely to be seen as a second hierarchy in tension with the first. Lawyers, like other staff members, avoid this problem by selling themselves as counselors; they emphasize that the line makes the decision and the staff only advises.[472] Even when the decision results from the staff's influence, the staff maintains the illusion it has not usurped the line's authority,[473] confirming managers' sense of their personal authority and responsibility.[474] In short, staffs function as "shadow hierarchies": gaining trust and exercising influence without diffusing managerial responsibility.[475] Mini-boards cannot so function. They will face managerial resistance and will not be able to become intimately involved in the manager's work. Consequently, like corporate boards, they are likely to defer excessively to the manager's expertise.

---

proposal implies that, for the legal staff to accomplish its mission, lawyers must gain power and influence within the corporation.

[470] *Ibid.*

[471] Research indicates that information blockages in organizations "are least likely to occur when the supervision function is structured into the system through the use of 'overlapping groups' linked by common members." *Ibid.*

[472] Allen, "The Line-Staff Relationship," 8 Mgmt. Rcd. 346, 348 (1955).

[473] M. Dalton, Men Who Manage (1953); Goldner, "The Division of Labor: Process and Power" in Power in Organizations 97 (M. Zald ed. 1970); Drucker, "Getting Control of Corporate Staff Work," Wall St. J. (April 28, 1982).

[474] V. Thompson, Modern Organization, 2d Ed., at 101 (1977).

[475] Professor Eisenberg uses the term "shadow hierarchies" in a quite different manner from this usage, which follows Harrison White. Responding to calls to enlarge the board's staff, Professor Eisenberg criticized such proposals as methods for instituting a "shadow staff" to "second-guess the management." Quoted in Coffee at 1154. This criticism is the one the text suggests as the problem of mini-boards.

The inevitability of diffused discretion within corporations gives rise to the proposal to create mini-boards. Mini-boards' weakness stems from the unwillingness of managers to yield their discretion to the authority of command. Rather than instituting new chains of command, it is better to use staffs, with their professional expertise and ability to influence decisions without second-guessing managerial actions, to limit managers' discretion.[476] The simple fact is that large corporations need both command and discretion. Hence, they build a constitutive organization of which the lawyer is part.

The second proposal directly alters the current corporate lawyer-client relationship. Instead of having lawyers serve the entity, the proposal recommends that they serve individual managers. Given the inevitability of conflict about who the corporate lawyer represents, let each involved corporate official or coalition have a lawyer.[477] Managers consider this proposal ridiculous.[478] Its weakness is that it denies the possibility of responsible exercise of managerial discretion. Even in conflict situations, the manager acts not in an individual capacity but in a corporate one. Normally, what a manager wants from a lawyer is support for his position. The manager wants the lawyer to help convince others in the corporation that his position best serves the corporation's interests. If the lawyer represents the manager individually, the lawyer's support will be of little value. At stake in the conflict is a corporate choice, not an individual one. For the lawyer, like the manager, to responsibly contribute to this choice, he must be familiar with the range of corporate interests, the extent of other interests, and the openness of the organization to change. To contribute to this decision process, the lawyer's allegiance cannot be to the individual manager, nor to the formal corporate hierarchy. The lawyer's allegiance must be understood by others, and by himself, as an "allegiance to the entity."[479]

---

[476] Although Professor Coffee is skeptical about the role of staffs, seeing internal staffs as captured and external staff as too distant, he does recognize that, for decisions within the ambit of the profession's expertise, professional expertise can substitute for mini-boards. *Id.* at 1187 (discussing accountants). He notes, however, that when there is a range of generally accepted accounting principles and that the client controls choice within this range the accountant's professional expertise is limited. *Id.* at 1188. When lawyers mix legal and business advice, this limitation can be overcome.

[477] G. Hazard, Ethics in the Practice of Law 55 (1978).

[478] *Ibid.* Hazard suggests that managers ridicule this proposal because it is a way to multiply legal fees while giving the lawyer a cop-out. *Ibid.* While it does increase fees, involved managers may be grateful to have the corporation pay for it. The key problem is that it is a cop-out to managers, who, like lawyers, have to balance conflicting interests and responsibilities.

[479] Model Code of Professional Responsibility, EC, 5-18 (1970). The Model Rules rejected this language. In the Model Rules, the lawyer "represents the organization." Rule 1.13(a). The potentially more inclusive duties of having an "allegiance to the entity" appear to be rejected.

THE IMAGE OF THE INFLUENTIAL LAWYER AND ITS CRITICS

These two proposals point to the corporation's need for lawyers who can influence the exercise of managerial discretion by drawing on their knowledge of the constitutive organization as well as their technical expertise. To some extent, lawyer-as-influential-counselor is the traditionally dominant image of the attorney.[480] This image recognizes that corporate decisions often result from a negotiated order between various corporate managers and the lawyer. It stresses that the lawyer should use his influence in this process to implement actions consistent with the law. The traditional image assumes that the lawyer, who has influence, arranges his practice so he can, without abusing his client's trust, advise against and work to defeat corporate plans or tactics that, even if not illegal, strike him as contrary to the public interest or violative of inchoate, emerging norms of socially responsible business behavior. It envisions that client goals are not arbitrary, subjective and incapable of public discourse. Consequently, the lawyer cannot retreat into expertise and claim that the only overriding norms are those of procedural justice.[481]

Today, the image of the influential counselor is in some disrepute.[482] For example, although Professor Hazard draws on the image in telling us that "[t]he practice of law largely involves persuading people to do things that are very unpleasant,"[483] he explicitly states that the "attorney-client relationship is not one of tutelage. The attorney is what is today called a 'resource person....'"[484]

Two factors propel this movement away from the influential counselor image. The first is a general social distrust of moral discourse. The second is a desire to minimize cognitive dissonance by re-writing professional norms to mirror current professional behavior.

---

[480] For a discussion, see Kagan & Rosen, "On the Social Significance of Large Law Firm Practice," 37 Stan. L. Rev. 399 (1985) [Hereafter cited as Kagan & Rosen]. In 1907, John Dos Passos, Sr. described the practice of the corporate bar in the following terms: "The lawyer boldly enters into the business end of his client's transaction—he sells him prudence and experience, sometimes even usurping the client's discretion and judgment." quoted in J. W. Hurst, The Growth of American Law 342 (1950). Chairman Wherry of the Committee on Professional Ethics of the N.Y.S. Bar Assoc., in 1948 stated: "The function of the lawyer is constantly developing. Today, he is called upon less often for dramatic forensic exploits than for wise counsel in every phase of life." Quoted in H. Drinker, Legal Ethics x, n.10 (1953). See also Model Code of Professional Responsibility EC 7-3—7-5 (1970) (but see EC 7-1); Smigel, The Wall Street Lawyer 4-5 passim (1964).

[481] Cf. Simon, "The Ideology of Advocacy: Procedural Justice and Professional Ethics," 1978 Wisc. L. Rev. 29, 59 n.70.

[482] This was the empirical finding of a survey done in connection with Kagan & Rosen.

[483] G. Hazard, Ethics in the Practice of Law 147 (1978).

[484] Id. at 138.

A confusion between the image of the influential counselor and that of the "community professional," whose influence is based on shared community values, partially explains the rejection of the former.[485] Given the disintegration of natural communities and the heightened sensitivity to pervasive social conflict, it is argued that a professional should not try to be influential. He is simply using "neutral" expertise to mask his dominance. The next section deals with this argument's lack of cogency in the corporate context.

The argument is also historically suspect. Professionalism emerged not in natural communities but in civil society.[486] Moreover, to predicate professional influence on the existence of natural communities is to forget that professionals create moral communities.[487] In the concluding section of this chapter, I argue it is precisely the corporation's differentiation, its lack of "community" and well-shared values, that requires lawyers to provide influential service.

The conditions of large firm practice also lead to the rejection of the claim that minimal corporate service demands an influential counselor. In large firms, the influential counselor style is likely to be extraordinary rather than ordinary.[488] To consider current practice valuable, one must deny that the lawyer has a duty to build a practice in which he has influence. Finding value in current practice, moreover, depends on justifying the market for corporate legal services, a market determined both by lawyers' willingness to offer certain types of practice and by clients' demands for particular types of service. This market can be challenged based on internal criteria, in terms of the "freedom" of the market, and on external criteria, in terms of the values maximized by the market. In discussing paternalism below, I will reject the claim that the lawyer has a duty not to exercise influence. By examining imperfections in the market for corporate legal services, I will then evaluate the market justification for not creating an influential practice.[489]

---

[485] Mindes, "Comment: Defining Professionalism in the Bar: Comments on Landon's Article," 1982 ABF Res. J. 1163, 1166-67.

[486] See M. S. Larson, The Rise of Professionalism: A Sociological Analysis (1977). Even Larson, who is skeptical about professionalism, sees its potential for creating moral discourse in civil society. *Id.* at 243-44.

[487] The clergy is the most obvious example. See also Mindes, *supra*, at 1172.

[488] See Kagan & Rosen, 37 Stan. L. Rev. 399 (1985). We there apply the argument, from sociology, that the organizational context of professional work determines the behavior of professionals to large firm corporate lawyers. For a review of the general sociological literature on this phenomenon, see Tuma & Grimes, "A Comparison of Models of Role Orientations of Professionals in a Research Oriented University," 26 Ad. Sci. Q. 187, 205 (1981). More generally, wherever problem-setting holds, or lawyers are risk analysis specialists, the dominant image of influential counselor is a rarity.

[489] This analysis is compatible with the most thoroughgoing extant critique of the influential lawyer: D. Rosenthal, Lawyer and Client: Who's In Charge? (1974) (analyzing the paternalism of personal injury attorneys). Rosenthal recognized that his discussion may not

PATERNALISM: ARE THERE STANDING OBLIGATIONS NOT TO BE INFLUENTIAL?

It is not difficult to imagine cases in which having the lawyer influence corporate decision-making would improve client service. The current organization of the market for corporate legal services, however, makes it unlikely that the lawyer will be influential even when it is desirable or necessary. To justify this result, it is argued that the lawyer has obligations that demand he resist using influence, regardless of the needs in individual cases. The argument asserts that the influential lawyer over-reaches his role, is irresponsibly paternalistic, and engages in a conflict of interest with the client.[490]

The argument that the influential lawyer is irresponsibly paternalistic builds on a rejection of the traditional social function of professionals. Professions traditionally have justified their privileged positions by claiming that professional standards, not merely client demand, govern what they produce. "The client, unlike the customer, is not always right."[491] Especially in the practice of law, where the client's law-related decisions and directives significantly affect third party and collective interests, it might be necessary and justified to override client demand. An influential lawyer might not only serve the client more effectively, he might also improve our decentralized system of legal control, by sensitizing the client to the demands of the law.

Traditionally, professions transcended the seller-customer relation because they met the challenge of moral difficulties, including evil, and emerged not only unscathed but triumphant.[492] Today, legal professionals,

---

apply to corporate lawyers. *Id.* at 148 (suggesting a study such as this one). According to Rosenthal, what it means for clients to "be active participants," "sharing responsibility," making "positive contribution[s]," that improve "[t]he caliber of professional service" and meet "[s]tandards of professional and client performance" will vary between different types of clients in different situations. *Id.* at 154. In other words, professional norms must be evaluated in terms of the organizational context of the profession's work. Professional norms must also be evaluated in terms of the external legitimacy of the different contexts. According to Rosenthal, the problem of lawyer control "advances or recedes according to the values, skills, interests, and experience which dominate the thoughts of men in particular societies and social settings." *Id.* at 152.

[490] Hegland, "Beyond Enthusiasm and Commitment," 13 Ariz. L. Rev. 805, 811-17 (1971); Lorne, "The Corporate and Securities Adviser, The Public Interest, and Professional Ethics," 76 Mich. L. Rev. 425 (1978).

[491] Marshall, "The Recent History of Professionalism in Relation to Social Structure and Social Policy," 158, 166 in Class, Citizenship and Social Development: Essays of T. H. Marshall (1965).

[492] Abbott, "Status and Status Strain in the Professions," 86 Am. J. Soc. 819, 829 (1981): "To see a crime, to converse with an insane person, to nurse a sick relative—these are defiling acts for an everyday conscience, mind, or body.... [T]hose who possess the cultural apparatus to touch and possibly control these social impurities assume their charismatic status.... [The professional] touches the problems and difficulties of our world without personal defilement."

fearing they cannot resist, let alone control, the moral pollution around them, retreat into technical virtuosity and specialized expertise.[493] Cleanliness has become the aspiration of the profession. Lawyers seek purity by defining their cases and their work solely in terms of the abstract norms of professional knowledge.[494] At the same time, they argue that to do anything else is dangerous and potentially immoral. To be anything other than a supplier of technical information is to dominate clients. At its best, it is paternalistic. At worst, it is power mongering. The claim is that there is no ethical way for the lawyer to meet moral difficulties.[495]

There are four principal reasons for developing standing obligations to guard against paternalistic judgments: (1) Individuals have different value priorities and are the best judges of their own interests; (2) Individuals have different access to information and therefore can best judge their own interests; (3) Maximizing individuals expectations generates creativity and self-realization; and (4) There is intrinsic value to self-determination.[496]

The first three reasons suggest that a lawyer, who is advising a corporate client, needs to understand the situation before he proffers advice. To be responsibly influential, a lawyer needs to develop a practice in which he has access to the range of value priorities within the corporation, information relevant to the decision, and knowledge of the scope of alternative actions.[497]

---

[493] The attack on professionals is not limited to lawyers. We live in a society that distrusts trustees. Corporate boards, for example, also are under attack. It is proposed that corporate boards contain directors representing various interests, rather than directors who can be trusted to balance the total picture. But, the lawyer cannot retreat so easily. The "purely" representative function is also under attack. Simon, "The Ideology of Advocacy: Procedural Justice and Professional Ethics," 1978 Wisc. L. Rev, 29, 51: "In becoming the tool of the client, the lawyer does not merely enable his client to vindicate expectations based on a determinate set of rights. Rather, he becomes an agency for the exercise of discretionary power."

[494] Thus, professionals who cannot retreat into expertise such as those who deal with emotional relations, have the lowest status in the profession.

[495] Interestingly, while lawyers make this claim, they also recall instances in which they triumphed over potential evil. See Kagan & Rosen, 37 Stan L. Rev. 399 (1985).

[496] This discussion follows A. Goldman, The Moral Foundations of Professional Ethics (1980).

[497] This precondition appears to justify today's lawyers' avoidance of influence. They say that they are ignorant about the business, the context in which the problem emerges, and everything outside their legal specialty. While, in many cases, "these arguments are used merely as rationalizations for the lawyer placing blinders on his own range of vision," Redlich, "Should a Lawyer Cross the Murky Divide?," 31 Bus. Lawyer 478, 481 (1975), as the discussions of large firm marketing practices, *infra*, and of specialization and problem-setting, *supra*, reveal, many a lawyer today is engaged in a practice in which he cannot be influential because of "the nature of the lawyer's involvement, his relationship with the client, his limited knowledge of the facts, and the narrow issue on which he has been asked for legal advice." *Id.* at 480. But, as Redlich concludes, this is "really directed to the weight of the evidence rather than to admissibility." *Ibid.* It is directed to how influential the lawyer should become. It admits that responsible influence is possible and desirable. It

These reasons do not justify an overriding prohibition on lawyers' exercising influence. Clearly there are instances in which the lawyer can be informed and offer productive suggestions.

The fourth reason for standing obligations guarding against paternalism is problematic in the corporate context. It assumes some sort of autonomy rights for corporations. Unlike individuals, corporations have no rightful claim to develop as outlaws. Compared to natural individuals, corporations have more restricted rights to self-determination.[498] For the lawyer not to try to further corporate legal compliance requires that the client have significant moral interests outweighing the value of obedience to the law. Managers' obligation to use their power legally and responsibly, however, limits their moral rights.[499] Consequently, the fourth argument, like the first three, does not support an obligation by lawyers not to pressure the corporation to abide by the law.[500]

---

simply cites features of the legal services market that hamper the rendering of influential advice. This argument's force depends on whether the lawyer has a duty to create a practice in which he can be influential. If so, then he has a duty to alter the conditions limiting his practice.

[498] See M. Cohen, Persons and Organizations: A Legal Theory (manuscript, 1984) (rejecting all autonomy rights for corporations). See also discussion of ALI draft, *infra*.

[499] See discussion of ALI draft, *infra*. This argument conflicts with the general rule that "[t]he client has ultimate authority to determine the purposes to be served by legal representation." Model Rules, Rule 1.2, Comment, at 4.

[500] The presumed existence of these standing obligations has furthered corporate and lawyer improprieties. At least in certain circumstances, reviewing courts have rejected the argument against paternalism, finding that minimal loyalty includes a duty to influence the client towards law compliance. In the National Student Marketing fraud, for example, the lawyers claimed that the asserted duties to influence the client was not within their job. They argued that SEC demands would "require lawyers to go beyond their accepted role." SEC v. National Student Marketing 457 F. Supp. 682, 713 (D.D.C. 1978). They argued that the decisions were not legal ones. They belonged to the corporate decision-making processes; they were business judgments. Consequently, requiring the lawyer to influence such judgments would inhibit "client's business judgments." *Ibid.* (quoting from Max E. Meyer and Louis F. Schauer, Post-Trial Memorandum and Proposed Conclusions of Law of Defendants Lord, Bissell & Brook, at 98). The court rejected both of these arguments. They concluded that the extent of the lawyer's role and his obligations to interject himself in corporate decisions depended on his duty to serve the corporation as an entity: "[A]ttorneys cannot rest on asserted business judgments as justifications for their failure to make a legal decision pursuant to their fiduciary responsibilities to client shareholders." *Id.* at 713-14.

In certain instances, the bar also has been careful to require lawyers participating in "business judgments" to fulfill their professional responsibilities. When, in connection with an illegal campaign contribution, the CEO of American Airlines argued his decision was made in his business capacity and was unrelated to his also happening to be a lawyer, the Committee on Grievances of the Association of the Bar of the City of New York rejected the claim, finding him subject to professional standards: "We cannot disregard the fact that you served for ten years as general counsel to the corporation and before that you were, for many years a member of a prominent law firm. This Committee holds that a line executive who is also a lawyer has an even greater obligation, as one who knows the law, to stand against practices that betray the trust upon which the very life of our business economy

The argument against paternalism's force derives from a subsidiary assumption implicitly rejected in the above discussion. The assumption is that lawyers and managers are morally isolated from each other. Lawyers can never understand client values because values are purely subjective and incapable of being communicated. No matter how informed the lawyer becomes, he cannot understand client values. This argument clearly is too strong. As stated, it would apply to managers as, well. This argument's implicit solipsism is incompatible with all forms of organization. Yet, a sense of lawyers and clients at odds remains. The traditional trust between lawyer and client that allowed the lawyer to advise against and work to defeat irresponsible corporate plans or tactics, seems to have disappeared. Clients only want lawyers to be conduits, sometimes helping them evade the law. For a lawyer to restrain clients requires him to be a policeman: external and authoritarian. A lawyer influential in corporate decision-making would as often help clients evade the law, as help them live up to it. Consequently, it is better for lawyers to avoid building a practice in which they have influence.[501]

This argument, which has some support in legal ethics' discussions, claims not to draw on a theory of autonomy rights, but on a theory of legal positivism: it is the corporation's choice whether to obey the law or face sanctions.[502] Whatever legitimacy legal positivism has for individuals, it holds little for corporations. The laws of corporate governance do not take a positivistic approach. Section 2.01 of the ALI Draft on Corporate Governance stipulates that "even if corporate profits and shareholder gain are not thereby enhanced, the corporation, in the conduct of its business...is obliged to the same extent as a natural person, to act within the boundaries of the law."[503] It explicitly rejects Holmesian positivism: "[D]ollar liability is not a 'price' that can ethically be paid for the privilege of engaging in legally wrongful conduct.[504] Furthermore, the corporation is told that it "should not rest

---

depends." N.Y. L. J. 1 (April 25, 1974), quoted in Forrow, "The Corporate Law Department Lawyer: Counsel to the Entity," 1797, 1827 (1979).

[501] This is a Pontius Pilate argument. Although it allows lawyer's hands to remain clean, it does little to help the corporations.

[502] Yet, when it is developed, this argument does draw on a theory of autonomy rights. No one argues that lawyers should be conduits for *malum in se*. It is only a theory of autonomy rights that allows one to violate *malum prohibitum*, but not *malum in se*, because only in the second are the autonomy rights of others overridden.

[503] American Law Institute, Principles of Corporate Governance and Structure: Restatement and Recommendations, Tent. Draft 1, Rule 2.01 at 17 (April 1, 1982).

[504] *Id.* at 24. In the commentary three exceptions are listed: where appeal is made to a higher law (*id.* at 25); where the law is not enforced (*ibid.*: Where "a departure from a legal rule is explicitly condoned by both popular morality and relevant government authorities." The Holmesian example, not specially sanctioning contractual breaches, is given as a separate example but appears to be explained, as in Holmes, by the issue of enforceability.); and where because of the consequences strong moral arguments argue against compliance (*id.* at 25-26: Where "noncompliance could be morally justified under the principle of necessity."). These exceptions may negate the rule's strong language. Cannot the corporation use the second exception to argue that inadequately funded regulatory bodies,

simply on past precedents or an unduly literal reading of statutes and regu-lations."[505]

To meet these duties, corporate managers must rely on lawyers. In guarding against paternalism, however many corporate attorneys base their opinions on just the type of cost-benefit analysis the ALI draft proscribes. Afraid to be paternalistic, many lawyers do not interpret laws in terms of their goals. The ALI draft denies that moral advice is purely subjective. By withholding moral advice, lawyers prevent managers from meeting their duties.[506]

Furthermore, corporate duties require the lawyer to help create pro-cedures that detect illegal and irresponsible exercises of discretion. The ALI draft requires the corporation to recognize and detect legal problems. When lawyers retreat into their craft expertise or accept problems as defined by the client, they inhibit the client's ability to recognize problems. The corporation has a duty not to wait until it is caught. Lawyers are not violating client rights, but helping them meet their duties, when they practice preventive law. Preventive law, properly understood, involves more than instituting formal compliance programs. Because corporate procedures are subject to loose interpretations and lax enforcement, the lawyer also must influence individual managers' exercise of their discretion.[507]

The corporate governance draft rejects not only the moral isolation buttressing the argument against paternalism, but also the organization theory in the Rules of Professional Conduct. The ALI draft begins with the assumption, as Eisenberg put it, that the "model of a pyramid is inadequate" to describe a corporation.[508] It seeks to create plural bases of responsibility. The corporation is conceived of not as a monarchy, but as a federal system in which actors' different moral perceptions are necessary for governance. According to the ALI draft, many distinct entities within the corporation have a duty to find the law and use it to guide their judgment. Given this

---

the rule not the exception in our society, provide a license for noncompliance? What can the corporation do but fall back on the explicitly rejected cost-benefit analysis to determine public commitment to enforcement? Cannot the corporation also use the third exception to return to cost-benefit analysis? If utilitarian analysis is possible in the case of necessity (and the discussion appears to say it is, *id.* at 26), how can we reply to the manager who claims violating an antitrust law is the only way to save the jobs of the people in his department?

[505] *Id.* at 25.

[506] Note, this does not relieve directors and officers of their duties to implement the aspirations of ALI Rule 2.01(a). See ALI Rule 4.01 and the Bar Chris decision where reliance on professional advice was deemed admissible, but not conclusive.

[507] This means that the current organization of legal practice, where the lawyer adopts a "wait in his office" routine, is inappropriate. "Compliance is often no once and for all matter but requires constant vigilance." E. Bardach & R. Kagan, Going by the Book: The Problem of Regulatory Unreasonableness 63 (1982) (quoting Steven Kelman).

[508] M. Eisenberg, The Structure of the Corporation: A Legal Analysis 1 (1976).

duty, lawyers do not abuse client trust by trying to influence the corporation's actions and by working to create decision processes that support legal aspirations.

THE MARKET ARGUMENT: THE NEED FOR FIDUCIARY STANDARDS

Large firms' marketing strategy hampers their abilities to be influential counselors. Because they sell highly specialized technical skills on a non-recurrent basis, they are often ignorant of conflicts within the corporation and of information relevant to policy choices. Nor do they develop the personal relationships with corporate actors that might help them to be agents for change. Furthermore, the financial advantages of not customizing their products and the security of retreating into a well-known technical role encourages large firm attorneys to avoid creating opportunities to exercise influence. They offer their clients craft-based skills, not consultation on corporate choices. They offer to supply information but not to become part of the corporate decision process.[509]

Since lawyers are client-serving professionals, the types of practice that lawyers supply can be tested by whether they meet client needs. Traditionally, because it was feared that the market itself would not create an appropriate supply of professional services, lawyers developed fiduciary duties to supply certain services. Because competition is muted in professional markets, professionals create demand and clients cannot effectively evaluate professional service.[510] Whether fiduciary standards will be reinvigorated, to offset a professionally generated incapacity to exercise influence, should depend in part on whether the existing market serves client needs. If it doesn't, the profession must engage in a process of self-criticism. As the provision of legal services to clients of ambulance chasers,[511] the poor, and the middle classes has been challenged,[512] so can the services provided to corporate lawyers.[513]

---

[509] For an elaboration of these points, see Kagan & Rosen.

[510] For a discussion, see Leubsdorf, "Three Models of Professional Reform," 67 Cornell L. Rev. 1021 (1982).

[511] Reichstein, "Ambulance Chasing: A Case Study of Deviation and Control within the Legal Profession," 13 Soc. Prob. 3 (1965). For historical materials, see J. Auerbach, Unequal Justice 48-50 (1976).

[512] L. Brickman & R. Lempert, eds., The Role of Research in the Delivery of Legal Services: Working Papers and Conference Proceedings (May 1976).

[513] In the context of corporate practice, the analysis of the delivery of legal services has largely been undertaken at an individual level. There are good and bad lawyers: "A main difference between a good attorney and a poor attorney is the number of roles and the sensitivity in determining which lawyer role to play in which situation, that a lawyer has at his command." D. Rosenthal, Lawyer and Client: Who's In Charge? 110 (1974) (quoting from a lawyer interview, describing general legal practice). It is also possible, however, to make general arguments about the ethical import of the market for the delivery of corporate

Because of corporations' sophistication, one might expect the delivery of corporate legal services could be left to the market. It might be argued that the profession need not impose minimal duties of service because corporate clients can easily bargain for the precise service they need.[514] In the six corporations studied, however, I didn't uncover any enhanced ability to integrate legal information. The utilization of lawyers demanded professional judgment to structure the relationship.[515]

Even sophisticated corporations cannot assess their demand function for legal services. As many corporations have learnt in developing corporate legal departments, they have bought more legal services than they really "need." Furthermore, they have also bought less than they really need. Operating under time, market and intra-corporate pressures, managers are likely to err in demanding legal services and in interpreting the information they receive.[516] Because control measures within corporations may slip and erode, lawyers who simply supply information, will generally not help the manager responsibly to apply his discretion.[517] Consequently, the actual demand for corporate legal services may reflect professionally created demand and fall short of what a perfectly informed, unified and prudent corporation would demand.

Does the availability of inside counsel justify outside counsel's failure to supply influential advice? Whether inside counsel well serve the corporation is an empirical question whose answer will vary from company to company.

---

legal services. For example, Lloyd Cutler describes those firms which have not "organize[d] their practice in a way that is designed to surface and resolve ethical issues" as having failed in their professional duties. Cutler, "The Role of the Private Law Firm," 33 Bus. Lawyer 1549, 1550 (1978) (arguing for the adoption of the two-partner rule).

[514] For decisions allowing parties who are capable of bargaining, such as sophisticated corporations, to replace professional duties with private bargains, see "Developments in the Law: Conflicts of Interest in the Legal Profession," 94 Harv. L. Rev. 1244, 1311-15 (1981); Boston Bar Ass'n Comm. on Prof. Resp., Op. No. 79-3, cited in Leubsdorf, "Three Models of Professional Reform," 67 Cornell L. Rev. 1021, 1031 n.73 (1982) (if client requests cursory opinion, lawyer may supply it).

[515] This result appears to seriously undermine the contract model of professional relationships. If any clients should be able to forsake the fiduciary model, large corporations should.

[516] Although the corporate lawyer's duty is to the organization, individual managers decide when to call on a lawyer and what services to request. Existing demand therefore, always falls short of real demand. On the problems of interpreting legal information, examine the case, *supra*. See also C. Stone, Where the Law Ends: The Social Control of Corporate Behavior 68 (1975): When the lawyer merely responds to managers' requests, all too often, "the law may be there, but it lacks the persuasiveness, reality, and immediacy of the other, competing aspects of the employee's environment" (emphasis omitted).

[517] Cf. E. Bardach & R. Kagan, Going By The Book: The Problem of Regulatory Unreasonableness 224 (1982): "Despite internal preventive rules, irresponsibility and dangerous actions continue to occur, stemming from the drift of managerial attention, conflicting goals and pressures, inadequate supervisory and reporting systems and insufficient power on the part of internal regulators."

Outside counsel must understand organizational dynamics to evaluate the corporate legal department's service. Unfortunately, outside firms' marketing practices mean that they are not well-situated to evaluate very much of inside counsel's advice. Outside counsel are too distant from the information and the managers.

In short, the current market doesn't meet client needs. The type of practice offered certainly doesn't meet the obligations stated in the ALI draft. Often it will not meet corporate economic interests either. Corporations are beset by bureaucratic pathologies, where managers displace corporate goals, and political pathologies, where decisions evade organizational controls. To serve their corporate clients, who are plagued by pathologies, lawyers must influence individual managers and improve the corporate decision processes' discipline.[518]

CONCLUSION: DIFFERENTIATION AND THE THRUST TO INTEGRATION

One reason it is difficult to determine who is the corporate client is that the corporation is not simply a hierarchical order. To be adaptive, the corporation must yield some discretion to those who work for it. To serve the corporation, lawyers must develop a practice that meets the interdependence engendered by differentiation.[519]

Because of differentiation, lawyers cannot be mere information suppliers. The organization may not consult a lawyer at appropriate times, may unduly restrict what it asks from the lawyer, and may not supply the lawyer with enough information. Similar problems face everyone who works for corporations. Like managers, lawyers face strategic choice questions; decisions are not given but are arrived at by individual and organizational choices.[520] As managers cannot rely on the invisible hand of the market or the controls of the organization to restrain them, neither can lawyers.

Because corporations are differentiated, the lawyer must exercise personal influence and cannot simply depend on the sanctions of hierarchical control. As Beckenstein and Gabel's survey of practicing corporate attorneys finds, formal rules are not only insufficient but also are counterproductive. They report that "procedures to reduce management discretion where there

---

[518] It could be argued that this section presents a challenge for corporations, not for their lawyers: Corporations must alter what they demand from lawyers. This overlooks imperfections in the supply market. It also overlooks the difficulties in controlling managerial use of lawyers. Consequently, responsible client service demands imposing fiduciary standards on lawyers.

[519] Cf. W. Kornhauser, Scientists in Industry: Conflict and Accommodation 197-99 (1962): "New goals for scientific activity have emerged in the course of the growing interdependence of research and industry."

[520] Strategic choice arises when the task transcends technique. Choice is a necessity. Thus, how the task is performed cannot be morally neutral. A. MacIntyre, After Virtue 74 (1981).

is a legal risk" and "veto power of counsel" over relevant decisions are "counterproductive" to legal compliance.[521]

In a differentiated corporation, the lawyer should be involved in guiding the exercise of discretion and in elaborating the processes of corporate decision-making.[522] Decisions are not determined solely by command. The threat of legal sanction is intertwined with judgments about business options, corporate policies, culture and character. However the lawyer acts, he will be a force in the immediate decision's politics. His advice will reshape corporate coalitions and decision processes. In a differentiated corporation, the threat of sanction does not do the lawyer's work; in fact, the possibility of punishment forces the lawyer to examine, in particular cases, how the organization determines its interests.[523]

---

[521] Beckenstein & Gabel, "Antitrust Compliance: Results of a Survey of Legal Opinion," 51 Antitrust L. J. 461, 462 (1983). They also were skeptical of risk analysis lawyering, reporting that "conscious avoidance of actions that are legal, but might attract litigation or investigation" was counterproductive. *Id.* at 464. Notwithstanding these findings, the authors suggest lawyers perform audit functions. They appear not to give great weight to the argument that lawyers avoid an auditing role "because it casts counsel in the role of a policeman rather than an ally in an effort to run the company profitably and legally." *Id.* at 477. In another article, they report that very few of the companies surveyed had reached the preferred "decision restructuring" compliance strategy, where "the company management integrates compliance with its normal management function." Beckenstein, Gabel & Roberts, "An Executive's Guide to Antitrust Compliance," Harv. Bus. Rev. 94, 101 (1983). They are at a loss to explain this result. The research here indicates that when lawyers act either as suppliers of information about legal risks (Beckenstein, Gabel and Roberts' "basic decision enhancing" strategy) or as auditors (the "advanced decision enhancing" strategy), they lose their ability to direct the corporation to the "decision restructuring" strategy, the strategy most likely to result in law compliance. The authors recognize that the "decision restructuring" strategy "stems more from a positive alliance...than from a negative policing effort" (*ibid.*), yet see the problem as all one-sided: "Managers have not integrated themselves in the process." *Id.* at 95. They fail to understand how lawyers can undermine corporate commitments to law compliance. They do not understand the organizational dynamics to which lawyers point when they eschew audit functions. Lawyers need to refrain from risk analysis and auditing to integrate themselves into the compliance process. Preserving commitments to law compliance demands influence not command. See discussion rejecting mini-boards and Chapter Three, *supra*.

[522] Stone reaches a similar conclusion with respect to the ambit of the law in C. Stone, Where the Law Ends: The Social Control of Corporate Behavior 121 (1975). The conclusion in the text appears to reflect the current practice of inside counsel. Survey materials reveal that inside counsel give advice on management decisions. Beckenstein & Gabel, "Antitrust Compliance: Results of a Survey of Legal Opinion," 51 Antitrust L.J. 462, 490 (1983)(17.3% of survey said inside counsel always give advice on management decisions, 53.4% often, 19.4% sometimes, 6.0% seldom, and 3.9% never. In the future, inside counsel should be even more involved in corporate decision processes: 64.7% reported an increase in advice during last decade and 1.0% reported a decrease. 95.5% reported that involvement in decision processes was "desirable" to "essential" for promoting antitrust compliance).

[523] A similar conclusion is reached in Palmieri, "The Lawyer's Role: An Argument for Change," Harv. Bus. Rev. 30, 31 (Nov.-Dec. 1978): "The biggest problem...is the corporate lawyer's traditional conception of his own role.... [T]he existence of tough standards on the books...is [un]likely to make an important difference in the quality of corporate governance

The differentiated corporation is not identical to the undifferentiated one.[524] To some extent this is simply because they contain different corporate actors. Although the values of corporate actors do influence organizational behavior[525] and a differentiated corporation does include actors holding legal professional values, this is only part of the story.[526] In a differentiated corporation, legal service affects the goals of corporate decision-making.[527]

The service of lawyers, like the work of other professionals in corporations, both reflects and fuels debureaucratization. The presence of lawyers poses problems of coordination and integration. The conflicts and tensions professionals generate within the organization cannot be eliminated because they improve the corporation's efficiency.[528] Nor can they be

---

unless counsel is ready, willing, and able to point out the problems in the context of specific situations." "The lawyer's traditional reluctance to be drawn into 'matters of business judgment' often insulates him from important informations and leaves him without sufficient understanding of the problems.... Corporate counsel has to be energetic in assisting the board to develop a philosophy of governance and a process so structured that, formally or informally,...[they] enhance...sound decisions...." *Id.* at 38.

[524] Professor Hazard observes that "[o]rganizational clients...seek legal advice...as a matter of routine." G. Hazard, Ethics in the Practice of Law 140 (1978). He does not see any moral implications in this development. For the emergence of fiduciary standards to integrate differentiated exchanges, generally, see Anderson, "Conflicts of Interest: Efficiency, Fairness and Corporate Structure," 25 U.C.L.A. L. Rev. 738 (1978). Professor Anderson pays no attention to the role of professionalization in developing fiduciary standards, as reflected in her conclusion that managerial discretion should serve only shareholders. *Id.* at 777. Her position envisions organization only as a transaction cost. It pays no attention to the moral lives of corporate actors. Business school literature on corporate social responsibility has been more attentive to the normative implications of management's professionalization, as has been the professed orientations of managers. In a survey of managers, only 1% responded with Anderson's view that "a corporation's duty is to its owners and only its owners." (41% responded that "a corporation's duty is to serve as fairly and equitably as it can the interests of four sometimes competing groups—owners, employees, customers, and the public.") Krishnan, "Business Philosophy and Executive Responsibility," in Managing Corporate Social Responsibility 23, 31 (A. Carroll ed. 1977).

[525] See studies of organizations in different cultures, e.g., R. Dore, British Factory-Japanese Factory: The Origins of National Diversity in Employment Relations (1973); H. Hartmann, Authority and Organization in German Management (1954).

[526] Because this is not the whole story, the argument does not turn on whether we have added "good" people, or people with higher or lower, ethical standards than is the norm in business.

[527] As Kornhauser found with the emergence of scientists in industry: "[T]he very act of establishing a research unit, and of hiring increased numbers of scientists with advanced degrees, engenders commitments to more fundamental research." W. Kornhauser, Scientists in Industry: Conflict and Accommodation 42 (1962).

[528] *Id.* at 197 and passim. Fuller explains this in his "Sixth Law of Associations": "In the normal course of its development an association tends to move toward dominance by the legal principle. At the end of this development, the principles of shared commitment sinks into a state of quiescence until some crisis, such as an external threat to the association, brings it back to life." The Principles of Social Order: Selected Essays of Lon L. Fuller 78 (K. Winston. ed. 1981). Professionals increase adaptive potential by anticipating crises as well

---

resolved by appropriate hierarchical ordering. As long as corporations employ professionals to serve staff functions, there will be "overlapping and crosscutting lines of authority and subunit mission."[529]

Differentiated organizations need professionals to control divisive conflicts. Managers' discretion enables them to evade command. A differentiated corporation is not a natural community. There is no homogeneity of values and procedures are subject to alterations. In this situation, corporations turn to professionals, including lawyers. They need professionals to exercise influence.[530] They want professionals to elaborate corporate interests and commitments. In short, professionalism "makes the use of discretion predictable."[531] But professionalism is in tension with inward-looking bureaucratization. It fights bureaucracy in the name of improved methods and professional autonomy. Professionalism means that "[d]issatisfaction with the structural limitations of one's work and the social uses of one's productive activity need not remain a private crisis of conscience."[532] Corporations must rely on professionals but they cannot totally constrain them. Hence, part of a profession's duty is to develop the standards for the influential service organizational clients require.

The lawyer's task, in exercising influence, is a difficult one. As in administrative agencies, the values to be upheld by the organization[533] often

---

as by dealing with them. In other words, professionalism is an antidote to the routinization of charisma and the iron law of oligarchy. Lawyers also improve efficiency by suggesting alternatives and mitigating the incidence of unreasonable regulations. "Legal rules are not an effective device for directing human energies to those places where they can be most creatively and effectively applied. In *Democracy in America*, Tocqueville observed that 'a government can only dictate strict rules.'... The real contribution of the private association may be to hold before the public possibilities it did not know existed..." *Id.* at 77-78 (from Fuller's "Fifth Law of Associations").

[529] Peterson, "Some Consequences of Differentiation," in Power in Organizations 144, 144 (M. Zald ed. 1970).

[530] E.g., outside management consultants do not only provide technical expertise. In a survey of executives, Seney found that only 23% cited "special skills and know-how" as the reason for using consultants. 11% used consultants to stimulate new definitions of the problem, 22% to change organizational operations, and 13% to train organizational personnel. (Consultants were used for services that outside counsel today perform in two areas beyond expertise: providing an independent review of corporate work (14%) and focusing on tasks to which management couldn't give sufficient attention (13%).) W. Seney, Effective Use of Business Consultants 17 (1963). Were lawyers to understand corporate reliance on professionals, they would offer a different set of services.

[531] M. S. Larson, The Rise of Professionalism: A Sociological Analysis 198 (1977).

[532] *Id.* at 243. Larson further claims that professionalism can support "the development of new norms and new criteria which are alien to the capitalist logic." *Id.* at 244. One need not agree with her assessment of capitalism's limiting and de-humanizing logic to recognize that professional principles can conflict with predatory capitalist principles.

[533] Which include accuracy, timeliness, consistency, equality, efficiency, and respect for individuals. See J. Mashaw, Bureaucratic Justice: Managing Social Security Disability Claims (1983).

conflict and any resolution of these tensions must take into account its practicality, implementability and cost. The task is to build on the ongoing machinery and commitments of the organization to make law compliance mesh with organizational routines and channels. The influential lawyer must educate, organize and respond. The influential lawyer must be a master of organizational analysis.534 In the discussion of problem-setting and salient conflict, I sketched the first elements of such minimal duties.

Although the profession prefers to avoid discussions of the influential lawyer, the growth of inside counsel has put it on the profession's agenda. Today, inside counsel must solve the dilemmas of how to gain, use and retain influence: "[I]t is clear that inside lawyers have no defined limits on their engagement."535 As a result, the inside counsel faces problems for which professional rules give him no guidance. How far should he probe for facts?536 Does he have any responsibility to create compliance programs? Should he take managers' problems as presented to him?537 Should he structure his practice to influence corporate decisions?538 A reprise of the traditional image of the influential counselor, but analyzed in terms of the

---

534 Without such analysis, arguing for the influential lawyer might have the result "that the lawyer is responsible to everyone and to no one." G. Hazard, Ethics in the Practice of Law 55 (1978). Professor Hazard fears this result is inevitable because the influential lawyer must be an "impartial arbitrator," "playing God." *Id.* at 62, 65. To Hazard, the lawyer, to have influence, must be able to harmonize the interests of all parties. *Id.* at 64-65. But Hazard derives the duty to be influential from a consideration of the lawyer's duties to others and the legal system. His discussion is one of the lawyer's maximal loyalty. To Hazard, the "lawyer is inevitably a moral actor" (*id.* at 59) because "he has duties to both his clients and others." *Id.* at 56. Unlike the current discussion, Hazard does not find that minimal duties of client service require the lawyer to be influential. (Hazard does not have a conception of the lawyer taking strategic organizational action. See *id.* at xii, where organizational variables are not listed as determinants of corporate action.) The argument here is that a lawyer is a moral actor because corporate structures are not given but must be built. Note, making the lawyer responsible to create a practice in which he can be influential does not imply that corporate and public interests always coincide. If the lawyer cannot influence the corporation, he still has to face the questions of withdrawing and maintaining client confidences. However, there is good reason to suspect that the lawyer can, in some cases, have some influence and prevent such tragic choices from arising or clarify them when they do.

535 Kennedy, "Professional Responsibility and the Inside Lawyer," 34 Bus. Lawyer 867, 868 (1979).

536 *Id.* at 868-69: "[I]nside lawyers cannot simply advise on the basis of facts furnished them by a client. In some cases they will know that the facts are different. In other cases, it will be relatively easy to check.... On the other hand, the lawyer cannot operate effectively as an auditor or investigator of every conceivably questionable situation. What are the proper boundaries...?"

537 *Id.* at 869: "Does the corporate lawyer with a continuing relationship to the client have an obligation to...[corporate] policies and procedures?"

538 Does the inside counsel have professional duties governing his reporting relations, his relations with managers, with the Board of Directors, the bar, with outside counsel?

organizational needs of differentiated organizations, is on the agenda of the profession.

ABOUT THE AUTHOR

Robert Eli Rosen is Professor of Law at the University of Miami. He earned an A.B. *magna cum laude* from Harvard College in 1974, an M.A. in sociology from the University of California at Berkeley in 1977, a J.D. from Harvard Law School in 1979, and a Ph.D. in sociology from the University of California at Berkeley in 1984. His dissertation committee consisted of Robert Bellah, chair, Philip Selznick, and Laura Nader. He joined the law faculty of the University of Miami in 1984.

During the 1987-1988 academic year, Professor Rosen was on leave at Harvard University as a fellow in Harvard's Program in Ethics and the Professions, and in 1994 he was a research scholar at Stanford Law School. He teaches courses in professional responsibility, business associations, sociology of law, and contracts. He consults with law firms and legal departments in addition to teaching and continuing research on lawyers and corporate governance.

Professor Rosen's most recent articles and essays may be found at his page at the Social Science Research Network:

http://papers.ssrn.com/sol3/cf_dev/AbsByAuth.cfm?per_id=270682

Quid Pro Books
www.quidprobooks.com

www.ingramcontent.com/pod-product-compliance
Lightning Source LLC
Chambersburg PA
CBHW061736270326
41928CB00011B/2257